MULTINATIONALS
IN CANADA

Multinationals in Canada: Theory, Performance and Economic Impact

Alan M. Rugman

With a Foreword by
A. E. Safarian

Martinus Nijhoff Publishing, Boston
Boston/The Hague/London

Distributors for North America:
Martinus Nijhoff Publishing
Kluwer Boston Inc.
160 Old Derby Street
Hingham, Massachusetts 02043

Distributors outside North America:
Kluwer Academic Publishers Group
Distribution Centre
P.O. Box 322
3300AH Dordrecht, The Netherlands

Library of Congress Cataloging in Publication Data

Rugman, Alan M.
  Multinationals in Canada.

  Bibliography: p.
  Includes index.
  1. Corporations, Foreign—Canada.
2. International business enterprises—Canada.
I. Title.
HD2809.R83   338.8'8'0971   79-25989
ISBN 0-89838-036-7

Printed in the United States of America.

To Andrew

CONTENTS

FOREWORD

Multinational enterprises have become one of the distinctive institutions of our times. Controversy over their economic and political effects, and over appropriate public policy responses, has become common in home and host countries and in international agencies. Much of this debate is reminiscent of the role of large corporations generally, particularly in their interregional and intergroup effects. The multinational setting, however, would have raised distinctive issues even apart from the strong surges of nationalism and anti-imperialism which have marked recent history.

Canada has a long and unusual experience with such enterprises. Foreign control of capital in the nonfinancial industries (manufacturing, petroleum and gas, other mining and smelting, utilities, merchandising) was already 20 percent in 1930 and 25 percent in 1948. It rose to 36 percent by the late 1960s, but has since receded to about 30 percent. In 1975, fully 55 percent of the capital in manufacturing was controlled outside Canada, as was 72 percent of that in petroleum and gas, and 58 percent in other mining. These figures exceed those of other developed countries, although there have been striking increases in recent decades. About 80 percent of the direct investment capital in Canada is from the United States. Recently, Canadians have become aware of a surge of Canadian direct investment abroad, which on a flow basis has exceeded inflows (exclusive of retained earnings) for most of the 1970s.

Public concern about the issues raised by multinational, especially American, investment has been evident since the mid-1950s. It has waxed and waned as particular issues came to the fore — concern over the balance of payments, cultural development, the extraterritorial extension of U.S. law, the impact on Canadian technological development, and the effects for resource development. In pressing for further regulation, leadership has come from many sources, but three have been prominent: (1) competing Canadian owners, or at least those whose interests were damaged by foreign direct investment, including prominent elements in the media; (2) those who saw the multinational as a threat to the power of government; and (3) more recently, proponents of a stronger, independent high-technology sector. Not surprisingly, governments have moved more slowly than such groups would prefer since they have had to reconcile group interests and take account of the benefits as well as the costs of a multinational presence. Nevertheless, a number of sectors have been declared off-limits to further foreign ownership; screening of foreign takeovers and of new entry has been instituted; a variety of incentives to Canadian ownership or to Canadian entrepreneurial activity have been developed; and government ownership or joint-ownership of industry have increased partly in response to questions about foreign control.

Professor Alan Rugman's contribution to the range of issues noted here can best be understood in the context of intellectual thought in Canada and elsewhere on this subject. It is a curious fact that the implications of the spread of such enterprise were neglected for so long. It was not until 1958 that a comprehensive empirical and theoretical work appeared on post-war developments, in the form of John Dunning's study of U.S. investment in U.K. manufacturing. It was some years more before the various social sciences took serious notice of the phenomenon. In Canada, the classic study of Canadian-American industry by Marshall, Southard and Taylor in 1936 was followed by a gap of twenty years before the publication of a few chapters in one of the studies for the Royal Commission on Canada's Economic Prospects. During the 1960s, both private scholarship and research directly sponsored by governments began to make up for this lack. At the same time, the debate on public policy heated up; the multinational enterprise had both critics and defenders, and there was room for dispute on appropriate policy responses.

Despite the subsequent outpouring of material on multinational enterprises in Canada, one is distinctly uneasy in considering its policy relevance. Policy will be determined by far more than the quality of Canadian writing on the subject. Canadian governments react to group pressures, and indeed, whatever their political hue, to highly pragmatic considerations. Yet, as Keynes reminded us in a famous phrase on the long-run importance of ideas as against vested interests, the former are by no means unimportant. Canadian writing on this subject has suffered for several reasons. Too often it has been divorced from the important literature on the subject elsewhere. Too often the issues, which go well beyond economics, have been left to economists to resolve, as best they can. Too much of the critical writing on this and related subjects has gone into analysis of the historic failures of Canadian private entrepreneurship, little into developing and testing counterfactual models or analyzing the constraints placed on such activity in Canada. And too many economists and noneconomists alike, including politicians and bureaucrats, treat the subject either as nonrational or self-evident, rather than as a complex and important aspect of Canadian life — and, increasingly, of life elsewhere — deserving the most careful theoretical and empirical analysis.

Lest this seem like a lament for the social sciences, let me add that Canadian economists in particular have made an important contribution to the subject. For example, Stephen Hymer placed the study of such enterprises squarely in the field of industrial organization, with emphasis on imperfect competition, in his influential doctoral thesis of 1960. Another Canadian, Harry Johnson, emphasized investment in knowledge as a critical aspect of the special advantages such enterprises enjoyed, and explored the welfare and policy aspects at length. John McManus analyzed the reasons for the existence of firms in general, and multinational firms in particular, as distinct from markets and contract. Kari Levitt raised a number of questions about the long-term developmental effects of heavy reliance on multinational firms. In addition, there has been outstanding work on Canada by non-Canadians. For example, Richard Caves, who gave a definitive statement of the industrial organization approach to this subject, has done several careful empirical tests for Canada.

In the meantime, a number of scholars, mostly associated with Dunning's group at the University of Reading, began extensive work emphasizing multinational enterprise as a response to the costs of organizing markets, particularly intermediate markets such as that for knowledge. A multinational enterprise is created when markets are internalized across national boundaries. Peter Buckley and Mark Casson have developed this internalization approach most fully in recent years. There are also other major explanations which partly overlap this approach. In particular, Raymond Vernon and his colleagues in the Harvard University project have put more emphasis on the stages and processes by which innovation-based oligopolies establish, then attempt to maintain, their multinational positions.

Rugman's work is mainly in the context of the Reading School. Some of his recent writings on the multinational enterprise have been brought together and extended in order to develop a major theme. His general objective in this study is to bring the theoretical developments on trade and foreign investment, especially the theory of internalization, to the forefront of public attention. More particularly, he has applied it to the debate on foreign ownership in Canada, and to issues of regulation of multinational enterprises generally. Several points might be noted on his contribution.

First, Rugman discusses at length the case for considering internalization as the most general theory of multinational enterprise and, hence, of the nature of alternatives to it. In the process, he adds precision to that theory, for example, in the case of the licensing alternative. Second, his work is explicitly based on economic analysis and directed to economic issues, not because he considers other issues unimportant, but because he believes the contribution of economics lies in its analysis of efficiency. Third, using these perspectives, he is sharply critical of the views of a number of Canadian writers on this subject, notably those in the political economy stream. In addition, he believes government industrial policies, including various forms of protectionism and of regulation of direct investment, are based on inadequate understanding of multinational enterprise and are therefore often counterproductive. To some extent the theory of internalization contradicts the conclusions about subsidiaries as "truncated" firms, a view which is central to much policy and thinking in Canada. At the same time, his position does not lead to a hands-off attitude to such enterprises' activities, in terms of the effects on national welfare. Rugman is careful to note that such matters as transfer pricing deserve more attention as trade grows within the corporation. He also underlines that the possible negative welfare effects from internalization are matters for empirical and theoretical inquiry, and attempts such in several instances in this study.

This is a stimulating book. It is likely to stir controversy in the challenges it mounts to some of the assumptions underlying public discussion of this topic in Canada. The framework and ideas of the study deserve attention by those concerned with the effects of multinational enterprises, wherever owned, and with the probable effectiveness of various types of policies towards them.

A. E. SAFARIAN

ACKNOWLEDGMENTS

The intellectual basis for this book was established during the eight years I taught economics at the University of Winnipeg. The advantage of holding a tenured position in such a liberal arts college is that it generates an atmosphere in which broad policy issues, such as the role of foreign investment in Canada, can be debated with colleagues and students on a cross-disciplinary basis. The persistent questions about foreign investment raised by political scientists, geographers, historians, sociologists, and other noneconomists inspired the analysis which appears herein.

In writing previous drafts of these chapters, and especially in rewriting them for this book, my thinking on the role of multinationals in Canada has been confined to making applications of economic theory using a precise methodology. This book attempts to push economic theory as far as it can reasonably go in the analysis of multinational activity in Canada. I have probably used it too much to satisfy many of my former colleagues in the other social sciences, but I believe it is the unique contribution of an economist to focus solely on the efficiency (or inefficiency) aspects of multinationals. This is what I attempt to do here. My major acknowledgment therefore goes to my former colleagues and students at the University of Winnipeg for stimulating my interest in the topic of foreign investment in Canada.

The most influential teacher I had was the late Harry G. Johnson, and the best advice about the use of economic theory that I received came from my doctoral dissertation supervisor, Herbert G. Grubel. The impact of these two intellectual tyros will be evident in what follows.

As my thinking about the role of multinationals evolved, I received valuable help from many other economists in understanding the modern theory of foreign direct investment. During my sabbatical year at the University of Reading, I enjoyed numerous helpful discussions about the theory of internalization with John Dunning and Mark Casson, while others in England such as Peter Buckley, Bob Pearce, and Paul Geroski helped clarify my thinking on the economic and financial aspects of multinationals. During an exciting academic year as a Visiting Associate Professor at Columbia University, I received constant help and good theoretical advice from Ian Giddy. Chapter 4 contains materials developed jointly with him, although the use of these ideas is my responsibility alone.

Helpful comments on various chapters have been made by Thomas M. Johnson, Wilson B. Brown, Anthony Scott, Hugh Neuburger, Solmaz Ayarslan, Evan Douglas, Sylvester Damus, and many others at various seminars and conferences. In addition to these people, I am indebted to the authors who have written on the theory of multinational enterprise and undertaken empirical studies of the effects of foreign direct investment in Canada and elsewhere. In particular, I should like to thank A. E. Safarian for very helpful comments at a late stage of the work. His valuable insights, and those of two anonymous reviewers, improved the work considerably.

Excellent research assistance for the empirical work was performed by George Manning, Gary Sawchuk, Ruth Kristjanson, and David Baril, all at the University of Winnipeg. Their efforts were supported by grants from the University of Winnipeg Research and Travel Committee and the Centre for Resource Studies of Queen's University, Kingston, Ontario.

The typewriters of Harriet Leonard and Debbie Goins at Columbia and of Marlene Lloyd in Montreal labored long in transforming this manuscript from anarchy to order.

I express my thanks to these individuals for stimulating my thinking and helping in the completion of this project. Naturally, I alone am fully responsible for any remaining errors in this book.

1 INTRODUCTION

PERFORMANCE AND EFFICIENCY

This study uses economic analysis to evaluate the performance of multinational firms in Canada. It is well known that the multinational enterprise (MNE) is a dominant force in the Canadian economy. The majority of manufacturing industry and most of the petroleum, mining, and other resource industries are foreign owned. The impact of the MNE on Canadian investment, growth, productivity, employment, and the international payments balance has been the focus of many academic and official studies. These studies are reviewed and synthesized below. In addition, the present analysis focuses on the performance of individual MNEs and evaluates their contribution to the Canadian (host) and foreign (home) economies.

Performance is measured by profit rates, after allowing for the effects of transfer pricing, taxation, concentration, and other relevant factors that influence the industry within which the MNE operates. Information on profit rates is available from corporation balance sheets and income statements, and can be supplemented by official corporation statistics, although the latter are normally reported for industry groupings rather than at the firm level used in this study.

1

This study is an exercise in the application of economic theory rather than one in political economy. I do not really believe that the complex nature of the MNE can be analyzed in a useful manner unless the basic premises of the methodology to be applied are made explicit. Here the efficiency aspects of MNEs are studied. Nothing is said about the distributional aspects of the MNE, although these excite many political economists and policy makers.

The distinction between efficiency and and distributional objectives lies at the heart of economic theory.[1] In a general equilibrium system it is possible to derive the conditions necessary for the attainment of a Pareto optimal situation; that is, one which is efficient subject to a set of assumptions such as perfect goods and factor markets, full information, homothetic tastes and so on. To simplify a very demanding analysis it may be stated that this general equilibrium model is all about efficiency and not at all about equity. Indeed, the neoclassical paradigm of general equilibrium ignores distributional issues. It shows the conditions for Pareto optimality for any given income distribution in a society[2] and argues that a system of taxes and subsidies can deal with any redistributional issues occasioned by the short-term adjustment process as the system moves to general equilibrium.[3]

The general equilibrium neoclassical paradigm is a powerful analytical vehicle because of its very simplicity. It is a limiting case in which only efficiency matters. It provides a first best theoretical solution against which real world situations can be compared. Therefore, by applying basic microeconomic theory to the MNE, it is possible to evaluate its efficiency and performance by an examination of profit rates. More specifically, profit rates of the MNEs can be compared to the norm or theoretical optimum for particular industries and non-MNEs in general. If MNEs are assumed to have market power, (that is, are monopolists), then their power should reveal itself in their economic performance, namely in excess profits. In this book, the profits of MNEs active in Canada are examined to test this hypothesis.

I use political economy in a pejorative sense since the practitioners of this art frequently confuse efficiency and equity issues.[4] It is tempting to do so when dealing with the MNE. Its very size, economic influence, and political power make it a target for many aspects of public policy. Yet the MNE is ultimately an economic creature. It exists primarily to produce and market the goods and services from which it can earn profits. It is argued in this book that it is not the function of the MNE to transfer technology, to act as a development agency, or to redistribute income. These are the policy goals of the governments of host nations in which the MNE operates. While there is clearly some interrelationship between the MNE and government, it is useful for the purpose of this analysis to separate these two powerful actors on the international stage. I therefore assume in this study that the nation state is not dead, but that it has a powerful independent government (or the potential for one) with the power to tax or regulate foreign investment if its electorate chooses.

The bulk of the literature on the MNE in Canada has not made this distinction between economic theory and political economy.[5] Many writers have confused efficiency and equity issues. Public policy toward foreign direct investment contains many elements which are self-contradictory or internally inconsistent. These failures of analysis and policy are evaluated. The one writer on the MNE in Canada who has managed to avoid these dangers is Harry G. Johnson. This study is written in the spirit of that great Canadian international economist.[6]

My work should be contrasted with that of such political economists as Kari Levitt (1970), Mel Watkins (1978), and Abraham Rotstein (1972). These writers have provided useful information on the extent of foreign ownership of the Canadian economy and have advanced many interesting proposals to help develop indigenous Canadian industry through subsidies, promotion of research, and other relevant policies. However, they tend to mix up such valid efficiency arguments with distributional ones, where the latter are along the lines of regulation and control of foreign investment. It is made clear in this book that restrictions on foreign direct investment will serve only to deny Canadians the net economic benefits of higher rates of growth and employment brought to Canada by the MNEs.[7]

Instead of controls and regulations, which have led to the establishment of such ineffective and misconceived bodies as the Foreign Investment Review Agency, it is more efficient to use tax policy to whittle away any excess profits earned by MNEs on their operations in Canada. Indeed this principle of attempting to enforce an optimal tax on MNEs, rather than controls, is of general application to all nations with foreign direct investment.[8] It is a solution that is soundly based in economic analysis rather than one based on the noneconomic goals of sovereignty and independence. The attainment of these latter objectives is not necessarily hindered by MNEs, despite the common perception to the contrary. Indeed the MNEs can be viewed as agents which provide a society with an expanded choice set, since these economic institutions increase national wealth and productivity. The critics of the MNE frequently attribute to it social and political problems which are characteristic of the nation at large rather than the MNE in particular. I believe that if attention is focused on the purely economic efficiency aspects of the MNE, then such potential errors in analysis can be avoided. To this end, this book examines the profits, performance, and economic impact of MNEs in Canada.

METHODOLOGY

This study of the MNE uses a theoretical framework which has been developed only recently. The modern theory of foreign direct investment (FDI) demonstrates that the MNE has a firm specific advantage which is exploited in foreign (host) as well as domestic (home) markets. In essence, the MNE is a response to exogenous market imperfections which can be internalized by the MNE. The theory of internalization is reviewed, developed, and used extensively in this study. It serves as a basis for the analysis of the economic efficiency of MNEs.

The methodology to be employed is based firmly in economic theory; that is, in the concept of efficiency and Pareto optimality discussed previously. The existence of market imperfections does not invalidate the neoclassical paradigm. Indeed, general equilibrium theory can be used to model the many facets of the MNE. Either the observed market imperfections can be assumed to be exogenous, to which internalization is then an efficient response of the MNE, or they can be assumed to be endogenous. In the latter situation, endogenous barriers to entry used by the MNE to close a market are clearly inefficient actions. Essentially it does not matter how the market imperfections are treated, provided they are modeled explicitly. Only then can economic analysis be applied to the MNE in a meaningful manner.

PLAN OF THE BOOK

This book has eleven chapters, divided into three self-contained sections.

Part I develops the modern theory of the multinational enterprise (MNE). Chapters 2 and 3 explain the concept of internalization and review key theoretical models of foreign direct investment in order to demonstrate that these theories are, in fact, subcases of the general theory of internalization. Having introduced internalization as a paradigm, Chapter 4 moves on to a consideration of three possible methods for a multinational firm to service foreign markets, namely by exporting, foreign investment, or licensing. Due to the firm specific advantage in technology, research, and knowledge enjoyed by the multinational enterprise, it is necessary to establish the conditions under which any one of these three options leads to the optimal rate of appropriation of rents for the firm. It is shown that the multinational enterprise is an efficient vehicle for international production and that its internal market allows it to overcome externalities in the sale of knowledge. Indeed the multinational firm is able to circumvent most exogenous market imperfections and concerns about its alleged market power are only valid if it is also able to close a market or generate endogenous imperfections. These and other problems are considered at the end of Chapter 4 in the context of the Canadian economy. This chapter develops a model of internalization in a rigorous manner and contrasts it with the prevailing but inadequate model of internationalization. It is found that the MNEs operating in Canada are explained by the theory of internalization.

Part II of this book is strictly empirical. It reports data on the profit rates of multinational firms active in Canada, and disaggregates the industry data which have been reported by others, by looking at individual corporations. There are separate sections on multinational firms operating in the resource sector, such as those in minerals and petroleum. Firms in manufacturing industry are also examined. Besides the level of profits, Chapter 5 also examines the risk of profits of multinational firms. This is proxied by the standard deviation of earnings over time of a firm and also by finding the beta coefficient of a firm (which measures the variability in earnings of the firm against the Canadian stock market average or some other proxy). In general, it is found that multinational firms do not earn excessive profits, but they do benefit from a more stable stream of earnings over time than do domestic firms. The latter advantage of multinationals is due to the benefits of international diversification.[9]

Chapter 6 demonstrates that U.S. multinational firms offer a social benefit to Canada when they pay Canadian taxes. Yet their home nation suffers a social loss due to the tax credits allowed U.S. multinationals for their taxes paid to Canada. Data are presented to substantiate this finding, which is correct even when disaggregated from manufacturing industry to the resource sectors. Next, Chapter 7 examines the issue of transfer pricing. It finds that, in theory, multinational firms can use transfer prices to increase the profits of the parent firm at the expense of Canadian subsidiaries. Yet, in practice, no evidence is found of transfer pricing in an examination of the performance of MNEs, even when analyzing data on the mining industry.

Finally, Chapter 8 looks at the wider macroeconomic impact of the multinational enterprise on Canadian investment, income, employment, international payments balance, and regional disparities. Again, the overall economic effects are beneficial, since the multinational enterprise is efficient. The issue of technology transfer is examined briefly and is shown to be a false one. I argue that the multinational enterprise is not a development agency and is not solely responsible for the growth of the host nation. This is the responsibility of the Canadian state and the elected federal and provincial governments. They have the authority to use taxes and subsidies to attack distributional issues and promote development objectives, while multinational firms clearly lack this power. MNEs are in the business of production. They are not social agencies.

Part III uses the theory of Part I and the empirical work of Part II to criticize existing federal government policy toward foreign direct investment. Chapter 9 reviews the reasons for increased Canadian nationalism and the objections to foreign ownership.[10] Chapter 10 castigates the Foreign Investment Review Agency and suggests that it is theoretically impossible for it to satisfy conflicting policy objectives. A distinction is drawn between equity and efficiency objectives, with regulation being an inferior solution to optimal taxes and subsidies as a method for solving distributional goals. Chapter 11 then examines some of the unforeseen implications of the regulation of foreign direct investment in Canada. A strong case is developed for the removal of tariff and nontariff barriers to trade. If these were eliminated there would be less foreign direct investment in the first place since U.S. firms could service the Canadian market by exports rather than subsidiary production. A final chapter draws conclusions and implications.

ENDNOTES

1. See any good textbook in intermediate microeconomic theory for support of this proposition. For example, Charles E. Ferguson and John P. Gould, *Microeconomic Theory,* 4th ed. (Homewood, Illinois: Irwin, 1975), especially Chapters 15 and 16 on the theory of general equilibrium and welfare economics; Edwin Mansfield, *Microeconomics: Theory and Applications,* 2nd ed. (New York: Norton, 1975), Chapters 14, 15, and 17; Robert Haney Scott, *The Pricing System* (San Francisco, Holden-Day, 1973), Chapters 1-6; and A. Asimakopulos, *An Introduction to Economic Theory: Microeconomics* (Toronto, Oxford University Press, 1978), Chapters 17 and 18.

2. For a diagrammatic derivation of a general equilibrium model for any assumed income distribution, see the classic article by Francis M. Bator, "The Simple Analytics of Welfare Maximization," *American Economic Review* 47 (March 1957):22-59, reprinted in William Breit and Harold M. Hochman, eds., *Readings in Microeconomics* (New York: Holt, Rinehart and Winston, 1968), pp. 385-413.

3. For a rigorous demonstration of the role of taxes and subsidies in solving the problem of income distribution, see the many imaginative examples in Melvyn B. Krauss and Harry G. Johnson, *General Equilibrium Analysis: A Micro-economic Text* (Chicago: Aldine, 1975). For discussion of the related problem of the compensation principle, see Ajit K. Dasgupta and D. W. Pearce, *Cost-Benefit Analysis* (London: Macmillan, 1972); and Vivian C. Walsh, *Introduction to Contemporary Microeconomics* (New York: McGraw-Hill, 1970), especially Chapter 11.

4. They also tend to confuse normative and positive economics, although this is very easy to do these days. Positive economics is more objective in principle than normative economics since it makes predictions from a stated model which can be tested empirically. See Milton Friedman, "The Methodology of Positive Economics," in his *Essays in Positive Economics* (Chicago: University of Chicago Press, 1953), pp. 3–43. For an authoritative discussion of methodology in economics, see Lawrence A. Boland, "A Critique of Friedman's Critics," *Journal of Economic Literature* 17 (June 1979):503–522.

5. Neither have the professional staffs which prepared the Watkins Report (1968) or the Gray Report (1972). For a critique of these reports, see Chapters 8 and 9 of this book.

6. Among the dozen books and over 400 academic articles written by Johnson in his career as an international economist, the strongest statements of his antipathy toward Canadian nationalism appear in Harry G. Johnson, *The Canadian Quandary: Economic Problems and Policies* (Toronto: McGraw-Hill, 1963, reissued by Macmillan of Canada 1978).

7. For supporting evidence of this general point, see the complementary works by Safarian (1973), Fayerweather (1974), and Daly and Globerman (1976).

8. Evidence of the barriers to foreign direct investment in the form of screening agencies and investment codes, imposed by fifteen nations, can be found in Richard D. Robinson, *National Control of Foreign Business Entry* (New York: Praeger, 1976).

9. The topic of international diversification is explored in Rugman (1979).

10. In 1975, foreign control of manufacturing capital in Canada was 56 percent; petroleum and gas, 75 percent; and other mining, 60 percent; see Safarian (1979).

I THEORY OF THE MULTINATIONAL ENTERPRISE

2 THE THEORY OF FOREIGN INVESTMENT

THE DETERMINANTS OF FOREIGN INVESTMENT

The theoretical literature on direct investment as relevant for the book is discussed here. In this section, a summary of the more recent and relevant literature on direct and portfolio investment is presented, followed by a review of some recent theoretical and econometric work, especially that related to Canada. For a fully comprehensive review of the literature, see Hood and Young (1979).

Consider the following production function in a two-country model:

$$Q = f(L, K, M)$$

where Q is output, K is capital, L is labor, and M is management (or technology). This is a normal neoclassical production function, except that management is explicitly included as a basic variable. When factor endowments are considered, it can be argued that the United States has a large amount of M relative to Canada and other countries. This means that the marginal product of M in the United States will be lower than in Canada, because the marginal product of a factor depends on the amount of other factors available. As there is a relative shortage of M in Canada, its

11

marginal product will be higher than in the United States. According to international trade theory, the United States should export the good that intensively uses its abundant factor, which is M in this case. Therefore the United States should export management- and skill-intensive products. In a rigorous model, countries trade goods not factors, yet here it may be useful to think of factor transfers themselves.

If the mobility of factors is considered, it would be expected that M would be more mobile than L or K. Labor is fairly immobile due to cultural ties, discriminatory immigration policies, and imperfect knowledge of wage opportunities abroad. Capital is more mobile than labor, with short-term capital movements being responsive to interest rate differentials and expectations of exchange rate changes. Long-term capital is less volatile, and may be considered as a joint factor of production along with management. Management is the most mobile factor of production because management skills, either embodied in executives or contained in technical papers, may be readily transported.

The three inputs of the production function are interrelated, such that an increase in any one of the inputs will increase the marginal productivity of the other two. Therefore, if Canada receives M from the United States, it would be expected that Canadian wages and profits would increase, because the marginal productivities of L and K respectively increase.

An implication of this model is that direct investment is beneficial if it allows the factor to move from a region of low rates of return, the United States, to one with higher rates of return, for example, Canada. In the case of management and skilled labor, the higher management rate of return in Canada may be revealed by a higher relative salary received by executives, due to their higher productivity relative to other factor inputs. The salaries need not be absolutely greater in Canada, but they should be greater than the return on the factors in wages and profits. Casual empiricism suggests that executives of foreign-owned firms receive a substantial salary differential within Canada, partly because wages and profits are lower in Canada, and the management return is commensurate with that in the United States.

Another way of looking at the effects of direct investment is to assume a two-country model with equal rates of return on capital and equal relative commodity prices under autarky. Opening up this simple model to international trade in goods provides the usual gain from free trade, as demonstrated in any trade textbook. For example, in a Heckscher Ohlin framework, each country specializes in the production and export of the good which intensively uses its abundant factor of production.

Instead of trade in goods, international factor movements can provide similar gains from trade. When dealing with capital flows, trade theorems have usually not considered the distinction between financial and nonfinancial investment. Neither have they considered the special role of the multi-national corporation as a vehicle for the international transfer of monopoly advantages such as technology, research, and management skills in a world of imperfect factor markets. If such market imperfections exist, there will be motives for foreign investment.

In addition, the risk of such foreign investment can be reduced if the factor markets (and/or goods markets) of the two countries are less than perfectly positively correlated. Such imperfect international correlations are themselves sufficient to induce trade and to yield gains from foreign operations that are potentially just as great as those from free trade in goods.

The motivation of foreign investment is determined by several variables. The theoretical literature summarized shows that authors have focused attention on different variables; hence, no general theory of foreign investment has emerged at this date. In this section, an attempt is made to analyze the theoretical literature more rigorously. This is done in order to introduce a new variable, risk, which is of concern in this section. It is not suggested that this risk variable will lead to a revision of the theory of foreign investment, but merely that it is an important variable worthy of consideration.

The theoretical literature on foreign investment can be summarized to suggest that the major independent variables are as follows:

$$\text{FI} = f(y, i, E)$$

where FI is foreign investment, y is income, i is rate of return of capital, and E represents exogenous factors. Direct investment is basically dependent on y, while portfolio investment is basically dependent on i. The contributions by writers such as Hymer, Kindleberger, Caves, Johnson, Vernon, and others have focused on direct investment and thereby on the income variable. Arguments about the size of the host country market, exploitation of monopolistic advantages in knowledge, economies of scale, lower production costs abroad, tax avoidance, and so on can be proxied by the income variable. The first partial derivative with respect to y would be positive in each case, since a larger income level would increase the benefits of foreign investment, other things being equal. The rate of growth of income would also be positively related to the level of foreign investment.

Portfolio investment is basically determined by the rate of return on capital, as has been argued by writers using the neoclassical model. More specifically, interest rate differentials between countries are relevant. These theoretical contributions[1] are not discussed in detail, as our main concern is with direct investment and with the introduction of a new risk variable.

This allows the equation to be reformulated as:

$$\text{FI} = f(y, i, E, \text{Var})$$

where the variables are defined as before, and the new risk variable of concern to us is shown as Var, representing the variance of an income stream over time. The hypothesis and model for risk is formulated more specifically in Chapter 3 of Rugman (1979). This book also reports on extensive testing of the risk of earnings of the multinational firms which undertake the foreign direct investment.

THE DETERMINANTS OF FOREIGN INVESTMENT IN A CANADIAN CONTEXT

In explaining international capital flows, Penner (1970) implies that direct investment may be regarded as exogenous to domestic stabilization policy, but that portfolio investment is induced by such policy changes. Consequently, direct investment may be ignored when policy decisions are made by the recipient economy, whether under a regime of fixed or flexible exchange rates. Penner demonstrates that portfolio investment is the volatile element in capital flows, while direct investment is a stable parameter. Certainly direct investment may be altered by peripheral types of government policy aimed specifically at it, such as the American Voluntary Restraint Programme, or changes in depreciation rules or tax rates. Yet on balance, general economic policy aimed at maintaining internal equilibrium does not alter direct investment, while it does change portfolio capital movements.

Penner uses a primitive one-sector Keynesian model in which home and foreign saving and investment functions make up the goods market. No equations are suggested for a money sector, although it is assumed that there are "monetary adjustments occurring in the background." Two countries are assumed — home and foreign. Domestic investment is determined by the interest rate, and domestic saving by the income level. Both domestic functions can be shifted through government policies. Foreign saving is attracted by a higher Canadian interest rate, given foreign interest rates. Foreign investment is a parameter, as foreign direct investment is assumed to be insensitive to home interest rates.

The domestic investment schedule is "moved to the right by the presence of direct foreign investment," and by this Penner implies a parametric shift. Apparently, large foreign corporations will find it profitable to make investments in Canada at a rate of interest which would fail to attract additional domestic investment. The reasons suggested are that foreign firms embody more technical and financial skills and are large enough to reduce risk by (international) diversification. Penner's treatment of foreign direct investment is inadequate. It is implied that the main variables determining it are level of income or profits in the foreign economy, and a scale economy concept, yet these are not specifically examined.

A final definitional equation is that international capital flows are identical to the sum of direct and portfolio investment. If foreign direct investment is a parameter, then only portfolio investment remains as an endogenous variable. I interpret Penner to mean that foreign saving inflow is portfolio investment, but this is not clear. Certainly foreign saving and the portfolio investment listed in his table (1970, p. 217) are both functions of interest rate differentials. He suggests that direct investment is exogenous, but that raising the domestic interest rates will attract more portfolio investment. This is consistent with a Keynesian distinction between autonomous (direct) investment and induced (portfolio) investment.

One of Penner's major objectives is to investigate the impact of foreign investment on domestic stabilization policy to reduce inflation and unemployment. He finds that, in general, foreign investment will worsen inflation and fail to reduce unemployment, whether Canada has a fixed or flexible exchange rate. Much of the reason for this is inappropriate government policies revealed by hindsight:

> During most of the 1950–56 period inflation was a serious problem and since the Caves-Reuber results indicate that the total capital inflow was probably inflationary on balance one might be inclined to blame foreign investors for intensifying the problem (p. 219).
>
> Given the misguided policies it is clear that Canada would have been better off in the long run without foreign investment during the 1957–62 period (p. 221).

One reason given for the inflationary impact of foreign investment (both direct and portfolio) is that it is most expansionary in boom periods, when one dollar of foreign investment will generate up to three dollars increase in Canadian capital formation. This is reported in Chapter 4 of Caves and Reuber (1971). At other times of high economic activity, the expansionary effect ranges down to half this, and the stimulative impact is lower in recession periods. In periods of economic slack, one dollar of direct foreign investment only produces eighty cents of Canadian capital formation, and assuming that portfolio investment does not offset this, total foreign investment is deflationary in such periods. On this basis, it appears that foreign investment "worsens" the trade cycle.

Distinguishing between direct investment as autonomous and portfolio investment as induced is inconsistent with a model such as Floyd's (September 1969, October 1969) that properly develops an asset sector as well as a goods sector. All capital flows are part of a stock adjustment as individuals attempt to move to portfolio equilibrium. In such a model, direct investment is not a parameter, but is part of the capital stock owned by domestic or foreign individuals.

In the context of Floyd's models, direct investment would have to be treated in the same manner as portfolio investment, as only two types of asset are assumed: monetary wealth in the form of real balances, and non-monetary wealth in the form of the perpetual income stream generated by the stock of capital goods. Capital flows take place between the two countries in order to achieve an optimal portfolio that maximizes utility over time.

Such capital flows are not continuous and permanent, but are stock adjustments from one portfolio equilibrium to another. This follows from the model's implication that capital flows and interest rates are determined simultaneously, whereas other models by Lee (1969) and Grubel (1968) had assumed that interest rates are exogenous and independent of capital flows. Therefore, in using a portfolio model there is no reason to distinguish between direct investment and portfolio investment because they must both be explained as stock adjustments.

In *flow* models, international capital movements are explained by the levels of other variables, such as the level of interest rates. This approach may give improbable results, for instance, by assuming a static system with fixed interest rate differentials it is possible for investors to continue to accumulate claims on foreigners indefinitely. There is a continuous flow of capital, although in a correctly specified static model there should be no capital flows at all, as with fixed interest rate differentials actual holdings of assets then equal desired holdings.

For this reason, a portfolio model of stock adjustment is better at explaining the reasons for capital flows. In *stock* models, the stock of claims of foreigners relates to the levels of variables, such as interest rate differentials and net worth. Changes in these explanatory variables call forth a stock adjustment to a new static portfolio equilibrium, and until this new portfolio is achieved there is a flow of claims. These capital flows are not continuous, but finite.

In his papers, Floyd develops a modified Keynesian two-country model to show that capital movements are not continuous flows over time, but are once for all stock adjustments as private individuals attempt to maximize asset portfolios. A portfolio consists of the real money balances of the resident's home country, plus a proportion of the resident's own capital stock, and, perhaps, foreign capital stock.

Making the small country assumption for Canada means that it cannot influence the foreign interest rate, and that Canadian residents will not hold any of the foreign capital stock. Foreigners may own a proportion of

Canada's capital stock, which implies that Canada will have a balance of indebtedness which may be reduced by an increase in the Canadian money supply, or by a decrease in the level of Canadian output. Such changes in the level of money or income, or, more accurately, changes in their rates of growth over time, give rise to portfolio adjust in the asset sector.

In the model there are two other markets: the goods sector and the balance of payments sector (for Canada). The goods market is cleared by the balance of trade plus government being equal to any excess of autonomous saving over investment. The balance of trade is a function of domestic income, the proportion of Canadian capital stock owned by Canadians, and the rate of interest (assuming that foreign real income and money stock are constant). The balance of payments equation is an identity as the trade balance plus net capital inflow equals the induced capital outflow. Thus, any excess of saving over investment must equal its total capital outflow (autonomous plus induced). Yet this does not determine the capital flow over time, as the statement is an identity with no behavioral significance.

As Floyd shows in his September 1969 paper, interest rates and capital flows need to be determined simultaneously. What, then, determines capital flows? They are stock adjustments in response to changes in the rate of growth of money supply or income in one of the countries.

We have examined two fairly recent theoretical explanations of capital movements as they may apply to the Canadian balance of payments. To some extent, the differences between the models have been exaggerated, but this was done deliberately in order to isolate their treatment of direct investment. In fact, Floyd's model does not mention direct investment at all and may be used in isolation to explain satisfactorily the portfolio items alone. If this is done, the potential value of Floyd's contribution is greatly reduced, as it points the way to a theoretical model that will allow an integration of real and monetary variables in explaining all components of the capital account of the balance of payments.

One such approach would be to specify a Patinkin type model with excess demand equations for the goods, money, and bonds markets, and the fully employed labor sector. Compared with Floyd's goods and money markets, such a model is an advance as it considers explicitly the bonds market, and allows the rate of interest to be determined by financial variables rather than as the marginal product of capital. At the same time, the model would retain the essence of Floyd's argument that capital flows are either stock adjustments when the level of money supply is changed discretely, or flow adjustments caused by continuous change in the rate of growth of income or money supply. Empirical testing of the model would indicate which wealth variables are significant in explaining specific capital flows. Recently there has been an abundance of econometric work on U.S.-Canadian capital movements which can be the basis for such a new theoretical approach. For a summary of some of these studies, with additional references, discussion, and analysis, see Pattison (1978).

THE EMPIRICAL LITERATURE

A comprehensive review of the recent empirical literature is beyond the scope of this chapter. There has been a proliferation of studies on capital flows between Canada and the United States, partly attracted by Canada as a case study of fixed and flexible exchange rates. For our purpose, it will be sufficient to report on the several representative studies which clearly indicate the major variables determining portfolio capital movements. This will clear the stage for the major focus of the book — direct investment.

Branson (1968) completely ignores direct investment in his pathbreaking analysis of the econometrics of capital flows. His quantitative results are the basis for further work, and were one of the first comprehensive tests of significant variables determining items in the capital account of the United States. His avoidance of direct investment was perhaps understandable on the grounds of scaling his thesis down to size. He defines financial capital flows as "all non-direct investment terms in the capital account." Foreign exchange theory under fixed rates is reformulated to yield a suitable model for testing. The model is basically one of portfolio equilibrium with flows of portfolio capital being determined by changes in the variables determining these equilibrium stocks of capital. Such variables are interest rate changes, changes in portfolio size, and changes in trade and output flows. The level of interest rate differential is unimportant. These changes in variables operate through a distributed lag stock adjustment process. Trade flows are determined exogenously, as are domestic interest rates. His specification manages to avoid the simultaneity problem.

The major results are: (1) interest rates have a powerful, but transitory effect on international capital flows, especially short-term capital flows; (2) long-term capital is affected by changes in the gross national product, trade flows, and changes in the U.S. government bond rate; and (3) the model suggests that when home output rises, with constant yields, then domestic investors will buy out foreign owners in the securities market.

The first application of portfolio theory to international monetary economics was by Grubel (1968). The empirical work is soundly based on a theoretical model which allows capital flows to respond not only to interest rate differentials, but also to differences in rates of growth of total asset holdings, where wealth can be held in three ways: money, bonds, and real assets. International diversification of bond holdings will reduce the riskiness of individual portfolios and give a welfare gain to wealth holders, whether under fixed or flexible exchange rates. In the empirical section, Grubel calculates rates of return and risk for stocks of eleven industrial countries from 1959 to 1966. Two efficiency loci are computed, one for the eleven countries, and one for the eight Atlantic countries, with risk being lower for each rate of return in the former case. Or for the same risk, an American investor can improve his or her expected return from 7.5 percent to 8.9 percent in the eight-country portfolio, or to 12.6 percent in the eleven-country portfolio.

Levy and Sarnat extend Grubel's work to investigate the possibility of risk reduction by international diversification of securities portfolios. For the period from 1957 to 1969, mean rates of return on common stocks and their standard deviations were calculated. Rates of return are in dollar terms, and are relevant only for countries with a constant exchange rate during 1951 to 1967, thus for example excluding the United Kingdom. Rates of return are the percentage changes in the dollar value of the index of common stocks. Results show that, in general, U.S. stocks had a high rate of return (12 percent) and moderate risk (12 percent standard deviation). The U.S. risk fell by diversification into an efficiency curve consisting of shares of other countries, especially those of some less developed countries and of Japan. Yet U.S. risk was not reduced by holding Canadian or European assets, as these were highly correlated with U.S. stock return. For example, Canadian stocks had a positive correlation of 0.81 with U.S. stocks, and were more risky. Therefore, U.S. stocks dominated Canadian ones, and thereby eliminated Canada from the efficiency locus. Other correlations with the U.S. stocks were: Belgium 0.83, Germany 0.43, Netherlands 0.53, France 0.34, Italy 0.09. The efficiency locus reduced risk greatly when twenty-six countries were included, but European stocks increased risks due to their positive correlation.

Michael Porter (1971) considerably advanced the analysis of short-term capital flows with his attempt to introduce uncertainty into international portfolio theory. From data on the term structures of interest rates in the United States and Canada, with capital assumed to be perfectly mobile, it was shown that variations in interest yield rates were due to differing expectations of the foreign exchange rate. This held under a regime of fixed exchange rates (1962–1968) as well as flexible (1953–1960) because in both periods interest yields revealed specific expectations of changes in the par value of the Canadian exchange rate, calling for higher Canadian interest rates to compensate for this exchange rate risk. In another section, Porter develops an intertemporal portfolio model on the premise that capital flows permit consumption by two countries to take place over time. There is not time to go into this model here, although it might prove a fruitful way to integrate real and monetary aspects of international theory.

The contributions to the empirical literature of Lee (1969) and Miller-Whitman can only be noted in passing. The former considers the possible reduction of securities risk by trading off the business cycles of various economies. The latter detect income to be a key variable determining the stock adjustment of long-term capital flows.

These studies generally confirm Mundell's theoretical contributions (1968) showing that a small open economy such as Canada is unable to pursue successfully an independent monetary policy with fixed exchange rates. For example, if Canada attempts to reduce the money supply through selling more bonds, the excess supply of bonds will cause the price of outstanding bonds to fall and the rate of interest to rise. The higher Canadian rate of interest will widen the interest rate differential and attract more foreign capital, which will increase the domestic money supply as the government mops up excess foreign currency to maintain the exchange rate. Under flexible exchange rates, the exchange rate itself appreciates in this situation to choke off the foreign capital inflows. Therefore, only under a flexible exchange rate will domestic monetary policy become effective. For example, unusually high unemployment in Canada in the winters of 1970 to 1972 followed the floating of the Canadian dollar on June 1st, 1970, as the previous restrictive monetary policy was suddenly made effective.

One of the more interesting econometric tests of foreign direct investment was reported by Scaperlanda,[2] using a neoclassical stock adjustment model. He suggests that the major determinants of foreign investment (FI) are:

M = size of host economy market,
ΔM = rate of growth of that market,
K = the stock of capital,
E = changes in host economy policy, for example, as revealed by fluctuations in the host economy's foreign exchange rate,
DUM = tariff policy, such as the Auto Pact Agreement.

This yields the following equation:

$$\text{FI} = f(M, \Delta M, K, E, \text{DUM})$$

The partial derivatives of the first three variables are positive, while that of the E variable is negative. Scaperlanda reported that testing of the model by least squares regression analysis had confirmed the signs and significance of the variables. Variable E for the foreign exchange rate is a financial proxy for real influences in the economy. For example, if there was a fall in the value of the U.S. dollar, which was offset by some strengthening of the Canadian market, this might lead to a greater inflow of American foreign investment, thus giving a negative relationship between foreign investment and the Canadian exchange rate.

The impact of the free trade agreement in automobiles is captured by a dummy variable, which significantly indicated that the recent efforts of the Auto Pact reduced the amount of foreign investment from what it would otherwise have been. Another dummy was used to measure the impact of U.S. mandatory controls on foreign investment imposed for a few weeks in early 1968. A negative relationship was postulated on the basis that uncertainty generated by the controls would reduce foreign investment. However, this variable was insignificant for manufacturing.

Another series of regressions was applied to aggregate investment instead of only manufacturing investment. The results indicated that the interdependencies between the U.S. and Canadian economies increased due to the inclusion of nonmanufacturing investment. Another variable was important — one which represented domestic cash flow factors. This variable was positively related to foreign investment.

In their 1969 article, Scaperlanda and Mauer tested three hypotheses as to the motivation of foreign investment. These were size of market in the receiving area, economic growth, and tariff discriminations. These were tested using various proxies by least-squares regressions on U.S. direct investment in the European Economic Community (EEC) from 1952 to 1966. U.S. direct investment is examined in aggregate across both industries and countries, which reduces the importance of specification errors, and cancels out some transitory investment elements. Transitory value might be higher with foreign investment; first, because of the uncertainty of international finance in the long term, and second, because of the lumpy and discontinuous nature of foreign direct investment.

The chief result of this study was that only the market size hypothesis was supported. The profit differential variable was unimportant, while the growth and tariff discrimination hypotheses were insignificant or even negative. From this, it can be concluded that greater domestic specialization in production is possible if U.S. firms invest in large foreign markets. Therefore, U.S. direct investment is undertaken in order to capture economies of scale that are unavailable within the home market.

Kwack[3] uses a stock adjustment model instead of the flow approach by Scaperlanda and Mauer, and finds that most U.S. direct investment is explained by output, home interest rate, and the initial value of U.S. direct investment itself. Furthermore, a rise in the home interest rate will reduce U.S. foreign investment, while a rise in foreign incomes will increase it. Government policies are also significant in altering U.S. direct investment in his model. Specifically, tax policies that increase the cash flow of U.S. nonfinancial corporations stimulate U.S. direct investment, but restrictive balance of payments programs temporarily reduce it.

One of the first attempts to use a portfolio model for direct investment rather than financial investment was by Prachowny.[4] He attempted to specify and test an optimum-stock equation for U.S. corporations in which the main explanatory variables are expected rates of return on foreign and domestic assets, risk (that is, variability) attached to these rates of return, covariance of these rates, and other external risk factors affecting foreign investment (such as expropriation and devaluation). The empirical results of this stock-flow portfolio balance model are "rather fragile," as data were not available for most of the desired variables, and even when proxies were used the risk variables were insignificant. Prachowny assumed that the corporation maximizes a utility function (u) of the rate of return on wealth (R),

$$U = U(R).$$

He assumed that the first partial is positive, and the second is negative.

In an earlier study, Stevens[5] made use of a two parameter utility function for the firm. He assumed that a firm engaged in direct investment will maximize a utility function which is positively related to the expected rate of return, and negatively related to risk. The empirical work by Stevens was also inconclusive, but again this was due to data problems rather than the utility function specified.

Richardson[6] has suggested a major distinction between two different stages of foreign direct investment. The initial investment abroad is likely to be motivated by the goal of market penetration, while continuing investments of established firms are due to the desire for growth and profit maximization on a global scale. There have been no tests of this distinction between an initial and a continuing investment by a multinational firm.

If it is possible to report a consensus of opinion as to the determinants of direct investment, it is that people in business assume that foreign investment is risky so they expect to make higher profits per dollar of foreign investment than they would on domestic investment. Other reasons may be given by them for undertaking foreign investment, but generally they are all subsets of this profit expectations hypothesis. Similarly, many factors may influence the foreign investment climate, but one proxy variable generally found significant in the academic literature is the market size of the host country.

The simplest indication of market size is GNP, preferably in real terms. It can reasonably be assumed that GNP determines the intensity of demand in the host country market for the output financed by the direct investment; and on average, most sales of foreign-owned subsidiaries are made in the local market, rather than being exported. It has been confirmed by Caves and Reuber (1971) that Canadian market size is a significant determinant of U.S. direct foreign investment. An identical conclusion was reached using European data by Bandera and White (1968).

In a related article, Bonomo and Tanner (1972) used spectral analysis to demonstrate that the Canadian business cycle was closely identified with the U.S. cycle, and specifically that there was a "strong dependence of Canadian investment on business conditions in the U.S.," as U.S. direct investment is nearly 40 percent of all new investment in Canadian plant and equipment. There were no significant lags before the U.S. cycle was transmitted to Canada, nor any evidence that the period of flexible exchange rates allowed more autonomy of domestic stabilization (especially monetary) policy to mitigate the pervading influence of the U.S. cycle. With such changes in U.S. income probably altering the rate of U.S. foreign investment, and with such direct investment accounting for two-fifths of total investment in Canada, then the rate of growth in Canada must be greatly affected by direct investment. This identification problem of simple regression models requires the use of techniques such as distributed lags or the specification of an integrated model.

A SUMMARY OF THE DETERMINANTS OF FOREIGN INVESTMENT

In summary, the possible determinants of foreign investment are:

1. the desire to overcome tariff and other barriers to trade,[7]
2. exploitation of monopolistic advantages, such as in the areas of technology, management, or research,[8]
3. large market size in the host economy, which may permit a firm to enjoy economies of scale and to engage in horizontal integration,[9]
4. lower costs of production abroad, for example, lower labor costs or lower borrowing costs,
5. possible tax avoidance by manipulation of profits among subsidiaries and by the use of transfer pricing,[10]
6. management reasons such as prestige and empire building.[11]

These above explanations represent a challenge to traditional economic theory because they emphasize factors that are not normally incorporated into neoclassical international trade theory.[12] In particular, they challenge the assumption of perfect competition because the multinational corporations themselves interfere with the movement of and return to factors of production, as well as being price makers. They also engage in trade, and, as Dunning has estimated, about one-eighth of the total of world trade is internal to the multinational companies.[13] A second assumption criticized is the traditional Ricardian one that factors are immobile between countries but mobile within countries in a trade theory model. The preceding approaches take, as a premise, the argument that multinational corporations move factors of production such as technology and management skills across national borders.

Noneconomic factors have also been suggested, for example, Galbraith's emphasis on political economy and the power exerted by multinational corporations on national governments.[14] The assumption that firms operate as price takers in a competitive world is inconsistent with the facts; consequently, the argument that firms maximize profits must be modified to take account of their incentive to act as pressure groups within the political process in democratic societies. It should be noted that multinational enterprises attempt to exert political influence in both the home and foreign countries, and that their influence is not confined to the host nation alone.

On the other hand, there is a substantial body of empirical work which supports the traditional approach that capital movements can be explained by models of neoclassical trade theory. Capital flows must be defined as either portfolio capital or direct investment; the distinction is that the latter involves control of the invested funds, whereas the former does not. There are many studies of the capital account of the balance of payments which examine portfolio capital and direct investment together, and distinguish between short-term and long-term items, rather than between portfolio and direct investment. According to traditional economic theory, foreign investment can be explained by the following:

1. Interest rate differentials between countries determine international capital flows. Short-term portfolio capital flows are particularly responsive to interest rate differentials, but there is also some sensitivity of long-term portfolio capital and direct investment to such differentials.[15] Exchange rate expectations may also affect short-term capital movements.[16]

2. Interest rate differentials are no longer assumed to be exogenous, but are determined endogenously in an appropriate stock-flow model.[17] Floyd's models are particularly interesting because they allow for the interest rate and capital flows to be determined simultaneously.[18]

3. Risk is specifically introduced as one of the determinants of international capital flows. This is done with the use of the theory of optimal

portfolio selection, but nearly all applications have been to portfolio capital movements and few to direct investment.[19] Rugman (1979) attempts the latter.

4. One element of risk — foreign exchange rate risk — has been applied to direct investment in two important contributions by Aliber.[20] There are different exchange rate risks associated with each currency and it is possible for the international firm to manipulate its overall portfolio in order to minimize expected changes in foreign exchange rates. In his first paper, Aliber implied that there was less risk associated with the American dollar, which gives an advantage to the subsidiaries of an American multinational enterprise compared with a local firm in the host country. In his second contribution, Aliber suggested other advantages enjoyed by subsidiaries, such as their ability to borrow cheaper capital, and the better capitalization rate on their shares.

The Aliber model can be applied to the MNE in Canada. He suggests that direct investment is significantly affected by foreign exchange rate risk. A nation with a strong currency will endow its entrepreneurs with a distinctive advantage over foreign local enterprise when the foreign country has a weaker currency. They can afford to pay more than domestic entrepreneurs for real assets or equity control. For example, an American-owned equity in a Canadian firm becomes an American asset, whereas the equivalent share owned by a Canadian remains a Canadian asset. The former has less risk than the latter, or at least this was the case for most of the 1960s due to the large and diversified nature of the U.S. economy, and the stability of the U.S. dollar.

During this period, the U.S. dollar was at a premium to the Canadian dollar, which, in Aliber's model, will lead to net foreign investment into Canada from the United States. The exchange rate premium enhances the income stream of an American-owned subsidiary in Canada, such a premium being required due to the uncertainty about the future forward exchange rate, and people's different subjective expectations about that exchange rate. In this case, the optimum amount of foreign investment will be explained by a portfolio theory model which incorporates the usual arguments of risk and expected return. In a world with different currency areas there will be different exchange rate risks, and market evaluations of exchange rate risks will cause direct investment to flow into risky countries (like Canada) from countries with stable exchange rates (United States). Aliber's is one of the first models to incorporate financial risk elements into a treatment of direct investment. Whether direct investment is influenced by exchange rate risk is, of course, an empirical question. So far, no known tests of Aliber's model have been made.

Aliber's model may be compared with that of Hymer (1976) who, in his doctoral dissertation at Massachusetts Institute of Technology in 1960, suggests that direct investment is due to monopoly elements; that is, decisions on the real side instead of the financial variables thought significant by Aliber. Similarly in his extension of Hymer's model, Harry Johnson (1970) indicates that the monopoly advantages of a firm with superior technology and knowledge allow it to maximize its return through direct investment. The social demand for knowledge is such that for its efficient use its price should be zero, but private firms are able to restrict supply through a monopoly ownership of this specific knowledge. Foreign-owned subsidiaries are extensions of the domestic monopoly, being mere replicas of the parent company. This implies that numerous foreign-owned firms in Canada must be of an uneconomic size due to the small size of the Canadian market. A policy implication of this might be that the Canadian government should insist on taxing away any excess profit or economic rent earned by foreign-owned subsidiaries in Canada.

In his own contribution to the Kindleberger symposium,[21] Hymer reports on an empirical test of the performance of American-owned firms in Europe. They grow by ploughing back profits and through mergers. From this evidence, Hymer argues that in the long run all multinational corporations will have similar relative market shares, which implies they will grow at the same rate regardless of national growth rates. The only variations will be due to random innovations.

T. J. Parry (1973) provided an elegant survey of the literature up to that date on the structure and role of multinational enterprise. Of particular interest here is his discussion of the motivation of foreign direct investment, a topic which has been surveyed earlier. Parry's explanation of foreign investment is that firms aim to maximize profits and that this proposition can be extended so that multinational firms attempt to maximize global profits. In doing so, they are constrained by a world characterized by market imperfections (such as tariffs, tax barriers, knowledge and information costs, etc.). These market imperfections necessitate a major reworking of conventional neoclassical microtheory which assumes perfect competition.

It is possible that the multinational enterprise is able to reduce these market imperfections. It can do so by introducing similar production operations in various world economies, and by stimulating homogeneous preferences among consumers in different nations. In this way the multinational enterprise is a vehicle of production and consumption decisions of the home economy. The foreign operations of a multinational enterprise permit it to exploit abroad any monopoly advantage it may enjoy in the product or factor markets. Such foreign operations yield economic rents, provided that there are limits to competition from oligopolistic rivals.

It is shown in this book that the motivation of foreign direct investment is at the firm level. The high profile of multinational firms, and their potential power to influence the policies of host nations, has led to a questioning of their economic role alone. The reason for this is that the objective of profit maximization by such firms may potentially conflict with the political objectives of host country governments. In general, the nation states are more concerned with self-sufficiency and domestic problems, whereas the multinational enterprises take a global view of their operations and tend to minimize the nationalist viewpoints of their consumers. This difference in outlook may lead to problems for the multinational firms. For example, in Canada there is evidence of an increase in public opposition to the influence of multinational firms, and even some indications in opinion polls that Canadians are willing to accept a reduction in their standard of living in return for more independence in their economic policies. Chapters 9 and 10 discuss this in greater detail.

This conflict between nation states and multinational firms is, in reality, an extension of the traditional economic theory problem of reconciling equity and efficiency objectives. The governments of nation states naturally place greater emphasis on noneconomic objectives; that is, objectives which do not emphasize efficiency. On the other hand, the firms are solely concerned with efficiency and therefore tend to neglect distribution of income effects. There is no way of reconciling this conflict between equity and efficiency unless the assumptions of general equilibrium theory are made, especially the assumption that there can be a costless tax-subsidy scheme to deal with income distribution problems. As economic theory itself has not yet solved this conflict, it is not surprising that there is no evidence of any solution to the equity versus efficiency debate in the subfield of international investment.

INTERNALIZATION AS A GENERAL THEORY OF FDI

Several of the concepts of the determinants of foreign investment need to be rethought once the theory of internalization is accepted as a general theory of foreign direct investment (FDI) as it is in this book. Internalization serves to unify and integrate many of the existing areas of the field. This common pattern emerges once attention is directed towards the imperfect nature of international good and financial markets.

The essence of the internalization theory is the recognition of market imperfections which prevent the efficient operation of international trade and investment. It shows that the multinational enterprise developed in response to exogenous government-induced regulations and controls, which have destroyed the reasons for free trade and private foreign investment. The process of internalization permits the MNE to overcome the externalities resulting from such regulations. In addition, the MNE has been an efficient response to nongovernment market failure in areas such as information and knowledge.

In his seminal article, Coase (1937) showed that a domestic corporation may bypass the regular market and use internal prices to overcome the excessive transactions costs of an outside market. Hymer (1976) applies the theory of industrial organization to explain the MNE. The first explicit treatment of the relationship between market imperfections and internalization is in Buckley and Casson (1976). There is also an excellent synthesis of the literature on the MNE, built around the concept of internalization, in Dunning (1977). The work of Buckley and Casson is reviewed in Giddy (1978). A more rigorous treatment of internalization appears in Casson (1979), while Rugman (1980a) explores the role of this theory for FDI.

The next chapter explains the logical development of the theory of internalization, while the final chapter of Part I develops a model of FDI and applies the internalization concept in a Canadian context. It is a central objective of this book to integrate the basic material of this chapter on the theory of FDI into a general theory of the MNE. It will be seen in the next two chapters, and in the ensuing empirical and policy sections, that the theory of internalization is such a general theory.

ENDNOTES

1. There is a brief review of some of the more important contributions below. For references and an analysis of the recent literature on both direct and portfolio investment, see E. Spitaller, "A Survey of Recent Quantitative Studies of Long Term Capital Movements," *IMF Staff Papers* (March 1971).
2. A. E. Scaperlanda, "Foreign Investment in Canada," unpublished address to the Society of Government Economists, Toronto, Ontario, 1972; see also, Anthony E. Scaperlanda and Lawrence Jay Mauer, "The Impact of Controls on United States Direct Foreign Investment in the European Economic Community," *Southern Economic Journal* (January 1973), and their related articles on "The Determinants of U.S. Direct Investment in the E.E.C.," *American Economic Review* (September 1969):558–568 (June 1971):509–510, and (September 1972).
3. Sung Y. Kwack, "A Model of U.S. Direct Investment Abroad: A Neoclassical Approach," *Western Economic Journal* (December 1972).
4. M. J. Prachowny, "Direct Investment and the Balance of Payments of the U.S.: A Portfolio Approach," in F. Machlup et al., eds., *International Mobil-*

ity and Movement of Capital (New York: National Bureau of Economic Research, 1972).

5. G. V. Stevens, "Fixed Investment Expenditure of Foreign Manufacturing Affiliates of U.S. Firms," *Yale Economic Essays* 9 (Spring 1969).

6. J. David Richardson, "On 'Going Abroad': The Firm's Initial Investment Decision," *Quarterly Journal of Economics and Business* 11 (1972).

7. T. Horst, "The Industrial Composition of U.S. Exports and Subsidiary Sales to the Canadian Market," *American Economic Review* (March 1972).

8. Stephen Hymer, "The International Operations of National Firms: A Study of Direct Investment," Ph.D. dissertation, M.I.T. 1960; and Harry G. Johnson, "The Efficiency and Welfare Implications of the International Corporation," in C. P. Kindleberger, ed., *'The International Corporation,'* (Cambridge, Mass.: M.I.T. Press, 1970).

9. A. E. Scaperlanda and L. J. Mauer, "The Determinants of U.S. Direct Investment in the E.E.C.," *American Economic Review* (September 1969); V. N. Bandera and J. T. White, "U.S. Direct Investment and Domestic Markets in Europe," *Economica Internazionale* (1968):117–133; and Richard E. Caves, "International Corporations: The Industrial Economics of Foreign Investment," *Economica* (February 1971).

10. L. Copithorne, "International Corporate Transfer Prices and Government Policy," *Canadian Journal of Economics* (August 1971).

11. Louis T. Wells and John M. Stopford, *Managing the Multinational Enterprise* (New York: Basic Books, 1972).

12. Many of these six reasons are interdependent, and have been reasonably integrated in the summary volume by Raymond Vernon, *Sovereignty at Bay* (New York: Basic Books, 1971).

13. John H. Dunning, ed., *The Multinational Enterprise* (New York: Praeger, 1972).

14. John K. Galbraith, *The New Industrial State* (London and Boston: Houghton Mifflin, 1967).

15. Richard E. Caves and Grant L. Reuber, *Capital Transfers and Economic Policy: Canada 1951-1962* (Boston: Harvard University Press, 1971). Robert M. Dunn, Jr., *Canada's Experience with Fixed and Flexible Exchange Rates in a North American Capital Market* (Montreal and Washington D.C.: Canadian-American Committee, 1971). Paul Wonnacott, *The Floating Canadian Dollar: Exchange Flexibility and Monetary Independence* (Washington D.C.: American Enterprise Institute, 1972). C. E. Lee, "A Stock Adjustment Analysis of Capital Movements: The United States-Canadian Case," *Journal of Political Economy* (July 1969).

16. Michael G. Porter, "Interest Rate Differentials Interpreted as Behaviour Towards Exchange Rate Expectations," Ph.D. thesis, Stanford University, 1971. Michael G. Porter, "A Theoretical and Empirical Framework for Analysing the Term Structure of Exchange Rate Expectations," *I.M.F. Staff Papers* (November 1971).

17. William H. Branson, *Financial Capital Flows in the U.S. Balance of Payments* (Amsterdam: North-Holland, 1968). Martin F. J. Prachowny, *A Structural Model of the U.S. Balance of Payments* (Amsterdam: North-Holland 1969).

18. J. E. Floyd, "International Capital Movements and Monetary Equilibrium," *American Economic Review* (September 1969). J. E. Floyd, "Monetary and Fiscal Policy in a World of Capital Mobility," *Review of Economic Studies* (1969).

19. Herbert G. Grubel, "Internationally Diversified Portfolios: Welfare Gains and Capital Flows," *American Economic Review* (December 1968). Norman C. Miller and Marina V. N. Whitman, "A Mean-Variance Analysis of United States Long-Term Portfolio Foreign Investment," *Quarterly Journal of Economics* 84 (May 1970):175-196. Haim Levy and Marshall Sarnat, "International Diversification of Investment Portfolios," *American Economic Review* (September 1970):668-675. Herbert G. Grubel and Kenneth Fadner, "The Interdependence of International Equity Markets," *Journal of Finance* (March 1971).

20. Robert Z. Aliber, "A Theory of Direct Foreign Investment," in Charles P. Kindleberger, ed., *The International Corporation* (Cambridge, Mass.: M.I.T. Press, 1970). Robert Z. Aliber, "The Multinational Enterprise in a Multiple Currency World," in John H. Dunning, ed., *The Multinational Enterprise* (New York: Praeger, 1972).

21. Charles P. Kindleberger, ed., *The International Corporation* (Cambridge, Mass.: M.I.T. Press, 1970).

3 TOWARDS A THEORY OF THE MULTINATIONAL ENTERPRISE

METHODOLOGY, ASSUMPTIONS, AND DEFINITIONS

The construction of a theory that captures the essential characteristics of the multinational enterprise (MNE) is a difficult task. Any such theory is bound to be a simplified abstraction of the complex interrelationships and decisions undertaken by the MNE. As an abstraction, the theory cannot hope to describe accurately and precisely every single detail of the MNE, yet it should be able to isolate the major variables which determine multinational activity and to predict in a general fashion how the MNE will respond to changes in the parameters of its environment.

Given that the environment of the MNE is a mixture of cultural, political and economic elements, it is necessary to state that these noneconomic elements are not considered explicitly in this analysis. Instead, an attempt is made to produce a theory of the MNE based on economic variables such as costs, prices, and technology where these are determined either within a regular market or are indeterminate under a situation of market failure. The focus on economic variables is broad enough to construct a satisfactory theory of the MNE since it permits the inclusion of managerial behavior, marketing strategy, and other activities inasmuch as these affect the economic and/or financial performance of the MNE. Any model requires a set of assumptions. The basic one made here is that economic variables alone can be used to build a powerful, predictive theory of the MNE.

Why does the MNE engage in international production? An MNE is defined as a firm with subsidiaries in six or more nations (Vernon 1971), one with income-generating activities in more than one nation (Dunning 1971, 1973), or one with a ratio of foreign to total operations above some arbitrary percentage (Bruck and Lees 1968; Rugman 1975). All of these definitions emphasize the essential ingredient in the mixture of the overall MNE process; namely that the corporation engages in foreign production and is thereby active in the goods and factor markets of many nations, rather than in one, as would be the case with a purely uninational firm or one that engages in free trade to supply foreign markets.[1]

Other definitions of the MNE focus on considerations such as the geocentric attitudes of their management team (Perlmutter 1969), or the transnational holding of equity capital (Robock et al. 1977). These definitions make it hard to distinguish between domestic and international enterprises or among purely trading, distributional, or producing activities. There is nothing wrong with such definitions, but they are of little use in building a theory of the MNE that will concentrate on economic questions. Again, the point can be made that the complex nature of the MNE requires that some simplifying assumptions are necessary. Having already assumed that economic variables are to be used in the theory, it is clearly necessary to focus attention upon the reasons for the formation and expansion of overseas subsidiaries of the MNE. This requires a theory of why international production takes place rather than exporting, licensing, or domestic production. For a similar argument developed in much more detail, see Dunning (1973).

The definition of the MNE as an international producer also permits treatment of Foreign Direct Investment (FDI). In fact, the MNE and FDI are the same when viewed in this manner. Hereafter these terms are used interchangeably, so the model of the MNE is also a model of FDI. Given that FDI involves control by the investors over the use of their funds, it is convenient to regard the MNE as a vehicle for FDI. The decisions about multinational activity need to be explained at the firm level, but these individual firm decisions sum up to explain the aggregate amount of FDI. The data on FDI are usually available at industry level, but can be used in studies of the MNE since some industrial sectors are clearly dominated by MNEs while others are not. The model advanced here can be tested using either FDI data or firm level data on the profits and financial valuation of the shares of MNEs.

WHY INTERNATIONAL TRADE?

To explain why international production takes place (why there is an MNE), it is first necessary to examine a world of free trade. If the conditions for free trade exist, then there is no point in international production — the latter only occurs when these conditions are removed. The rationale for free trade, as explained in any textbook on international economics, is that there is a difference between the foreign and domestic relative goods price ratio, in a model with two factors, two goods, and two nations.

In the simple Heckscher-Ohlin world of the textbooks, a sufficient reason for this price differential is the existence of nonidentical supplies of factor endowments within the nations. In fact, this difference in factor endowments (where these can be classified into broad groupings such as labor, land or resources, capital and technology) is the only relationship required to generate trade. Thus, the nations can have identical production functions, identical tastes, and be identical in every other respect, but there will still be available a welfare gain from trade compared to autarky. The Heckscher-Ohlin model assumes perfect goods and factor markets, and essentially sets all other conditions equal to zero. This means that items such as tariffs, quotas, taxes, and transport costs are all assumed to be zero and that scale economies are ignored. Thus, none of these items can affect the ratio of foreign to domestic prices and thereby determine trade patterns.

The simple Heckscher-Ohlin world is, however, not the only model of trade, and a variety of other trade economists have relaxed these conditions with interesting results. It has been demonstrated by Melvin (1969, 1970), for example, that increasing returns to scale is a reason for trade, or that taxes (but not transport costs) can also generate trade. Similarly, differences in tastes, or distortions such as a monopoly, will also lead to trade. The basic reason is that each of these items generates a differential in the ratio of foreign to domestic prices, in the same way that different factor endowments do in the basic Heckscher-Ohlin framework.

The manner in which these conditions are modeled affects the implication of gains from trade but, in general, serves to make trade theory fairly robust since there are clearly many determinants of trade. The predictions of trade theory in explaining the direction of trade, the welfare gains from trade compared to restricted trade, and the overall efficiency of a trading economy are of great importance in acting as a basis for the theory of FDI. Only if the theoretical reasons for free trade do not hold, is it necessary to have a model of the MNE. Thus free trade is seen to be the converse of FDI.

WHY INTERNATIONAL PRODUCTION?

In the Ricardian model of comparative advantage, it is assumed that factors of production are fully mobile within a nation but immobile between countries. This assumption carries over to the Heckscher-Ohlin model and most other theories of free trade. It makes comparative advantage into an international theory, for without it regional comparative advantage within a nation would determine domestic trade in the same manner as foreign trade.

In a similar fashion, some extra assumptions are required to build up a theory of international location or international production. Location theory suggests that the spatial allocation of plants and subsidiaries is determined by the costs of factor inputs in various regions together with the transport costs involved in linking the production process with the firm's marketing strategy. Yet to advance location economics from a purely domestic theory to an international one, an extra element is required. This will distinguish the location of a uninational or exporting firm from that of an MNE. The extra element is that the MNE has a firm specific advantage. Since a firm specific advantage is the reason for internalization by the MNE, a model that explains why international production takes place will also explain why international location takes place. For support of this point, see Dunning (1977), Buckley and Casson (1976), and Casson (1979).

International production takes place once the MNE has secured a firm specific advantage. As Hymer (1976) first demonstrated in his 1960 doctoral dissertation, and Caves (1971) confirmed, these advantages can be one or more of several types: scale economies, managerial expertise, a technological or knowledge advantage, monopoly, product differentiation, and financial strength, where this includes the benefits of international diversification (see Rugman 1979). Such firm specific advantages encourage the MNE to seek worldwide markets through the process of FDI, rather than by licensing. The latter method is inferior to production by wholly controlled subsidiaries since it nullifies the relevant advantage.

Licensing will dissipate the information monopoly of an MNE that has incurred a private cost in funding research and development into a new technology, which is not practical to defend by use of a patent. In this case, property rights are assigned to the MNE in order to overcome the externality associated with the production of knowledge. A firm specific advantage in the production, distribution, or marketing of a product which embodies the new knowledge enables the MNE to appropriate a fair return for its investment. Only at a later stage in the "technology cycle," will it pay the MNE to license use of what by then is a "standardized" technology. For a formal development of this last point, see Magee (1977).

WHY INTERNALIZATION?

The classic example of a market imperfection leading to the creation of a firm specific advantage is that of knowledge. The creation of knowledge involves an expenditure on research and development, or other outlays which introduce innovations into the production or marketing process of a firm. These expenditures are private costs since the scientists, researchers, and members of the production or management team have to be compensated for their labors. Yet once a genuine research discovery is made, it becomes a public good. A public good is defined as a good for which consumption by one party does not reduce the consumption of others.

Knowledge is a public good in this theoretical sense because it can be applied by any person or organization to a specific problem without destroying the ability to apply the knowledge to another use. Public goods should be contrasted with the private goods and services that are more familiar in trade and investment theory. The consumption of a private good, such as an apple or cigarette, by one person destroys the consumption of another. Even with a good such as an automobile, which has several characteristics in its use, the consumption of it by one person, at any point in time, prevents its use by another party. Similarly, when one person is consulting a physician, another is denied the privilege. In contrast, the consumption of television signals by one person does not deny consumption to others, so these signals are public goods. In the context of this book, an invention, new idea, or other discovery, once made, is a public good.

A private good can be priced in a market according to the conditions of aggregate supply and demand for the product, or if the market is monopolized through the discriminatory pricing of the monopolist. A public good cannot be priced by the market. Indeed, the price of a public good is zero. Only if there is some intervention in the market, or if property rights are assigned, is it possible to overcome such a case of market failure. For example, a government agency can provide the services of a public good and determine the efficient amount to supply by using marginal cost pricing, or it can use some other method to calculate the net social benefit of the good. Alternatively, property rights can be assigned, either through a patent, a political edict, or through the intervention of a firm or organization, which acts as sole supplier of the product. It is to this last solution to the externality that the MNE is particularly suited.

Knowledge is also an intermediate product, so its pricing must take place through the monopolization of a final good or service. A firm can overcome the missing regular market for knowledge by internalization. The internal market of a firm permits production of final products which uses knowledge as an intermediate input, and the monopoly use of the knowledge advantage permits the firm to appropriate a return for its initial outlays on research generation. While any firm with a monopoly in information can service the domestic market, or in a situation of free trade the world market, only the MNE is in practice able to overcome the barriers to free trade that exist today.

WHY THE MNE?

The role of the MNE as an agency for the internalization of markets arises since it is necessary to exploit, on a worldwide basis, the production of the good using the knowledge advantage. The MNE is a superior device to other potential solutions such as licensing or patents since it is able to regulate and monitor the use of its information advantage. With licensing there is a risk of dissemination of the information monopoly, especially at the early stages of a research or technological advance. Similarly, international patent law does not permit the effective transmission of one national patent to another jurisdiction. The MNE can exploit its property rights to knowledge by either exporting to nations that do not impose barriers to trade, or by setting up subsidiaries in nations that do. Its internal cost conditions determine the provision of, and profit from, the supply of the good using the information. Servicing of foreign markets depends on the relative costs of exporting versus FDI versus licensing.

The MNE needs a closed market to service demand for the product using the new information since this is frequently the only practical method of financing production. The internal organization of an MNE permits *de facto* transfer prices to be charged. These transfer prices are only means to an end — the production of goods that embody the knowledge. It can be seen that the process of internalization is an inevitable response to the externality in the generation of knowledge. The MNE is the most suitable vehicle for appropriation of the private costs of research, since its internal costs are less than for any alternative method and only through international production can a firm overcome trade barriers and service the world market.

The MNE will also typically engage in price discrimination. Charging different prices for a product to different users is facilitated by the establishment of overseas subsidiaries. This process of FDI permits the MNE to segment national markets and provides additional information on the local demand curves for the products of the MNE. One problem with exporting to supply foreign markets is that a uniform world price is likely to be established, if not at the firm's volition, then to satisfy the requirements of consumers and governments in other nations. For example, many nations have anti-dumping laws under which the importing nation attempts to calculate if the good sold to them is priced below the costs of production. To avoid such nontariff barriers to trade, an MNE is better off by servicing foreign markets through subsidiary production.

The very success of MNEs in foreign production and sales has recently led to the establishment of agencies in host nations which are charged with the task of monitoring new FDI to see if it provides net social benefits to the host nation. These agencies ignore the process of internalization and instead attempt to evaluate the impact of the MNE in various economic and social areas. Attempts to unbundle the package of technology which the MNE brings to the host nation are doomed to failure if they proceed in this partial and self-contradictory manner.

The social benefits and costs of FDI cannot be evaluated in any precise or meaningful fashion since the technique of benefit cost analysis, being derived from the theoretical welfare economics of a general equilibrium system, does not lend itself readily to the measurement of intangible political goals such as independence and sovereignty. It would be more efficient for host nations to recognize the concept of internalization and accept the economic benefits of FDI in its own right. The MNE is a complex organization which has developed in response to the practical difficulty of servicing world markets with a new technology.

CONCLUSIONS AND IMPLICATIONS

This chapter presented a modern theory of foreign direct investment. To understand why FDI takes place, it is useful, and probably necessary, to examine the two basic alternatives to FDI in servicing foreign markets: exporting and licensing.

Exporting is the preferred alternative when no substantial barriers to free trade exist. Firms can then supply foreign markets from their domestic production bases and the location of economic activity will be determined according to the principles of comparative advantage. If world markets are denied to firms once nations impose tariff and nontariff barriers to trade, then such firms may have to turn to FDI. Viewed in this light, FDI is an alternative to exporting.

FDI is made necessary by the barriers to free trade that exist in the real world and restrict access to foreign markets. By engaging in foreign production (that is FDI), a firm can circumvent barriers to imports imposed by host nations, since production by its foreign affiliate escapes customs duty and other trade restrictions. The multinational enterprise will engage in international production for a variety of reasons, but ultimately all of these collapse into a single calculation which shows that FDI is a better way of servicing foreign markets than either exporting or licensing, given the constraints on the latter two alternatives. The main constraints on exporting are trade and other barriers, but the constraints on licensing are more subtle and require an analysis of the concept of internalization.

Licensing is a feasible method of servicing foreign markets once the firm with a knowledge, technological, or other advantage is assured of receiving a sufficient return for the use of its internal advantage. In practice, this is a difficult condition to satisfy. There are ever present dangers of the firm's information monopoly being compromised by the licensee. Once the firm's knowledge advantage is lost, it becomes impossible for the firm to receive a fair return for its previous investment in research and development. It is to prevent this potential knowledge dissipation through licensing that the MNE will, in general, always prefer to retain direct control over the use of this intermediate product rather than to license it. More generally, licensing takes place when the potential revenues exceed the costs of policing the use of the license plus the discounted risk of dissipation of the firm specific advantage.

The major qualification to this analysis arises once consideration is given to the possibility of segmenting markets. Then the MNE could use licensing as a viable alternative to FDI without the fear of knowledge dissipation. The MNE will always favor price discrimination as a method of maximizing returns on the sale of the good which uses intensively its knowledge advantage. If foreign markets are fully segmented, the MNE is encouraged to license its technology, since it does not have to worry about the elimination of its information monopoly by the subsequent sublicensing of its licensees. Further, the assumption of fully segmented foreign markets permits the MNE to use discriminatory charging for licenses.

In practice licensing is unlikely to be a viable option. Foreign markets are not perfectly segmented, so there is always a risk of knowledge dissipation by licensing. It will be very difficult to set an appropriate price for the license, one which meters the use of the knowledge advantage. There is too much uncertainty in licensing. The preferred method of servicing foreign markets is likely to be by FDI where control over the technological advantage is secure.

In conclusion, this chapter has explored some of the conditions under which foreign markets can be serviced by a firm endowed with a technological, knowledge, or some other type of significant advantage. The three options open to the firm in theory are to export, to engage in FDI, or to license. In general, exporting takes place when there are no barriers to free trade and FDI takes place when there are such barriers.

Furthermore, the modern theory of FDI places emphasis on the firm specific advantages enjoyed by the MNE, and it implies that such advantages are best exploited via foreign production rather than by either exporting or licensing. The condition for successful licensing, namely that foreign markets are fully segmented and that dissipation can be avoided, are unlikely to be realized in practice, so this is not a viable option. Therefore, the theory of FDI is really a theory of the MNE. In turn, the firm specific advantages of the MNE are best explained by the new concept of internalization.

Further research is required before a full theory of the MNE can be developed and used in practical applications. This research should probably focus on the theoretical and empirical conditions that determine either exporting, FDI, or licensing as the optimal method for servicing foreign markets. It should also examine how such conditions may vary over time. Until such an integrated model of foreign trade, investment, and licensing is available, it is necessary to speculate about the MNE along the lines of this book. The theory of the MNE is basically a theory of FDI, and this interrelationship is explained by the process of internalization.

APPENDIX

THE ORIGINS OF INTERNALIZATION

In 1937 Ronald Coase developed a model in which intrafirm transactions replaced market transactions. He found that profit-maximizing firms create an internal market and they operate it by administrative decisions when this is more efficient than using a regular market. Frequently there is no such market in any case, as with the problems of pricing intermediate products or public goods.

It is only in recent years that the fundamental insight of Coase has been applied in an international context. The work of Buckley and Casson (1976) and Dunning (1977) has placed internalization at the center of the modern theory of the multinational enterprise. These authors are the first to consider explicitly the use of the internal markets by the MNE as an explanation of the reasons for foreign direct investment. In an earlier work, Stephen Hymer (1976) has applied industrial organization theory to the MNE, but his treatment of internalization as the central reason for FDI is implicit rather than explicit. The emphasis in his 1960 dissertation is on the existence of market imperfections as an explanation of FDI. The MNE is able to set up an internal market to bypass imperfect markets.[2]

The story about the delayed publication of Hymer's seminal work is probably familiar to most specialists in international business. As reported in his laudatory introduction, Professor Kindleberger recommended Hymer's doctoral dissertation for publication by the M.I.T. Press in 1960. The publication committee of the Department of Economics at M.I.T. rejected publication of the thesis, one of the reasons being that "the argument was too simple and straightforward." Hymer apparently did not bother to have the thesis chapters submitted for journal publication, and so it was left to Kindleberger to advertise the thesis in his textbook on international economics. (Professor Kindleberger is too modest to mention that his own first rate book on *American Business Abroad* is a brilliant summary and extension of Hymer's theoretical work). In any case, the 1960 Hymer thesis became a basic reference in all subsequent work on the multinational enterprise, but one which many readers found hard to acquire. Its recent publication is to be welcomed, and it is a belated recognition by M.I.T. of the importance of Hymer's thesis.

The seminal nature of the book lies in its now classic statement of the theory of foreign direct investment. The modern theory of FDI with its emphasis on market imperfections and the concept of internalization is clearly stated by Hymer. He explains that the MNE uses its international operations either to remove competition, or to exploit some advantage due to an imperfect market — a situation that is preferable to licensing from the viewpoint of the MNE. He states that the MNE "is a practical institutional device which substitutes for the market. The firm internalizes or supersedes the market" (p. 48). It is the imperfect market "which leads the possessor of the advantage to choose to supersede the market for his advantage" (p. 49). Hymer believes that the MNE is an organization that allows for "centralized decision making" and that "whether or not this will occur depends mainly on whether the markets are perfect" (p. 37). Hymer emphasizes that the basis for the theory of international operations by the MNE is its "motivation to separate markets and prevent competition between units . . . " (p. 67). He repeats "that many of the reasons for choosing not to license arose from the imperfect nature of the market for the advantage. These imperfections prevented the appropriation of all the returns to the advantage" (p. 87). The importance of these quotations cannot be over-emphasized. They have led to the subsequent theoretical expositions of FDI by Caves (1971), Kindleberger (1969), Johnson (1970), Buckley and Casson (1976), Magee (1977), and others.

In another area, Hymer provides the genesis of the concept of international diversification. He suggests "that profits in one country may be negatively correlated with profits of another country . . . " (p. 94), and that "an investor may be able to achieve greater stability in his profits by diversifying his portfolio and investing part in each country. This investment may be undertaken by shareholders of the firm, and not the firm itself . . . " (p. 95). Hymer does not go on to make the point that the degree of segmentation of world capital markets and the existence of barriers to international portfolio diversification are crucial problems facing an individual investor and that these barriers can be overcome by investing in the MNE. Neither does he attempt any empirical work to support the concept of portfolio diversification. In fact, he does not seem to grasp the vital distinction between international diversification and the product diversification he discussed earlier. Further, his discussion of cross-investments in his Chapter Four is in error, since he does not discuss risk. I have the impression that Hymer did not really understand the full implications of his statement on portfolio diversification, and indeed these have only become clear with the subsequent development of modern finance theory.

Hymer was the first economist to apply the theory of industrial organization to the international sector and FDI. The market advantages of the MNE result from four possible factors: (1) lower cost in acquiring factors of production, (2) control or special knowledge of the process of production, (3) better marketing and distributional facilities, (4) a differentiated product. It is also made clear in his Chapter Five that an additional market advantage accrues to the MNE in the money markets, since it is better able to finance itself and may be a better credit risk than rival, domestic firms. Hymer thinks that nearly half of the capital for FDI is raised in the host nations when subsidiaries of the MNE are given loans or make equity issues. This phenomenon has been especially irritating to Canadians concerned about the almost total foreign control of their resources and manufacturing industries. It has led nationalists in many countries to complain that the process of FDI involves the host nation in financing its own sell out. Hymer attempts some very rough calculations of the net benefits of FDI and concludes that "international operations from 1946 to 1958 have provided a net gain of foreign exchange for the United States" (p. 205). However, he does not stray into the area of political economy by attempting to evaluate social and political factors — an omission which he corrected in his later academic career.

The weakest parts of the book are the empirical sections. Hymer's Chapter Four uses secondary sources and presents very elementary tables. No econometric work of any sort is attempted. Hymer relies very heavily on work done by Professor John Dunning. In fact, Dunning is quoted so often, both in the theoretical and empirical sections, that one wonders how far Hymer would have gone had Dunning's 1958 work not been available. The other major sources used by Hymer are Brecher and Reisman on Canada, Phelps on Latin America, and Southard on Western Europe. Virtually all of the seventy pages of the "empirical" Chapter Four reproduce tables and statistics from these sources. Yet the evidence chosen by Hymer supports his theoretical work very well and he did manage to "put it all together" for the first time. Although the departmental committee at M.I.T. was probably correct in rejecting publication on the grounds of inferior empirical work, we now know, with the benefit of hindsight, that some latitude should be allowed to pioneers. The brilliant theoretical conception of Hymer has become clearer with the passage of time.

ENDNOTES

1. Most scholars in the field of international business writing about the theory of foreign direct investment define an MNE as either: (1) having subsidiaries in six or more nations, or (2) having a ratio of foreign (F) to total (T) operations (i.e., sales, employees, etc.) greater than some arbitrary number, for example, (F/T) 10 or (F/T) 25, etc. Vernon (1971) and Dunning (1973) use the first method; while Bruck and Lees (1968), the U.N. studies (1963, 1978), and Rugman (1976) use the second. The essence of being multinational is international *production*. Otherwise, foreign markets could be serviced by exports and trade theory would suffice to explain world supply and consumption patterns.

   The Perlmutter (1969) model is derived from behavioral theory and management science rather than economics. Not surprisingly, it does not emphasize that the unique aspect of being multinational is international production, as it should. Instead, the definitions of firms as ethnocentric (home oriented), polycentric (host oriented), or geocentric (worldwide oriented) describes a management philosophy only. Yet managers need to be evaluated on their performance rather than their attitudes, since the latter are unimportant in themselves. For example, while an ethnocentric firm is clearly nonmultinational, either a polycentric or a geocentric firm could have many foreign subsidiaries and thus qualify as a multinational on the grounds of international production. A distinction between these latter two groups is of little value in defining multinationality.

2. The remainder of this section was first published in the *Journal of International Business Studies* 9 (Fall 1978):103–104. Reprinted with permission.

4 A THEORY OF THE MULTINATIONAL ENTERPRISE IN A CANADIAN CONTEXT

INTRODUCTION

This chapter explores the conditions under which foreign markets are serviced by a multinational enterprise (MNE) in one of three ways: international trade, foreign direct investment (FDI), or licensing. This extension of Chapters 2 and 3 builds upon previous work by Horst (1974), Hirsch (1976), and Casson (1979). It is assumed that the MNE has a monopolistic advantage in the production and marketing of a knowledge intensive good. The MNE has to determine an appropriate strategy to service both home and foreign markets in order to maximize profits. The model that is developed is applied to the special conditions of Canada in the final section.

THE NEW GENERAL THEORY OF FDI

There are two major elements in this theory of the MNE. First, I focus on the assumed firm specific advantages possessed by an MNE which encourage it to service world markets by exporting in a situation of free trade, or by either FDI or licensing in a situation of restricted trade. The most interesting example of a firm specific advantage is when the MNE has a monopoly in the use of knowledge or some other type of technological information. This externality can be internalized by the MNE as explained in the new general theory of FDI, For more information, see Rugman (1979) and Chapters 2 and 3 of this text.

The research expenditures incurred by the MNE as it produces knowledge are a private cost, yet once a research discovery is made it takes on the characteristics of a public good. The externality of a public good, defined as a good where consumption by one person does not deny identical consumption by another, arises when a regular market is unable to price the good. In fact, since the knowledge is potentially available to all consumers, once it has been discovered, the social price should be zero. Yet the firm has incurred a private cost in its manufacture. Thus, the firm faces an appropriability problem. It can attempt to protect its knowledge advantage through a patent or by using the knowledge as an intermediate input into the production or marketing process of the firm. In either case, the problem of knowledge as a public good is overcome by assignment of property rights. The MNE is able to internalize an externality and set a price for knowledge by the denial of its unlimited consumption.

Second, I make use of the idea that technology is not homogeneous over time to introduce some dynamics into the choice between FDI and licensing. The notion of a technology cycle over time has been introduced into the theory of FDI by Magee (1977), which is itself an extension of Johnson (1970). Here I argue that the technology cycle encourages the MNE to set up foreign subsidiaries in the early life of the technology, since the process of internalization will prevent loss of its information advantage to potential rivals, while only at a much later stage is the MNE willing to license the technology. Then there is less to lose by dissipation of its knowledge advantage since most of the rent from the information monopoly will have been appropriated.

The MNE is also likely to engage in price discrimination, and will prefer to operate in segmented foreign markets whenever possible in order to maximize profits on its firm specific advantage. In general, production by overseas wholly-controlled subsidiaries achieves the task of servicing separate foreign markets and increases the opportunity for the MNE to use non-uniform pricing. Licensing will only be of similar value to the MNE when foreign markets are fully segmented for exogenous reasons, such as capital controls or prohibitive taxes on international direct investment. Such controls or taxes will make it impossible for the MNE to appropriate a rent in the use of its knowledge advantage which is embodied in the MNE itself as it undertakes FDI. Once the rent has been extracted, however, any extra foreign sales, or fees for licences, are an additional benefit to the MNE and demands for licenses are then more likely to be accomodated. This occurs when the product of the MNE has become standardized; that is, where there are no more rents to be realized.

The authoritative article by Caves (1971) on industry specific foreign direct investment in an oligopolistic structure deals with licensing in but one brief paragraph. He argues that smaller firms have an incentive to engage in licensing and that a technological advantage is a one-shot affair which is easily transferred by the MNE. I demonstrate here that it is difficult for the MNE to appropriate a return on investment in knowledge unless it engages in FDI, since a premature licensing agreement will dissipate its information advantage. This principle applies as much to small as to large MNEs. The risk of dissipation is particularly strong if markets for knowledge are integrated.

Casson's work (1979) is the first significant analytical treatment of the internalization of knowledge by an MNE. He shows that the MNE is able to exploit its proprietary information in an efficient manner through the use of its internal market, a point first explored in Buckley and Casson (1976), when they built upon the seminal work of Coase (1937) on the theory of the firm. Conceived of in a domestic context, Coase showed that a firm can use administrative fiat to organize production in situations when high transactions costs either prevent a regular market from doing so, or make it inefficient to do so. The MNE is also likely to use price discrimination (charging a nonuniform price to consumers), in order to maximize its rent on the information monopoly it has created. Magee (1977) makes the same points, but he does so in terms of a technology cycle of three stages: invention, innovation, and standardization of the technology. He also argues that there is a high correlation between new technology and highly concentrated industry structures. The technology advantage is greatest in its early stages and is exploited through the MNE.

To summarize, the contribution of this chapter is its extension of the static models of Horst (1974) and Hirsch (1976) into a temporal dimension and the specific consideration of licensing as a third option for the MNE to evaluate as it determines the optimal strategy for servicing foreign markets. The chapter also uses the internalization of markets explanation of FDI advanced by Buckley and Casson (1976), which was shown to be a general theory of FDI in Chapters 2 and 3. Finally, the appropriability problem raised by Magee (1977) and Casson (1979) is reconciled with the concept of internalization by focusing attention on the firm's choice between the three possible methods of servicing foreign markets over time. The optimal strategy for the MNE may change over from exporting to FDI to licensing in a regular and predictable fashion. If this occurs, then the MNE will appropriate all the possible rents available from its firm specific advantage in technical knowledge. In so doing, the MNE will be operating in an efficient manner.

In the next section, the model of Hirsch (1976) is reviewed and extended to incorporate the third option of licensing. Then a more general model is developed, along slightly different lines from Hirsch. The relevant literature is not discussed here in any more detail since there are excellent surveys of the theory of FDI and the role of internalization available elsewhere, for example in Hood and Young (1979), Brown (1976), Buckley and Casson (1976), Casson (1979), and Dunning (1977). The final section applies the new model to the Canadian situation. An earlier attempt to apply Coasian analysis to the theory of the MNE, with reference to Canada, was made by McManus (1972).

AN EXTENDED MODEL OF INTERNATIONAL TRADE, INVESTMENT, AND LICENSING

In an interesting paper, Hirsch (1976) developed a model of international trade and production. In it he explores the conditions required for exporting or foreign direct investment by a firm endowed with a firm specific knowledge advantage, K. Although not stated explicitly, the model treats K as an intermediate product which is internalized in the structure of the multinational enterprise. Here I extend the model in two ways and consider explicitly the conditions for licensing, an important addition to the options of exporting or FDI considered by Hirsch.

The two areas ignored by Hirsch are: first, the dynamic nature of technology, that is, the changing conditions under which the MNE can appropriate its firm specific advantage in K; second, the possibility of licensing as opposed to exporting or FDI. I find this third option — licensing — to be viable at the end of the firm's technology cycle rather than at an early stage of foreign activity, as is sometimes argued in the literature on international business.

The model assumes two nations, H and B, and a knowledge-intensive firm, F, which is based in H (the home nation). Firm F has to determine how to service B (the foreign nation's market). Notation:

K is a firm specific knowledge asset of Firm F, which is located in Country H (the home nation). K is a sunk cost to F, but a real cost to a potential rival firm in Country B (the foreign or host nation). K can be obtained by firms in Country B through investment in research, or (in theory) by paying an appropriate license fee — if Firm F is ever willing to license (an unlikely event in practice due to the difficulty of finding the correct fee for this intangible intermediate product).

M is the export marketing cost differential, i.e., basically transport costs, insurance, and information costs of servicing a foreign market (Country B) by exports (from Country H).

A is the additional costs of foreign operations compared to domestic ones; these costs affect subsidiary production and sales; they are costs of control, coordination, and direction in a foreign cultural environment ($A = C$ in Hirsch).

P is the normal total costs of production of the good made by Firm F. Costs are P_H in Country H and P_B in Country B.

Note: K, M, A, and P are all expressed in present value terms; that is, these are the present values of costs incurred over a time horizon t-T for a specific investment project, where r is a discount rate. Therefore we have these definitional relationships:

$$K = \sum_{t}^{T} \frac{K_t}{(1 + r)^t};$$

$$M = \sum_{t}^{T} \frac{M_t}{(1 + r)^t};$$

$$A = \sum_{t}^{T} \frac{A_t}{(1 + r)^t};$$

$$P = \sum_{t}^{T} \frac{P_t}{(1 + r)^t};$$

Case 1

Assume $K + M + A = 0$, then Firm F exports to Country B if $P_H < P_B$

Assume $K + A = 0$, $M > 0$, then Firm F still exports if $P_H + M < P_B$.

Case 2

Assume K, M, A are all > 0.

Trade:

Firm F will *export* to Country B if:

$$P_H + M < P_B + K$$

(In this case there is a gain of exporting over foreign indigenous production.)

and

$$P_H + M < P_B + A$$

(In this case there is a gain of exporting over FDI.)

FDI:

Firm F will engage in FDI in Country B if:

$$P_B + A < P_B + K$$

(In this case there is a gain of FDI over foreign indigenous production.)

and

$$P_B + A < P_H + M$$

(In this case there is a gain of FDI over exporting.) Although this is the end of the Hirsch model, it can be extended as follows:

License:

Firm F may license to a firm in Country B if:

$$P_B + K < P_B + A$$

(In this case there is a gain from licensing, that is foreign indigenous production, over FDI.)

and

$$P_B + K < P_H + M$$

(In this case there is a gain of licensing over exporting.)

The extension to licensing is very tricky since K is, in practice, a difficult product to price. It is an intangible intermediate good, here treated as a sunk cost to the MNE (Firm F) but an actual cost to be paid by any potential rival firm in the host economy. Either the rival firm will spend K, perhaps helped by a government subsidy, or it may attempt to secure a license. In the latter case, it is extremely difficult to negotiate the correct license fee, since the MNE risks the loss of its knowledge advantage if the licensee sells it to another firm in its own or another nation. Thus, it is necessary to keep the model simple by either assuming a two-country framework or by assuming that the market for knowledge is segmented, such that the licensee cannot resell the knowledge. Neither assumption is all that realistic, although they do generate some general predictions, for example, that the MNE can license if it is cheaper to service the foreign market by this method than by either exporting or FDI. The great difficulty of finding a mutually acceptable license fee between the MNE and host country firm may well imply that FDI is the preferred method of entry by the MNE to the foreign market, at least when exporting is denied it by tariff and other trade barriers.

This is potentially a very useful model in understanding the method by which a firm with a monopoly advantage in knowledge chooses to service a segmented foreign market. Naturally, for such a simple model to be useful it has to be based on many assumptions. The more restrictive assumptions — those concerning the static nature of the model and those confining the analysis to only two countries, the home and host nations — are relaxed in a paper by Giddy and Rugman (1979).

Some empirical work on technology transfer by Teece (1976) has found that the marginal cost to the MNE of applying its knowledge advantage abroad is not zero. Yet the argument that knowledge is a public good did not deny that there are start up costs for foreign production. The parent firm can charge fees for the use of its knowledge advantage. Teece overestimates technology transfer costs, however, by also including actual production and operating costs in his estimates.

Teece has argued that, in practice, the marginal cost to the MNE of applying knowledge abroad is not costless, as is assumed by writers such as Johnson (1971) in a theoretical context. The classical theoretical position has been to state that knowledge is a public good with a zero price, and as it stands this proposition is correct on its own terms. Yet clearly the physical activity involved in the transfer of technology abroad must incur some costs. Knowledge is not merely an abstract idea but is usually embodied in a particular technique, innovation or production process. Therefore its application abroad would seem to involve transactions and start up costs, not only in the equipment itself but in the selection, training and adaption of the host country labour force. Teece finds the costs of technology transfer to be considerable. His empirical work is open to criticism, however, since he includes what I believe are operating costs as part of the technology transfer costs. The actual royalties and license fees paid for technology and information are almost insignificant given his own figures. Clearly, more empirical work is required on this sensitive subject before a definitive conclusion can be drawn.

TRADE, FDI, AND LICENSING:
THE RELEVANT COSTS OVER TIME

The optimal strategy for the MNE to follow in choosing either trade, FDI, or licensing as the appropriate method for servicing one or more foreign markets will depend on the relative costs and benefits of each method. Assuming benefits, in the form of total revenues, to be constant, the analysis will then focus on the relative costs of trade, FDI, and licensing, especially the manner in which these costs vary over time.

The previous notation can be continued with M being the extra costs of exporting and A the additional costs of FDI. The K costs need to be considered explicitly in order to evaluate the licensing option. Whereas previously K is best viewed as a sunk cost, now K represents the additional cost to be paid by a potential rival firm both to purchase a license, and to finance the ongoing research costs required to retain the monopoly advantage in knowledge over time. From the viewpoint of the MNE, which needs to prevent dissipation of its knowledge advantage, K can be thought of as the insurance and policing costs required to protect this knowledge advantage. There is a risk of rival firms securing the knowledge, and of its value thereby being reduced substantially. These costs are now discussed in greater detail.

A SIMPLE MODEL OF FDI, TRADE, AND LICENSING

Assume an MNE based in Country A, producing and marketing a product in that country on the basis of knowledge generated by that firm itself. The firm then chooses to exploit that advantage in a second country, B, although later a third country, C, is introduced. The two-country model is equivalent to assuming that national factor markets for knowledge and technology, or goods market for products which use such intermediate inputs, are fully segmented. This means that there is no risk of loss of the knowledge advantage possessed by the MNE once it starts to service foreign markets, since there is only one such market, in Country B.

The firm has three means of exploiting its product or process advantage in knowledge at time t. These methods are: exporting from Country A; foreign direct investment in Country B; or licensing a local firm in Country B. In the first two cases, the MNE faces potential rivalry from local firms, since they do not face the additional costs of marketing (M_t) or producing (A_t) at a distance. On the other hand, local firms would have to produce or buy the knowledge in order to compete effectively, and in doing so face knowledge costs of (K_t).

The choice will be made at the initial time and in all future periods on the basis of which method maximizes the net present value (NPV) of servicing the market of Nation B. We now consider each NPV and how it may behave over time. For the sake of simplicity and for consistency, we assume identical sales revenues (R_t) and production costs (C_t) for each method of entry. The latter assumption is relaxed in the section on licensing. The profits from each method will differ due to the varying impact of the special extra cost of either export marketing, overcoming the disadvantages of FDI, or paying for knowledge.

Exporting

Exporting will be chosen on the basis of the relative production and marketing costs associated with manufacture in Country A and Country B. In this case, the MNE is a purely exporting firm. It will face its own (Country A) production costs plus the additional costs of marketing abroad:

$$\text{NPV}_E = \sum_{t = t_e}^{T} \frac{R_t - C_t^A - M_t}{(1 + r)^t} \tag{4.1}$$

where

R_t = total revenues from sales of the final product in foreign country B

C_t^A = total costs of producing the good in the MNE's home country A

r = rate at which stream of revenues will be discounted to the present

M_t = additional marketing costs to a firm associated with exporting; transportation, tariffs, information costs, etc.

t_e = date of entry into foreign market.

In making the choice of exporting, the major element of interest is the additional marketing costs, M_t. In this model, M_t has two components (see curve EE' of Figure 4-1). There are initial costs (aE) which arise from gathering information about the foreign country and its potential total market. These are "one-shot" costs which diminish over time as familiarity with the new market increases. These initial costs eventually fall to zero. In addition, there are fixed costs (oa), invariant with time, arising from transportation, insurance, tariffs, and other barriers to international trade. These costs are

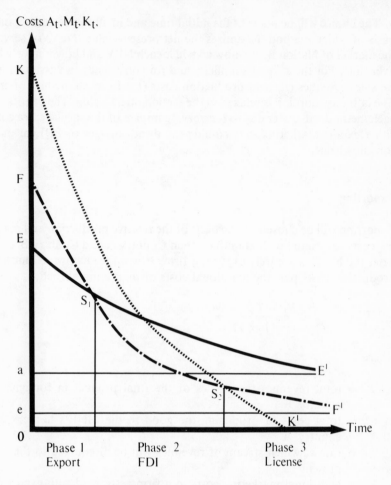

FIGURE 4-1. Additional costs of exporting, foreign direct investment, and knowledge

incurred as each unit of the good using knowledge as an intermediate input crosses the border of Country B or as it goes there. From t_e, the period of entry, therefore, the marketing costs behave as follows:

$$M_t = a + bt^c \quad a > 0, c \leq -1, t \geq t_e \tag{4.2}$$

Here the parameter a represents the fixed costs and b is a coefficient representing the variable marketing costs, which decline over time at the rate c.

Foreign Direct Investment

The distinguishing feature of FDI is that it occurs if the MNE possesses an internally generated advantage A_t sufficient to overcome the cost of being a foreigner. The internal appropriation of the rents from a firm's specific knowledge advantage occurs through direct investment in preference to exporting when local production by a subsidiary of the MNE is more efficient than local lost country production, taking into account the special costs of each. The MNE must also find that it can best appropriate the value of A_t within the firm rather than through markets (i.e., by licensing). The net present value to the MNE of FDI will be:

$$\text{NPV}_{\text{FDI}} = \sum_{t=t_e}^{T} \frac{R_t - C_t^B - A_t}{(1 + r)^t} \tag{4.3}$$

Here the variables are as defined previously with the new variables being:

C_t^B = costs of producing in host Country B

A_t = additional production, marketing, and "distance" costs associated with being a foreign rather than a domestic investor in Country B. These costs are borne by the subsidiary(ies) of the MNE located in Country B.

The additional costs of being a foreign investor, A_t, behave in a fashion similar to the additional costs of exporting, M_t, which were discussed previously. A_t, too, has a (low) fixed component and a variable one that diminishes over time. However, since direct investment requires much more detailed local information, personal contacts, and access to official channels than does the prior option of exporting these additional costs, A_t will commence at a much higher level and diminish more slowly than M_t (see curve FF' of Figure 4–1). In other words, the following equation applies:

$$A_t = e + ft^g \qquad t \geq t_e$$

and

$$e < a, g > c \tag{4.4}$$

Here there are high fixed additional costs (oe) of starting to produce in a foreign environment while the variable f represents the additional costs (eF) which change over time at the rate g.

Licensing

In contrast to the first two cases, licensing is one in which the MNE seeks a return on its information or special advantage by selling it to a third party instead of internalizing the market. Here it is useful to relax the assumption made in the two preceding cases, namely that production costs are the same for foreign (MNE) and local (host) nation firms, and to introduce a third nation, C. Initially the markets of the three nations are assumed to be fully segmented (to avoid dissipation of knowledge), but the problems of integrated markets are addressed later.

A licensing option occurs when the returns from the present sale of information and future sale of ongoing R&D exceed the returns from exploiting the knowledge through exporting or FDI. Whereas exporting and FDI are each affected directly by the special costs of these forms of entry, no such special costs arise from selling the knowledge. Instead, the cost of licensing is best viewed as an opportunity cost. The act of licensing may well sharply accelerate the dissipation of the firm's knowledge advantage and accordingly diminish its appropriability. Other things being equal, therefore, licensing is likely to occur only when

1. the special costs to the MNE (E_t and A_t) of internalizing the market for information are very high; or
2. the knowledge can be differentiated or the market for knowledge otherwise segmented in such a way as to forestall dissemination of the knowledge by the licensee; or
3. the knowledge has been disseminated to the point where licensing it will result in little or no more dissipation of appropriability, a situation which occurs when the product has become standardized.

In this model, it is assumed that the two components of knowledge — existing and ongoing R&D — are tied products, so that the revenues from the rents on licensing knowledge necessarily include both. For simplicity, these two components are defined as K. Since the marginal cost to the MNE of providing a license is essentially zero, the present value to the MNE from licensing is:

$$\text{NPV}_L = \sum_{t = t_e}^{T} \frac{K_{t_e}}{(1 + r)^t} \tag{4.5}$$

where K_{t_e} equals the market price at time t_e, of the knowledge possessed by the MNE; t_e is, as before, the date of entry into the foreign country. Other terms are as defined previously.

K_{t_e} are revenues to the MNE but these are, of course, the costs paid by the host country licencee firm (HC). Therefore in order for licensing to occur, not only should it be the choice of the MNE to do it in preference to other entry methods, but another condition is that the local firm must also be able to exploit profitably the knowledge at that price; that is, a second condition for licensing is required. It is also necessary to relax the assumption that production costs (C_t) are the same in both home and host nations — now they can differ. Therefore, the second condition for licensing is:

$$\text{NPV}_{\text{HC}} = \sum_{t = t_e}^{T} \frac{R_t - C_t^{\text{B}} - K_{t_e}}{(1 + r)^t} \tag{4.6}$$

where HC is the local (host) country licencee firm, C^{B} is the costs in Country B, and other variables are as defined previously.

The behavior of the price of firm specific knowledge advantage of the MNE depends on the stage of the industry technology cycle, a concept introduced by Magee (1977). The cycle itself depends on the extent to which the knowledge has already been sold to purchasers within the relevant market, or whether it has been retained within the firm. When once the knowledge is sold outside the firm, the price and hence the appropriability of the knowledge falls rapidly — much faster than M_t or A_t. At the standardization stage of the technology cycle, the license for the original knowledge or for patent rights thereto is priced at a low level or is even zero. Hence, the cost curve for knowledge is:

$$K_t = h + qt^{\text{P}}$$

and

$$P > c, h = 0, \qquad t \geq t_f \tag{4.7}$$

where t_f equals the date of first license for the knowledge sold in the relevant market. Clearly, $t_f \leq t_e$ where t_e is the date of commencement of any particular licensing arrangement.

Observe that K_t is undefined for values of $t < t_f$. The KK' is a cost curve for the MNE in the sense that it represents the (intangible) risk of knowledge dissipation and the (tangible) costs of policing the potential license to avoid excessive dissipation. Both of these costs are assumed to fall over time; the dissipation cost due to greater standardization of the technology over time and the policing cost due to the reduced incentive for a rival firm to isolate the knowledge advantage.

The time path of K_t is depicted graphically in Figure 4-1 as line KK'. Here the fixed costs (oh) are zero, while the knowledge costs (to the potential host country rival firm) of OK decline at the rate p over time. Although KK' is the cost curve for a rival firm's access to knowledge, for simplicity it can be regarded as a cost of licensing to the MNE (i.e., it represents the risk of dissipation of knowledge, and policing costs.)

In terms of the three cost curves it is possible to derive a Vinerian least cost envelope curve ES_1S_2K'. This determines two switchover points at S_1 and S_2. The interdependencies of the cost curves reveal that the MNE should export in Phase 1, do FDI in Phase 2 and license in Phase 3. This is a simplified solution to the model, in which it is assumed that each cost is independent of the other. The MNE does not solve for all three cost curves simultaneously in this version of the model, a simplification which is justified for my purposes since it still permits the concept of relative choice between exports, FDI, and licensing to be illustrated, albeit in more of an intuitive than a rigorous fashion.

CONDITIONS FOR EXISTENCE OF EXPORTING, FOREIGN DIRECT INVESTMENT, AND LICENSING

The form of international business that will prevail when an MNE has a supply of original and ongoing internally-generated knowledge will be determined by the relative value of each to the MNE. In summary, these conditions are:

1.   Export when $\text{NPV}_E > \max(\text{NPV}_{FDI}, \text{NPV}_L)$ (4.8)

2.   FDI when $\text{NPV}_{FDI} > \max(\text{NPV}_E, \text{NPV}_L)$ (4.9)

3.   License when $\text{NPV}_L > \max(\text{NPV}_E, \text{NPV}_{FDI})$ subject to $\text{NPV}_{HC} \geq 0$ (4.10)

In order to determine the periods in the industry and product cycles during which one form or other will prevail, the behavior of each NPV over time must be examined. This behavior depends crucially on assumptions concerning the degree of international segmentation of the market for knowledge. Here it is assumed that $t_f = t_e$; that is, if the MNE licenses the knowledge it is the first to do so. It is necessary to solve for:

1. t_1 such that $\text{NPV}_E^{t_1} = \text{NPV}_{FDI}^{t_1}$ (4.11)

2. t_2 such that $\text{NPV}_E^{t_2} = \text{NPV}_L^{t_2}$ (4.12)

3. t_3 such that $\text{NPV}_{FDI}^{t_3} = \text{NPV}_L^{t_3}$ (4.13)

This procedure can be undertaken but it is unnecessary to do this here since no new information emerges from such solutions. It is more useful to relax some of the assumptions, such as those concerning the independence of each cost curve and the lack of simultaneous relationships in the decision of the MNE to choose each phase separately. Some of these complications to the model are explored in Giddy and Rugman (1979).

In a related piece of work, Ray (1977) has demonstrated that, under monopoly conditions, a firm owning a patent must determine the amount of direct sales and licensed sales jointly. The two types of sales are interdependent under monopoly. In general, the patent-holding firm can increase its quasi rents by extension of its total market through licensing, provided that the choice between direct sales and licensed sales is determined by the usual profit maximizing conditions of setting marginal revenue equal to marginal cost for the firm. In Ray's model, the markets for direct sales and licenses are not segmented, so the decision to choose either mode is endogenous to the patent-holding firm.

Ray also shows that, in the long run, direct sales are preferred by the patent holder. This allows the firm to save the extra policing costs which are unique to licensed sales. In the long run, it is assumed that any capital constraint is removed so the patent holder has the physical capacity to produce sufficient units of the product itself. In practice, Ray argues that accumulation of sufficient capital takes time and that "licensing can be viewed as an alternative means of extracting rents in the short run" (p. 3). Ray derives conditions under which licensing is chosen instead of FDI. An examination of his cost curves reveals that he does not have additional costs of FDI nor other costs specific to a mode of supply. Therefore, his analysis is complementary to this model rather than a substitute for it.

SUMMARY, CONCLUSIONS, AND IMPLICATIONS OF THE MODEL

This chapter developed a Coasian model of the firm in which imperfect factor or product markets, especially for the production and marketing of technological intensive commodities, are internalized within the organizational structure of the multinational enterprise. The concept of internalization of externalities is a familiar one in economic theory, following the seminal work of Coase (1937). It has been extended to an international dimension by Buckley and Casson (1976), Dunning (1977), and Casson (1979). Unfortunately, most theoretical work on the multinational enterprise continues to ignore the powerful explanatory nature of internalization. It can be read into the classic work of Hymer (1976), but it is not recognized explicitly by Hufbauer (1975) or in Agmon and Kindleberger (1977). Only recently has it been shown that internalization is a potential paradigm for the modern theory of foreign direct investment. See Rugman (1979) for further details.

The model by Hirsch (1976) is the first explicit treatment of the theoretical reasons for a multinational firm to either export or engage in international investment. This chapter extended the static Hirsch model in two ways: first, it considered another possible method of servicing foreign markets, namely licensing; and second, it studied the temporal conditions of the evolution of the form of multinational activity. Furthermore, the concept of internalization is at the heart of the model whereas it was only implicit in the paper by Hirsch.

The only other attempt to model the international operations of a multinational enterprise along the lines of internalization that is familiar is that by Horst (1974). Again his model is confined to the choice between exporting or foreign direct investment, and it ignores licensing. Horst recognizes that a multinational firm can profit by price discrimination if it can segment foreign markets. The multinational firm has an investment in technical information which helps it generate a firm specific knowledge advantage. The main thrust of the Horst paper is to demonstrate that both a profit-maximizing and a sales-maximizing strategy will yield similar decision rules for the multinational firm, namely that a foreign investment phase will follow the export phase. Using the analysis here, the Horst model could be extended to show that licensing will follow the foreign direct investment phase if the cost conditions warrant it.

In conclusion, the major contribution of this chapter is its explicit development of the changing cost conditions over time for a multinational firm faced with the problem of how to service foreign markets in an efficient manner. Previous theoretical work has been largely static in nature and has dealt only superficially with the choice between exporting and foreign direct investment. Here the net present values of these two methods of servicing foreign markets were derived, and the third option — of licensing — was also introduced for consideration.

The main finding of this approach is that the optimal strategy for a multinational firm to follow in servicing foreign markets is determined by the relative net present value of each of the three options of exporting, foreign investment, or licensing. In turn, the net present values of these options depend on the assumptions made about the firm's method of appropriating its technological or knowledge advantage, and the degree of segmentation or integration of international factor markets, especially the market for such technology or knowledge.

Since the degree of segmentation of international factor markets is a parameter in the model, the essential issue examined is the method by which the multinational firm can service foreign markets in order to achieve full appropriability of its firm specific technological advantage. It is found that no one method is sufficient for this purpose, but that the multinational firm must carefully evaluate the net present values of the three interrelated options of exporting, foreign investment, or licensing. Therefore, the operation of internalization is not a mechanical process but one which raises many subtle problems for a multinational firm as it seeks to service foreign markets in an efficient manner.

THE THEORY OF INTERNALIZATION
IN A CANADIAN CONTEXT

How does the theory of internalization in general, and the model developed here in particular, apply to the Canadian situation? Canada, after all, is one of the primary examples of a host country (recipient of FDI) rather than a home country from which the MNE originates. This dependence on net FDI is, in fact, being reduced and Canada today engages in substantial international production and sales through its own MNEs. As the Canadian economy increases its wealth, such multinational activity by its firms, and especially its banks, is also likely to increase, perhaps even at a faster rate. However, for the purpose of this analysis, it is useful to picture Canada in its traditional guise as a large net importer of foreign capital and as a repository for the branch plants of MNEs, over 80 percent of which have historically been of American origin. In the sense of Agmon and Kindleberger (1977), Canada is a "small" nation, open to trade, MNEs and foreign influence. Other examples are Australia and Switzerland.

The basic fact of Canada's being a host nation to the MNE demonstrates the relevance of the theory of internalization. For example, it reveals that the original research and development, and indeed the ongoing knowledge generation, is most likely centered on the parent firm of the MNE, based in the United States. The MNE sets up and maintains subsidiaries in Canada in order to service the local market. For a hundred years, the Canadian tariff has been an effective additional cost of export marketing facing the U.S. firm. The tariff has consequently not protected indigenous Canadian industry, but instead has attracted American FDI. Potential rival Canadian firms are only likely to license technology and knowledge advantages from U.S. firms at a stage in the technology cycle when there is little risk of the MNE losing these advantages through dissipation. Due to the difficulty of setting the correct price for a license, the MNE may well prefer FDI to licensing. It avoids the risk of undercharging the license as well as dissipation of knowledge. These are some of the implications to be drawn from the model of the last section. Others will undoubtedly be apparent to the reader.

Possibly other factors can be identified as important causal events attracting FDI. Yet, apart from the obvious geographical proximity of Canada to the United States (which is as much an advantage for potential Canadian exporters as it is to American ones), most of these can usually be identified as subordinate explanations to the generalized theory of internalization developed here. For example, international tax rate differentials, or an occasional period of effective currency exchange controls, may have induced the MNE to use transfer prices in order to maximize its earnings. Such internal prices are an efficient response by the MNE to exogenous market imperfections imposed by government regulation. Canada is unlikely to be used for offshore assembly of goods by U.S. MNEs (as its labor costs now exceed those of the United States), but the assembly argument is another example of the use of administrative fiat by the MNE.

The nature of the Canadian federation is also partly responsible for the large amount of American foreign ownership of its industry and resources. The federal government is not as powerful as the national governments of Britain or the United States. Many economic powers, especially the control of land, minerals, and other resources reside with governments of the provinces. Unfortunately, there is insufficient harmony of tax policy (and other regulations affecting corporations) between federal and provincial governments. This leads inevitably to a morass of market imperfections and the now classic response of internalization by the MNEs.

The nonuniform nature of the Canadian economy and federal-provincial efforts to reduce regional income disparities have led to industry location incentives and other policies for regional economic development. These and other subsidies to industries have encouraged MNEs to open branch plants, which they probably would have been happy to establish anyway. Provincial governments have tried to outbid each other in fighting for the establishment of a subsidiary in their own territory. Their political leaders are aware of the benefits in terms of employment creation, tax revenue, and output generation provided by the MNE subsidiary. These provincial leaders have many economic levers to pull in order to attract the MNE — possibly too many for the good of the country as a whole. The regional and trade aspects of the regulation of foreign investment in Canada are developed in greater detail in Chapters 8 and 11.

In the area of research and science policy, there are similar lessons to be drawn by application of the theory of internalization. The majority of

Canadian industry is foreign owned. If the theory of internalization tells us anything, it is that the initial and ongoing knowledge generation takes place in the U.S. parent firm and not in the Canadian subsidiaries. Yet Canadian science policy attempts to encourage research and development by Canadian industry at large. It is therefore doomed to failure, since the majority of firms receiving funding are the subsidiaries of U.S. MNEs. These subsidiaries, by definition of their role, are not geared for original or even innovative research. Neither are they likely to have a comparative advantage in knowledge generation, although Canada itself may have.

The failure of Canadian science policy to generate any substantive indigenous technology advantage has been documented by McFetridge (1977), and is related to tariff policy in an imaginative study by Daly and Globerman (1976). The recent xenophobic report of the Science Council of Canada has been criticized by Safarian (1979). An implication of the theory of internalization is that Canadian funding for research should be directed toward independent local firms only, or to universities and specialized research centers. Basic research can be stimulated in the latter and can conceivably be generated in truly indigenous firms. In turn, these will become prototypes for the Canadian MNEs of the future.

The foregoing is a type of infant technology argument for a subsidy. It is related to the infant industry argument for a tariff, but it actually has a better economic rationale. The infant technology argument is in the form of a subsidy rather than a tariff, so it avoids the secondary distortions that arise once a tariff alters the relative prices of traded to nontraded goods. As Johnson (1971) and Corden (1974) have shown, the unforeseen byproducts of the tariff on a general equilibrium system are to be avoided whenever possible. Therefore, if the objective of Canadian public policy is to promote industry, then the correct economic way to proceed is by a direct subsidy to indigenous industry rather than by the tariff.

In the case of technology, it is possible to apply the theory of internalization in a Canadian context to demonstrate that a public subsidy may conceivably generate a firm specific knowledge advantage. In time, the incipient Canadian-based MNEs may rival the more established U.S.-based MNEs, which continue to dominate the Canadian economy at the present time. Future empirical work using internalization as a seminal base is required before the implications drawn in this section can be accepted with greater certainty.

In the interim period, public policy in Canada would do well to recognize the special role of the MNE in Canadian industry. It is an organization with a knowledge advantage, and Canada is just one market to be serviced in an efficient manner. The Canadian tariff has denied exporting to the U.S.

firms, and licensing is perhaps a risky option, so the firm is left with FDI. Over the years, Canada has maintained market imperfections which have, if anything, encouraged the MNE to internalize markets. Unless there is a dramatic change in the direction of Canadian public policy, it would appear that FDI will continue and that the MNE will use the process of internalization to service the Canadian market.

II PERFORMANCE OF MULTINATIONALS IN CANADA

5 AN EMPIRICAL ANALYSIS OF PROFITS AND RISK IN CANADIAN MULTINATIONALS

INTRODUCTION[1]

This chapter reports the most arresting results of two research projects which have examined the level and variability of profits in two Canadian industries dominated by multinational enterprises (MNEs). The major findings are that profits of MNEs and their Canadian subsidiaries are not excessive, but that parent MNEs enjoy more stable profits than their Canadian subsidiaries. This has important policy implications for the taxation policy of the host government. The techniques used to measure risk include applications of portfolio theory in an international context, in which the mean and standard deviation of profit rates are examined.

In the next section, the mean profit rate and the risk of earnings, where the latter is proxied by taking the standard deviation of the earnings stream over specified time periods, are examined for the largest Canadian petroleum firms. This procedure is then repeated for the largest multinational mining corporations active in Canada. Data over the period 1960–1977 on profit rates are reported and analyzed.

The oil and mining industries are chosen as examples of two major areas of the Canadian economy dominated by multinational firms, mainly of

U.S. origin. The Canadian resource sector is clearly worthy of study in its own right, given the dominating role it plays in the Canadian economy and balance of payments. It is assumed that the findings of this study are of general application, but a definitive statement on the earnings of all multinational firms active in Canada awaits further study of the other major sectors, especially manufacturing.

PROFITS AND RISK OF CANADIAN OIL FIRMS

This section examines the profits of major petroleum corporations operating in Canada.[2] Such a study is necessary given the spate of legislation and public discussion covering Canadian energy policy in general and the activities of oil firms in particular, as outlined elsewhere in this book. There are two major themes in this section.

First, the average level of profits is examined in order to find some factual basis for the common allegation that oil firms realize excessive profits. As most of the Canadian petroleum industry is foreign owned, the profits of U.S. parent firms are used for comparison. Second, the variability of profits is analyzed. Such a test of the risk of the rate of return is required, for it is argued frequently that oil production is a risky business. Exploration in frontier regions is regarded as a gamble; high cost methods of extraction are anticipated in the future. There is also a climate of uncertainty surrounding both federal and provincial government policy in the energy field. Of course, the oil industry can incorporate these problems into its calculations of total cost of production and attempt to apply a suitable discount factor against such uncertain outcomes. Here it is assumed that the oil industry does operate in such a rational manner, and that firms attempt to maximize profits and to minimize risk. Therefore, an examination of flunctuations in profits will be a suitable method of investigating the risk of the operations of oil firms.[3]

For the purpose of this research, the largest Canadian petroleum firms are found by size of sales. The leading fourteen Canadian petroleum firms are identified in Table 5-1, with the largest eleven plus two others being used in subsequent testing. The firms are ranked by size, where the size indicator is usually total operating revenue, which in turn is a measure of total sales. Thirteen of these firms have sales of over $100 million. The largest firm by far is Imperial Oil, which is over twice as large as Shell and Gulf. In turn, these are twice as large as Texaco, while this fourth-ranked firm is twice as large as BP, Petrofina, Irving, and Husky. Texasgulf has been included in this table, but it is excluded from subsequent tests since it does not

TABLE 5-1. Rates of return (E/K) for the major Canadian petroleum firms, 1960-1977

	1977	1976	1975	1974	1973	1972	1971	1970	1969
Imperial	15.13	15.21	15.84	21.0	18.07	13.49	13.10	10.81	10.08
Shell	12.57	12.01	13.85	14.94	12.03	9.72	8.13	7.20	6.97
Gulf	14.36	14.40	17.12	17.92	12.95	8.68	7.64	5.81	6.89
Texaco	8.78	7.24	13.23	18.11	16.19	13.63	12.14	11.45	12.17
Texasgulf	6.15	8.11	16.24	26.32	16.79	7.93	5.51	12.37	17.93
BP Canada	11.07	9.64	9.84	13.59	10.43	7.60	6.79	7.73	9.30
Petrofina	11.72	9.11	13.82	14.68	13.50	10.41	10.55	9.31	8.80
Husky	15.74	13.92	18.60	19.48	11.83	8.73	8.36	5.79	6.68
Irving	N/A	N/A	N/A	N/A	N/A	25.08	10.78	11.68	
Pacific	18.18	16.48	16.16	14.46	10.62	9.02	7.24	6.02	5.52
Hudson Bay Oil and Gas	24.26	23.27	24.33	24.23	19.63	15.80	14.46	13.57	14.01
Total	11.42	8.92	8.55	1.92	5.35	4.24	3.00	2.72	3.71
Home	7.48	6.91	11.68	6.84	7.56	5.23	3.65	3.09	3.91
Candel	13.66	10.61	22.97	11.54	10.36	10.18	12.09	11.36	13.16

	1968	1967	1966	1965	1964	1963	1962	1961	1960
Imperial	11.05	10.98	11.13	10.8	10.29	9.57	9.61	9.99	9.43
Shell	8.36	7.49	7.07	6.29	4.99	3.87	1.46	(9.52)	(13.05)
Gulf	7.40	7.81	7.00	7.68	7.68	6.67	7.02	7.15	7.07
Texaco	10.85	9.94	9.27	8.47	8.47	8.38	7.91	8.61	9.78
Texasgulf	24.00	26.75	15.87	12.69	7.28	7.21	9.75	10.67	11.00
BP Canada	10.39	9.10	8.75	2.76	(4.87)	(6.02)	(6.63)	(7.25)	(25.86)
Petrofina	8.87	7.68	6.92	6.53	5.54	5.52	5.36	4.49	.98
Husky	7.35	10.73	10.18	11.23	8.50	7.72	.45	(3.88)	(8.26)
Irving	11.12	7.60	4.49	5.68	.59	4.48	5.38	7.99	8.58
Pacific	5.21	4.51	2.90	2.39	1.98	1.69	1.70	.75	(2.17)
Hudson Bay Oil and Gas	15.18	13.80	14.68	15.19	13.77	13.29	13.12	9.76	1.47
Total	3.09	1.79	3.20	3.11	(.72)	(5.48)	(6.45)	(12.17)	(7.0)
Home	5.07	8.47	8.44	10.99	11.17	9.19	3.55	(.81)	(3.83)
Candel	14.05	23.57	(27.01)	(34.15)	75.53		(201.67)	(2.19)	(4.17)

Sources: Various company annual reports; The Financial Post Survey of Oils.

have any major oil-producing operations in Canada. Data are gathered on the major financial indicators of these firms for as long a period as possible, namely the years from 1960 to 1977. The data were found by searching in annual issues of the respective company reports, supplemented by data from the Financial Post's *Survey of Oils*.

Table 5-1 also reports the rate of return on stockholders' equity for the largest Canadian firms over the last eighteen years (1960-1977). The ratio E/K is a conventional indicator of the profit rate, where E represents net income after taxes, and K represents the net worth of stockholders' equity, recorded at book value. In Table 5-1, figures in brackets indicate losses. The figures from the E/K ratio are percentages, and it can be observed that there was a large increase in profits in 1974. This point becomes clearer upon examination of Table 5-2.

In Table 5-2, the mean rate of return is recorded for each firm, along with the risk of profits. Risk is shown by the standard deviation of the E/K ratio for each firm over the eighteen years and for three subperiods of six years each, this latter breakdown being used to trace trends and significant deviations over the longer period. It has been observed that the recorded E/K for 1974 was well above the mean E/K for the total period, for all firms. Indeed, the 1974 profits are completely out of line and were clearly due to special factors associated with the energy crisis which were magnified by the Arab oil embargo and sudden increase in the world price of oil. Another problem is that the out-of-trend profits for 1974 result in a distortion in both the mean return and in the risk measure for the 1972-1977 period. The standard deviation for the entire period from 1960 to 1977 is also slightly pushed up by this outlying year.

It can be observed in Table 5-2 that the mean rate of return for Canadian oil firms is generally greater than 5½ percent with a risk in profits generally lower than 7 percent. The larger Canadian oil firms enjoy more stable profits; for example, the standard deviations for Imperial Oil, Gulf, and Texaco are just over 3 percent while it is just over 4 percent for Shell. The smaller Canadian oil firms (including the second fifteen not reported in the table) are, in general, more risky. This table tends to support the portfolio theory model which suggests a tradeoff between risk and return. However, there are some firms that have both high mean returns and low risk — such as Imperial, Texaco, and Hudson Bay Oil and Gas. The twofold benefits enjoyed by these large firms are to be explained by their market power and special factors which cannot be examined further at this stage. The present study merely presents basic data on risk and return. It suggests that further analysis of the balance sheets of some of the larger oil companies may provide interesting reasons for their good performance.

TABLE 5-2. Largest Canadian petroleum firms mean return and risk, percentages

	1960–1965		1966–1971		1972–1977		1960–1977	
	Mean	S.D.	Mean	S.D.	Mean	S.D.	Mean	S.D.
1. Imperial	9.95	0.52	11.19	1.01	16.46	2.67	12.53	3.30
2. Shell	-0.99	8.20	7.45	0.58	12.52	1.79	6.35	7.34
3. Gulf	7.21	0.40	6.93	0.63	14.24	3.30	9.46	3.93
4. Texaco	8.60	0.62	10.97	1.18	12.86	4.19	10.81	2.98
5. Texasgulf	9.77	2.17	17.07	7.74	13.59	7.70	13.48	6.77
6. BP Canada	-7.98	9.50	8.68	1.26	10.36	1.97	3.69	10.03
7. Petrofina	4.74	1.95	8.69	1.27	12.21	2.17	8.54	3.58
8. Husky	2.63	7.75	8.18	1.96	14.72	4.09	8.51	7.04
9. Irving*	5.45	2.86	9.13	3.04	N/A	N/A	8.62*	6.11
10. Pacific	1.06	1.67	6.15	2.08	14.15	3.59	6.81	6.07
11. Hudson Bay Oil and Gas	10.93	4.90	14.28	0.60	21.92	3.50	15.66	5.74
12. Total	-4.79	5.32	2.92	0.64	6.73	3.50	1.62	6.03
13. Home	5.04	6.41	5.44	2.42	7.62	2.16	6.03	4.07
14. Can Del	-33.33	102.48	7.87	17.66	13.22	4.95	-2.36	56.22

*1960–1973 only.
Source: Financial Post of Canada: Survey of Industrials, Annual Issue.

69

TABLE 5-3. Largest U.S. petroleum firms mean return and risk, percentages

	1960–65		1966–71		1972–77		1960–77	
	Mean	S.D.	Mean	S.D.	Mean	S.D.	Mean	S.D.
1. Exxon	11.53	1.08	12.20	0.97	15.28	3.03	13.01	2.48
2. Mobil	7.83	1.39	10.35	0.53	13.12	2.01	10.43	2.60
3. Texaco	14.97	0.51	14.37	1.30	12.57	3.54	13.97	2.32
4. Gulf	9.55	4.66	11.88	1.30	10.97	4.09	11.47	2.38
5. Standard (Calif.)	11.58	0.28	10.67	0.79	13.27	2.19	11.84	1.69
6. Standard (Ind.)	6.68	1.43	9.60	0.39	14.13	2.98	10.27	3.44
7. Shell	11.45	1.42	11.28	2.27	13.27	3.09	12.00	2.40
8. Continent.	10.38	1.05	10.63	2.19	14.35	2.49	11.79	2.66
9. Atlantic	6.52	0.86	8.07	1.15	11.15	3.27	8.58	2.77
10. Phillips	9.58	0.47	8.87	1.73	13.92	3.50	10.79	3.13
11. Occident.	N/A	N/A	16.78	3.96	12.92	7.93	14.46	6.64
12. Union	7.55	0.59	9.93	1.94	11.95	2.61	9.81	2.58
13. Sun	8.40	0.89	9.80	1.07	12.13	3.06	10.11	2.42
14. Ashland	12.52	2.21	12.15	4.36	16.08	1.40	13.58	3.31
15. Standard (Ohio)	9.97	1.90	9.57	4.21	8.90	2.31	9.48	2.84
16. Getty	N/A	N/A	9.14	0.91	11.12	3.47	10.22	2.72
17. Marathon	10.67	1.27	11.75	1.42	14.73	2.79	12.38	2.55
18. Universal	N/A	N/A	4.40*	5.08	12.77†	1.36	7.80‡	5.36
19. American	4.02	2.69	14.73	3.38	13.98	5.55	11.32	6.22
20. Clark	12.18	10.77	17.48	7.31	12.86	8.78	14.53	8.50

*1968–1971.
†1972–1974.
‡1960–1974.

Source: Fortune 500: Annual Issue.

Table 5-3 identifies the twenty largest U.S. petroleum firms, ranked in decreasing order of size. Mean rates of return and risk (standard deviation) of profits are reported for the same time frame, 1960 to 1977, and the same three subperiods, as for the Canadian oil firms. It can be observed that the mean profit rates are usually higher and risk is considerably less for the U.S. parent multinational firm when compared to their Canadian subsidiaries. I suspect that the main reason for this is the more stable nature of the U.S. economy itself, and the relative novelty of the Canadian oil industry compared to the more established U.S. oil industry. The relative weights of these two explanations (or other ones) unfortunately cannot be determined from my data.

TABLE 5-4.   Risk and return by six-year subperiods, 1960-1977

	1960-1965	1966-1971	1972-1977	1960-1977
14 Largest Canadian Petroleum Firms				
Mean	1.64	8.93	13.12	7.84
S.D.	11.58	3.59	3.80	4.76
20 Largest U.S. Petroleum Firms				
Mean	9.73	11.18	12.97	11.39
S.D.	2.68	3.01	1.67	1.89

It can be observed from Table 5-4 that the average rate of return (E/K) for the major Canadian oil corporations, from 1960 to 1977, is 7.84 percent. This is over one-third lower than the average profit rate for U.S. oil firms, which was 11.39 percent in the same period. Canadian oil firms are also more risky than their U.S. parent firms, as they exhibit a higher standard deviation in rate of return of 4.76, compared with 1.89 for U.S. oils. Therefore, Canadian oil firms have both lower profits and greater risk than U.S. oil firms. However, this is not unusual, for Canadian industry in general is more risky than American industry. A sample of Canadian non-oil firms, of the same size as the oil firms, was found to have profits of 8.24 percent and a slightly higher risk than the Canadian oils, with the latter difference not being significant.

PROFITS AND RISK IN THE
CANADIAN MINING SECTOR

The largest corporations active in the Canadian mineral resource sector are listed in Table 5-5, ranked in decreasing order of size as measured by assets. The profit rates (E/K) for these firms for the period 1960 to 1977 are reported in Table 5-6. These mining firms, and their performance over this time period have been analyzed in detail in Chapter 11 of Rugman (1979).

Since most of the larger firms are U.S. multinationals (such as Amax, IMC, Texasgulf, Rio Algom, and JMC) or exist to serve the U.S. market through exports of resources (Inco, Falconbridge, Asbestos), for the purpose of this study it can be assumed that this group of corporations are representative of multinational mining activity in Canada. The rapid increase in assets of Kaiser, which would rank twelfth in size in Table 5-5, for 1977,

TABLE 5-5. Leading corporations in the Canadian mining industry, ranked by size indicators, 1977

Rank (by Assets)	Name	Assets	Revenue	Net Income
			Thousands	
1	Inco*	4,065,764	1,953,328[a]	99,859
2	Amax*	2,966,160	1,337,700[a]	68,990
3	Noranda	2,152,881	1,386,516[b]	67,176
4	Texasgulf*	1,477,879	49,155[d]	46,285
5	IMC*	1,368,360	1,296,500[c]	108,200
6	JMC*	1,333,800	1,461,432[a]	102,627
7	Cominco	1,052,277	759,242[f]	62,248
8	Falconbridge	888,153	381,684[e]	(29,223)
9	Rio Algom	682,645	486,587[b]	42,815
10	Hudson Bay M&S	618,736	346,346[g]	4,413
11	Placer	333,369	177,100[f]	20,753
12	Kaiser	312,755	307,727[j]	57,282
13	Patino	302,197	1,930,972[h]	5,863
14	Sherrit	233,684	178,604[b]	4,166
15	McIntyre	232,963	119,761[i]	(9,499)
16	Asbestos	288,676	145,344[f]	21,021

*U.S. dollars. Loss shown by parentheses.

[a]net sales; [b]production revenue; [c]net sales, interest, and other income; [d]net sales, royalties; [e]total revenue; [f]sales; [g]production sales; [h]net sales, other income; [i]coal production, metal production, dividend revenue; [j]sales, other revenue.

Source: Annual Reports.

TABLE 5-6. Profit rates (E/K) for leading corporations involved in the Canadian mining industry, 1960–1977, percent

Year	Inco	Amax	Nor-anda	IMC	JMC	Txs. gulf	Falc. Brdg.	Co-minco	Rio Algom	Hud. Bay	Patino	Placer	Mc Intyre	Sher-ritt	As-bestos
1977	5.2	4.0	8.9	16.7	13.8	6.2	-7.6	12.8	12.3	1.7	5.4	9.4	-6.5	3.8	15.3
1976	12.6	9.6	6.5	23.3	7.9	8.1	4.6	10.3	9.8	1.4	5.3	8.6	8.2	3.9	16.9
1975	12.6	9.8	7.3	35.3	6.6	16.4	1.0	18.2	9.9	6.8	2.3	4.9	7.6	10.4	7.4
1974	21.7	15.8	22.4	18.6	9.0	26.3	7.2	22.6	16.7	17.8	20.8	19.9	7.1	22.3	12.8
1973	18.5	12.5	21.0	10.2	11.0	16.8	16.5	12.3	22.4	25.7	11.2	34.7	-12.6	23.4	0.9
1972	10.1	10.1	13.4	8.8	10.3	7.9	2.3	6.4	8.9	7.9	1.0	11.2	-8.1	6.5	1.8
1971	9.0	8.9	13.8	6.0	10.0	6.8	6.0	4.0	5.4	2.6	2.6	5.2	2.6	10.7	7.9
1970	19.8	13.7	14.4	2.3	8.2	12.3	15.4	8.0	8.7	13.1	-6.9	9.1	3.6	26.9	8.8
1969	12.3	12.5	14.2	-10.4	10.8	17.8	18.1	9.0	9.2	21.1	13.1	14.0	5.8	19.5	8.8
1968	15.7	13.1	15.5	4.2	10.9	21.9	11.1	11.0	8.2	17.0	5.4	12.6	5.4	9.8	7.4
1967	16.4	12.7	16.9	7.1	9.3	23.7	13.1	13.6	7.5	16.1	5.1	18.8	6.0	9.1	6.4
1966	14.6	16.9	18.0	13.8	1.3	13.8	14.8	18.4	9.0	19.4	5.4	11.3	7.7	6.1	10.8
1965	18.7	17.1	16.7	12.7	10.5	10.1	16.1	22.8	10.0	18.5	5.1	12.0	7.0	9.9	8.5
1964	19.0	14.5	16.6	10.9	10.4	7.0	15.4	19.0	9.8	16.2	4.9	14.0	5.6	9.7	7.2
1963	16.2	12.9	11.6	8.6	9.3	5.9	9.8	15.8	13.3	15.2	5.2	9.3	4.7	5.6	8.0
1962	26.5	10.4	9.8	7.6	8.3	8.0	13.9	12.9	11.0	15.2	5.6	9.6	6.3	4.1	13.2
1961	15.6	14.5	16.0	7.7	8.4	8.7	24.8	12.3	16.5	15.3	23.1	10.0	4.8	7.9	22.8
1960	15.5	16.9	16.0	7.9	9.6	8.9	28.0	13.8	8.2	15.0	4.3	6.0	4.4	7.7	19.5

illustrates the strength of the new Japanese market for Canadian resources but does not change the overwhelming dependence of Canadian resource exports on the U.S. market.

Table 5-7 reports the mean return and risk of earnings for each of the fifteen largest mining corporations in the period 1960 to 1977. The average profit rate for this group of predominantly multinational firms is just over 11 percent, while the risk of earnings is high, as shown by an average standard deviation of nearly 6 percent. There is less evidence of a size bias for the mining than the oil firms. Here the larger mining corporations (with the exception of Inco) do not seem to earn higher profits or have less variation than the smaller firms in the sample. Indeed the mining sector is subject to considerable risk in earnings and all corporations suffer from the cyclical variability of profits in the mining industry. No evidence is found of windfall profits, nor of economic rent being reflected in the performance of these MNEs.[4]

Table 5-8 further illustrates the large annual variation in earnings of the Canadian resource firms. During the period 1960-1977, the mean profits for the largest fifteen firms averaged around 12 percent, but moved from about 7 percent in 1971, up to 17.4 percent in 1974, down to 7 percent again

TABLE 5-7. Canadian mining firms; mean and standard deviation of E/K by firm, 1960-1977

Firm	Mean	Standard Deviation
Inco	15.56	4.95
Amax	12.55	3.36
Noranda	14.39	4.32
Texasgulf	12.59	6.45
IMC	10.63	9.40
JMC	9.20	2.52
Cominco	13.51	5.22
Falconbridge	11.69	8.56
Rio Algom	10.93	4.07
Hudson Bay	13.67	6.87
Placer	12.26	6.90
Patino	7.37	6.01
Sherritt	10.96	7.11
McIntyre	3.31	5.98
Asbestos	10.24	5.66
Mean	11.26	5.83

TABLE 5-8.   Mean and standard deviation of E/K for group of fifteen largest corporations in Canadian mining, by year, 1960-1977

Year	Mean	Standard Deviation
1977	6.76	7.21
1976	9.13	5.40
1975	10.43	8.28
1974	17.40	5.97
1973	16.94	8.30
1972	7.61	3.70
1971	7.06	3.20
1970	11.41	6.27
1969	13.30	4.50
1968	11.28	4.89
1967	12.12	5.49
1966	12.75	4.45
1965	13.05	5.01
1964	12.01	4.72
1963	10.09	3.92
1962	10.83	5.38
1961	13.89	6.16
1960	12.11	6.52
Mean	11.57	5.52

in 1977. It appears that mining firms are subject to the specific risk of the resource section and that they are insufficiently diversified to enjoy as stable earnings as oil firms.

CONCLUSION

It has been found that the profit rates of multinational firms active in the Canadian petroleum and mining sectors are not excessive. Indeed they are very close to the normal, average observed profit rate of about 12 percent on equity. There is considerable variation in earnings for mining firms, but in comparison, less risk in earnings of oil firms. For both oils and mines, there is greater variation in profits from their Canadian operations than in U.S. operations. This variation is probably explained by the economic structure of these two nations and illustrates the lack of "power" of the multinational enterprise. It is responsive to economic forces rather than a determinant of them. The performance of oil and mining multinationals is normal, so their influence on the Canadian economy can be regarded as neutral.

ENDNOTES

1. This chapter was originally presented at the North American Economic Studies Association joint meetings with the Southern Economic Association, Washington, D.C., November 8-10, 1978.
2. For critical analyses of the profits of multinationals see:
   R. J. Barnet and Ronald Muller, *Global Reach: The Power of the Multinational Corporation* (New York: Simon and Schuster, 1974).
   R. D. Cairns, "Ricardian Rent and Manitoba's Mining Royalty," *Canadian Tax Journal* 25 (Sept.-Oct. 1977):558-567.
   Winston G. Chambers, "Transfer Pricing: The Multinational Enterprise and Economic Development," mimeo, EMR, Ottawa, 1975
   Wallace Clement, *Continental Corporate Power* (Toronto: McClelland and Stewart, 1977).
   Alexander Dow, "International Minerals Policy Should be Adopted by Canada," *International Perspectives* (Nov.-Dec. 1977):19-25.
   E. Kierans, *Report on Natural Resources Policy in Manitoba* (Government of Manitoba), 1973.
   Kari Levitt, *Silent Surrender* (Toronto: Macmillan, 1970).
3. For a more detailed analysis, see "Risk and Return in the Petroleum Industry," paper presented to Academy of International Business, Dallas, Texas, published in Chapter 9 of Rugman (1979).
4. For a discussion on windfall profits and rents in the context of probability theory, see Herbert G. Grubel and S. Sydneysmith, "The Taxation of Windfall Gains on Stocks of Natural Resources," *Canadian Public Policy* 1 (Winter 1975):13-29.

6 PRIVATE AND SOCIAL RATES OF RETURN FROM U.S. FOREIGN DIRECT INVESTMENT IN CANADA

INTRODUCTION

This chapter presents and interprets the result of an empirical investigation of the private and social rates of return on U.S. foreign direct investment in Canada. Three areas of high foreign ownership are chosen for study: mining, petroleum, and manufacturing sectors. Private return means the return to an individual investor, whereas social return incorporates tax effects and represents the return to society at large. The methodology of this investigation follows that of Grubel (1974).

In an interesting empirical paper, Grubel (1974) has demonstrated that U.S. foreign direct investment abroad realized a net social loss over the 1960–1969 decade. The main reason for this surprising finding appears to be the exemption from U.S. taxation granted to corporations on their operations taxed abroad. The institutional and legal process by which double taxation is avoided can lead to unexpected economic consequences, and to unfair criticism of the multinational enterprise, which is not the cause of this exogenous market imperfection. The MNE is obliged to operate in an environment characterized by international tax rate differentials, which serve to complicate its internal organization and may give an incentive to use transfer pricing.

This study extends the work of Grubel to update his findings for U.S. manufacturing and also attempts a new disaggregation to the mining and petroleum sectors. Attention is confined to U.S. foreign direct investment in Canada since the activities of the MNE in that nation are the concern of this book. Several minor corrections to the Grubel article are made, but no alternative interpretation of his results is required since the magnitude of the numbers and the conclusions to be drawn from them have not changed.

METHODOLOGY

The objective of the study is to calculate the effective tax paid to the Canadian and U.S. governments by foreign-owned oil and mineral resource firms active in Canada. These figures permit a comparison of the private and social rates of return of foreign investment in this industry, and provide a framework for subsequent evaluation of host country taxation policy towards multinational mining firms. In addition, the manufacturing sector is examined.

The existing literature on foreign investment, the role of the MNE and MNE-related tax revenues does not support the popular view that the MNE avoids taxation or is favorable for the nation's economic growth. For example, the seminal theoretical article by MacDougall (1960) on the advantages of FDI has been extended by Corden (1974). Corden demonstrates that the advantages of free trade and capital flows still persist when the neoclassical assumptions of the MacDougall model are replaced, and that there is no theoretical case to be made against FDI by the MNE on efficiency grounds. Economic analysis should separate efficiency from distributional questions as attempted here.

The MacDougall model has been tested by Grubel (1974) and by Jenkins (1973b) in his 1972 Chicago University doctoral dissertation, entitled "Analysis of Rates of Return from Capital in Canada." They find that there is no social loss to Canada from the activities of MNEs. In fact, Grubel argues the opposite case — that the United States suffers a social loss since its MNEs are not subject to double taxation, and thus do not pay tax in the United States once it is paid by a subsidiary in Canada. Evidence in a similar vein has been found by Horst (1977).

In the Canadian context, several writers have argued that multinational mining corporations active in Canada earn excessive profits (Kierans 1973, Chambers 1975, Cairns 1977, and Dow 1977). Implicit in the first three papers, and explicit in the fourth, is the argument that Ricardian rent exists on the mineral deposits of successful mining firms. It is the allocation of this rent — to the firm, the consumer, or the state — that is the subject for dispute in current policy. This issue about the distribution of mining profits is clarified by this research.

Even if the MNE were able to exploit Canadians, it is not clear that excessive profits could be realized at home. Examination of existing tax codes by Musgrave (1969) and others shows that the U.S. government has the power to impose "arm's length" (market prices) for intracorporate prices. This power of the internal revenue service should be a check against possible transfer pricing policies of U.S.-based MNEs. It is, of course, necessary to extend this work by an examination of Canadian tax legislation as it affects the MNE. In any analysis of transfer pricing, it is necessary to consider the impact of taxes, tariffs, profit controls, and other regulations that affect the profits of an MNE.

In his paper, Herbert Grubel (1974) found that the United States realized a net social rate of return of −9.2 percent in direct investment in Canadian manufacturing, mainly due to the double taxation agreement between Canada and the United States. Under this agreement, taxes paid by corporations to the Canadian government are taxes foregone by the United States despite the initial outflow of funds from the United States.

Grubel did not study the 8 percent of U.S. direct investment which goes into mining and smelting, but using data from the U.S. Department of Commerce *Survey of Current Business,* it was possible to find these rates of return. The interaction between tax policy and transfer pricing is examined using these findings. The results of this research reveal a divergence between social and private rates of return, due to government legislations, which prevents the free movement of international capital. It is found that Canada, on the whole, enjoys a net social benefit from foreign investment in the mineral resource industry, and that the U.S. experiences a social loss through foregone tax revenue. In this case, the economic role of minerals in the Canadian economy appears in a different and more favorable light than in an analysis which fails to make the vital distinction between private and social costs.

CRITICISM OF THE GRUBEL-JENKINS APPROACH

The papers of Herbert Grubel (1974) of Simon Fraser University and Glenn Jenkins (1973b) of Harvard University are important contributions to the literature on taxation and FDI. It is a useful contribution of both papers to focus attention on the crucial role of the government itself since taxation policy is a very important element influencing international capital flows.

Traditional textbook models of foreign investment that ignore the existence of government taxation policy are of little use in a world characterized by capital controls and other restrictive devices. There has not been a perfect international capital market since the early 1930s.

Both papers are based on the theoretical work of MacDougall (1960). He demonstrated in his classic article on the benefits and costs of foreign investment that the host economy made a social gain in the form of tax revenue paid to it by foreign subsidiaries established and financed through foreign investment. On the other hand, the donor country suffered a social loss of tax receipts which were foregone due to intergovernment agreements not to engage in double taxation of corporations. Thus, when corporation taxes are paid by an American subsidiary in a host economy such as Canada, there is no need for the parent corporation to pay further taxes to the United States on the profits of its Canadian subsidiary. These two papers offer empirical support for the theoretical argument advanced previously by MacDougall, and they are the first such detailed evaluations to appear.

The results of the private and social rates of return on foreign investment made by each author are strikingly similar. Grubel approaches the problem from the viewpoint of an international trade economist, and makes an aggregative evaluation of the portfolio (bond and equity) and direct investment effects. Jenkins undertakes detailed calculations of the private and social rates of return of each sector in the Canadian economy. His work is disaggregated by industry classification, for example, including twenty manfacturing industries and about another twenty nonmanufacturing industries.

In general, Jenkins finds that the private rate of return on private investment is about 6 percent and that the social rate of return is significantly higher at about 9 percent. Grubel finds similar rates of return for direct investment in Canada. Grubel, however, takes the argument further than Jenkins by demonstrating that the U.S. social rate of return before taxes on such investment in the manufacturing sectors is about 19 percent. Therefore, the net social rate of return on U.S. direct investment is negative 10 percent. The negative social rate of return is entirely due to the U.S. tax credit given the MNE under the double taxation agreement. The resulting social loss of taxes to the United States is clearly a social gain to Canada from U.S. FDI.

Two major questions arise when one examines these papers. First, it is possible that the private rates of return have been underestimated. There may be additional unrecognized advantages to the MNE from foreign investment. Using a portfolio theory model based on the work of Tobin and Markowitz, it can be postulated that direct investment allows an American

MNE the chance to reduce the risk of its earnings stream over time. This will be possible if the economies of foreign countries are not perfectly correlated with the U.S. economy itself. This principle of international diversification is explained in Rugman (1979). Once the utility of an investor is assumed to depend on the stability of earnings as well as the absolute level of earnings, then it becomes an important consideration for the firm to look for a stable pattern of sales since these are likely to generate stable earnings and a favorable stock market evaluation. The sales into foreign economies are realized, for example, by the MNE through its direct investment abroad. It could also, of course, be achieved through exports, but this depends on there being reasonably free entry to foreign markets.

Second, the papers do not include any analysis of the determinants of foreign investments, and they just accept the existence of such foreign investment when the calculations are being made of private and social rates of return. A theory of the motivation of foreign investment is required before any firm policy conclusions are drawn from this work. It may be that the private benefits to the MNE from FDI are impossible to earn in the home economy so the opportunity cost of U.S. FDI is negligible. Both papers calculate rates of return on FDI, which implies that they are examining only one motive for foreign investment, namely the neoclassical one where performance is reflected fully in the profit rate of the firm. Here other variables may be important. For example, the modern theory of FDI suggests that market imperfections should be considered. Such market imperfections are the public good nature of new knowledge and research that are internalized by private corporations in an attempt to appropriate a fair return for private expenditure on knowledge generation. Yet the social price of knowledge should be zero. Such firm specific advantage to the MNE should be offset against any considerations of a social loss to the home nation from U.S. FDI. In conclusion, both the principles of international diversification and internalization imply that there are substantial benefits to the U.S. MNE from its FDI. These benefits are not captured fully by examination of the private (or social) rate of return.

Both authors discuss the role of the tariff as it has affected Canadian economic development. However, the full implications of the tariff are not drawn out in the papers, and the methodology employed in deriving the social welfare gain to Canada of foreign investment is somewhat suspect. On the one hand, it is suggested that there is a social gain to Canada from (mostly U.S.) foreign investment of some 2 percent per annum of GNP (Jenkins 1973b, p. 20; Grubel 1974, p. 26). On the other hand, there is a well-known literature on the costs of the tariff to Canada, including the work of John Young (1957), Wonnacott and Wonnacott (1967), and Eastman (1964). A good summary of this literature can be found in the summary volume of the *Canada in the Atlantic Economy* series, edited by English, Eastman, and Wilkinson (1972). In general, the costs of the tariff, in terms of industrial inefficiency and the resulting higher prices of manufactured goods due to the lack of economies of scale in the too small Canadian protected market, have been established at between 4 percent and 12 percent of GNP per annum. Therefore, the social gain to Canada from the taxation received from foreign subsidiaries established and financed through U.S. direct investment must be weighed against the established social loss resulting from protection of inefficient manufacturing industries.

In fact, Canada is doubly unfortunate in the sense that the historical reliance on the tariff to build up domestic industry has resulted in a greater volume of FDI which took place in order to avoid the tariff wall. Such foreign ownership is disliked by many Canadians with nationalist feelings and a concern for Canadian political sovereignty. The tariff has a cost in terms of inefficiency, and the resulting foreign investment has a cost in terms of offending the preferences of Canadians. If Canada had relied on a free trade policy, then through comparative advantage it could have exported resource intensive goods in return for imports of industrial products. In doing so, Canada could have been better off in terms of income per capita, and also in terms of less foreign ownership.

Both authors have anticipated this type of criticism and argue that their estimates of the social rate of return are biased downward so that their main conclusion that there is a social loss to the United States from foreign investment will hold up if, in fact, the social rate of return is greater. I have argued that the private rate of return may be somewhat underestimated, which implies that there is less of a social welfare loss to the United States than is indicated by Grubel and Jenkins. However, the negative social rate of return on direct investment will remain if the spread between private and social rates of return holds up due to a downward bias in the calculated social rates of return.

Finally, on this particular subject it is questionable whether a social rate of return (in terms of welfare economics) has been calculated. Only tax rates have been included in order to distinguish social from private rates of return. This leads to some odd implications. For example, in a related paper, Jenkins (1973a, p. 2) found that the private rate of return on tobacco products was at a conventional level of 7 percent, but that the social rate of return was 133 percent. This is, of course, simply due to the high rate of taxation on tobacco products, but does indicate the danger of calling this a social rate of return.

Despite these problems, it is a worthwhile exercise to use the methodology (of Grubel especially) for an updated analysis of the private and social rates of return from U.S. FDI in Canada. The results of such an analysis are reported in Table 6-1. To understand this table, it should be noted that the procedure of Grubel (1974) was exactly replicated, to the extent of checking all his original data sources before updating the figures. Grubel only examined manufacturing, but, with some reservations, the identical technique can be applied to the petroleum and other mining sectors.

One of the reservations Grubel had in mind is that the domestic (U.S.) opportunity cost of FDI in mining and petroleum "is impossible to establish reliably" since it is dependent on specific natural deposits. Yet this argument is a half truth since the financing of foreign or domestic mineral deposits by an MNE should be determined by the firm's overall cost of capital — which does not vary by project but is that of the parent firm. See Giddy (1977) and Shapiro (1978) for more details. Second, Grubel states that "special treaties with foreign governments about royalties, special accounting, and depreciation rules . . . makes it impossible to estimate rates of return which would be theoretically appropriate. . . . " Again we know now that these imperfections are explained by the theory of internalization and that the MNE can overcome such externalities.

RESULTS

Rows 12 and 13 of Table 6-1 reveal that there is a negative social rate of return to the United States for its FDI in the Canadian mining, petroleum, and manufacturing sectors over the 1966–1976 period. In mining, the net social loss is about 10 percent, and in petroleum it is about 6 percent. There is a social loss of around 5 percent from U.S. FDI in the Canadian manufacturing sector. If an adjustment for royalties and fees received is made, as in row 13, then these net social losses to the United States are reduced by about 3 percentage points in each case.

What do these figures imply for Canada? They indicate that if U.S. FDI realizes a social loss, due to foregone tax revenues, then the converse must hold. The converse is that Canada realizes a social gain from U.S. FDI. Canada receives the tax revenues so it should interpret these results as indications of some social gain from U.S. FDI. The precise numbers may not be too relevant, but the direction of the sign — positive — is relevant. The implication that Canada has a social benefit from U.S. FDI is an important one. It is consistent with much of the other theoretical and empirical analysis of this book.

The social losses to the United States of its FDI in Canada clearly result from the structure of the U.S. tax system. The tax credits allowed to U.S. MNEs for taxes paid abroad are the single most important cause of the social loss. It may be more accurate, in fact, to refer to the social loss as a tax loss. In any case, the social losses from U.S. FDI may be offset, in part, by gains from net FDI by Japanese, European, or Arab direct investors. The rapid growth of such FDI in recent years will mitigate considerably the social losses from U.S. FDI itself. Thus, the net impact on the U.S. economy

TABLE 6-1.   Average rates of return from U.S. direct investment in Canada, 1966-1976

	Manufacturing		Petroleum		Mining	
(1) Book Value, 1976, $ million	15,984		7153		3200	
Before-tax rates of return:						
(2) Book value	22.08		21.02		15.8	
(3) Equity	30.38		28.92		21.8	
(4) Effective corporate tax rates	50		50		50	
After corporate tax rates of return on:						
(5) Book value	11.04		10.51		7.9	
(6) Equity	15.19		14.46		10.9	
(7) Ratio of dividends to earnings	0.35		0.41		0.66	
(8) Tax rate on dividends	15		15		15	
(9) After corporate and dividend taxes rate of return, equity	13.60		12.68		8.7	
	(x)	(y)	(x)	(y)	(x)	(y)
(10) Exchange rate adjustment	0.00	+0.80	0.0	+0.80	0.00	+0.80
(11) Gross social rate of return (9) + (10)	13.60	14.40	12.68	13.48	8.70	9.50
(12) Net social rate of return (11) − 19.3%	−5.70	−4.90	−6.62	−5.82	−10.60	−9.80
(13) After adjustment for royalties and fees (12) +2.89	−2.81	−2.01	−3.73	−2.93	−7.71	−6.91

Notes:
Column (x) is assumption of parity in exchange rate between United States and Canada.
Column (y) is exchange rate adjustment. See note (b).

from FDI is unknown at the moment. In the other attempts to examine the tax effects of U.S. FDI by writers such as Bergsten, Horst, and Moran (1978) a different approach was followed, so this work should be thought of as complementary to theirs, rather than a substitute for it.

Furthermore, the concept of a social gain or loss is pretty nationalistic. It does not refer to welfare gains or losses, but only to the effect on an economy's tax receipts; that is, a distributional effect. The existence of different national tax laws is therefore another example of a market imperfection

Notes to Table 6-1

(a) Line (5) is the average rate of return on United States direct investment in Canada calculated from data available in an annual article entitled, "U.S. Direct Investment Abroad" which appears in the U.S. Department of Commerce *Survey of Current Business.*

(b) The exchange rate adjustment (line (10)) is total appreciation of the Canadian dollar over the period expressed at an annual rate

$$\left(\sqrt[ii]{\frac{(1966)}{(1976)}} - 1 \right) \times 100 \times (-1)$$

(c) The "Book value" includes liabilities to parents, using Grubel's methodology to obtain the rate of return on equity (Grubel 1974, p. 483).

(d) Effective corporate tax rate was taken from the table "Corporation Tax Rates" based on Canadian Tax Foundation data.

Following Grubel's methodology:

(1) Source: *Survey of Current Business.*

(2) $= (5) \times \left[\dfrac{100}{100 - (4)} \right]$

(3) $= (2) \times 1.376$ (see note (c) above)

(4) (See note (d) above)

(5) (See note (a) above)

(6) $= (5) \times 1.376$ (see note (c) above)

(7) Source: *Survey of Current Business.*
     Average ratio of distributed to after tax earnings.

(8) Same source as (4) (d).

(9) $(6) = \left[\dfrac{(8)}{100} \times (7) \times (3) \right]$

(10) See note (b) above

(11) (9) + (10)

(12) (11) − 19.3 (see note h in table 4 of Grubel 1974)

(13) (12) − 2.1 × 1.376 (see Grubel 1974, p. 485)

We are not assuming that the ratios used in line (13) which applied to the 1960–1969 period hold for our period as well, i.e., it is assumed that the ratio of royalties and fees to book value averages 2.1% so that the ratio of royalties and fees to equity would be 2.9 (i.e., 2.1 × 1.376). Source: U.S. Department of Commerce, *Survey of Current Business.*

confronting the MNE. It is criticized for not paying enough taxes to the home nation when the source of this problem (if it is a problem) lies in the U.S. tax legislation which is beyond its control. If national tax rates were harmonized and the substantive differences in national tax codes eliminated, then the MNE would be in a position where it would pay taxes in a socially (welfare) efficient manner.

In this first best situation, the MNE should pay taxes to the host nation (Canada) for the use of the infrastructure and other government-subsidized services provided to the MNE, and to domestic corporations as well. It should pay for the use of these services by paying its corporation tax on the profits of the subsidiary of the MNE. For tax purposes, the subsidiary has to be regarded as an independent profit center. In general, this is a bad assumption to make since the MNE is operating according to the theory of internalization, and since this theory indicates that it is the overall performance of the MNE which is of relevance, rather than that of an individual subsidiary. Yet here it was assumed that tax rates and tax codes are harmonized, and in such a world of one less market imperfection there is less sense in having independent profit centers than in a world with tax rate differentials.

In conclusion, the empirical work reported in this chapter is very exploratory and should be treated with caution. It is worthy of attention only as a suggestion for future, more detailed, research. The results of this section are of some interest, given their limited nature and the restrictive methodology, only inasmuch as they provide a little more support for the basic premises of this book. These state that the MNE is an efficient vehicle for FDI and that the performance of the MNE, in terms of profitability and risk, does not reveal any evidence of excessive market power or influence. In turn, this implies that individual U.S. investors are not enjoying excessive returns on their holdings of foreign assets, nor is U.S. FDI contributing in any exceptional manner to the wealth of that nation.

7 TRANSFER PRICING IN THE CANADIAN MINING INDUSTRY

INTRODUCTION

It is frequently alleged that the multinational enterprise has the market power and managerial ability to engage in transfer pricing. Both critics of the MNE, and even its supporters on occasion, have argued that the MNE can use its internal organizational structure to charge nonmarket prices for intermediate inputs. It can thereby influence the net revenues earned by the parent firm and the various subsidiaries. Here I argue that the extent to which the MNE uses its own internal market to manipulate intracorporate prices of intermediate goods will be influenced by external factors such as the taxation policy, tariffs, and capital controls of national governments.

Transfer prices and tax rates are interrelated. International tax rate differentials on both final goods and on the inputs for the MNE affect its profitability and its costs. Thus, the normal costs of factors such as labor and capital in each subsidiary need to be amended to account for tax effects. If there are no tariffs and international tax rates are uniform between nations,

87

then there would be no incentive for transfer pricing by the MNE. If there were no market imperfections, then "arm's length" prices would exist within the MNE. However, the need for internalization and the observed exogenous market imperfection of international tax differentials act as incentives for transfer pricing. The MNE responds to market imperfections by manipulation of prices within its internal market and organization. This is yet another example of internalization. It is also an efficient response by the MNE to an exogenous market imperfection. If another imperfection exists, such as restrictions on dividend remittances, blocked funds, or other types of capital controls, then the MNE will have additional incentives for the use of transfer pricing.

While in theory the MNE can engage in transfer pricing, in practice there is little evidence of such an activity. There have been few empirical studies of transfer price manipulation by the MNEs except for the influential but inadequate work of Vaitsos (1974) and Lall (1973). Both authors focus on an unrepresentative group of MNEs. They use data on the pricing of pharmaceuticals by MNEs active in Colombia and (on occasions) three other South American nations. Yet data based on customs duties paid are not available for public scrutiny to check out their results, since they were provided by government agencies on a confidential basis. The industry itself is perhaps not representative of MNEs. The work has been criticized by Vernon (1977) and Lessard (1977) on these, and other, grounds.

An alternative approach to that of Vaitsos is followed here. We choose to evaluate the performance of the MNEs active in the Canadian mining industry. The ultimate criterion of economic performance is profitability. Therefore, the profits of both parent and subsidiaries are calculated and examined for significant differences. If transfer pricing is being used by the MNE, it should show up in excessive profits of either the parent or one or more of its subsidiaries. However, if profit rates are found to be virtually identical for all parts of the MNE, it is hard to live with the idea that transfer pricing is in operation.

It should be noted that this investigation of profitability examines the breakdown between parent and subsidiary. Naturally, an MNE can use any market power it may possess to normalize profits or even set a target profit rate (presumably close to the average for all manufacturing firms). If this procedure is followed, then the MNE manipulates the costs and revenues of various subsidiaries to stabilize the profit rate of the consolidated MNE. The approach followed here permits us to go behind the screen of consolidated balance sheets and potentially stable profits. The profit rates of individual subsidiaries, and of the parent, are examined for significant differences.

THE TRANSFER PRICING LITERATURE

Vaitsos (1974) provides a good survey of the literature on the determinants of foreign investment and also reports tests of the transfer pricing policies of multinational firms operating in Latin America. His survey of the motives for foreign investment emphasizes oligopoly theory and the market imperfections model advanced by Hymer, Kindleberger, Caves, and others in recent years. His most important contribution, however, is in the empirical work reported in his book. This provides a fascinating insight into the distortions which result from overpricing of the products of foreign-owned companies.

Vaitsos was able to assemble data on transfer pricing policies for four industries for four Latin American countries. The industries studied are pharmaceuticals, chemicals, rubber, and electronics. These are all studied for Colombia with some supporting work from Ecuador, Chile, and Peru. Vaitsos found that, on average, the pharmaceuticals industry in Colombia was overpricing its products by 150 percent; chemicals by 25.5 percent; rubber by 40 percent; and electronics by 16 to 60 percent. Similar results were found for the other countries.

Overpricing is defined as the FOB price paid by the purchasing nation less FOB prices quoted in different markets around the world, all divided by the latter times 100. It is alleged that transfer pricing operates in two ways — exports being underpriced when sales are made in Latin American subsidiaries to their parent firms in the USA, and imports being overpriced when sales are made from the parent to the subsidiary. Vaitsos summarizes his argument: "Foreign subsidiaries in the cases investigated apparently use transfer pricing of products as a mechanism of income remission, thus significantly understating their true profitability" (p. 50).

Other findings are that there is a large balance of payments effect, as much as 80 percent of potential export revenue being lost. In addition, there is a tax loss from corporation taxes which are never realized. This amounts to as much as 50 percent of the total tax bill. Both these balance of payments and tax situations have adverse effects on growth. Further, there are losses of efficiency since foreign-owned sectors are promoted at the expense of potentially efficient sectors.

While this evidence on the practice of transfer pricing is limited to four industries, Vaitsos thinks the results are of sufficient generality to apply to all developing countries. Vaitsos goes so far as to suggest that foreign subsidiaries negotiate with national governments for favorable tariff and tax provisions, and that they benefit from patents, licenses, and other protective devices.

Vaitsos argues that monopoly profits earned by subsidiaries are not captured by the government since declared profits at the subsidiary level are understated. In his own words, "declared profits . . . grossly understate the effective profitability resulting from foreign operations" (p. 61). Vaitsos finds that in Colombia declared profits are only 6 or 7 percent in the pharmaceutical industry, but he calculates the effective profit rate to be 136 percent. The effective profit rate for electronics is 50 to 80 percent, whereas the subsidiary in this industry reported a "loss" of 18 percent in 1967. Vaitsos also finds that subsidiaries negotiate favorable terms in financing. The debt equity ratio for foreign-owned firms was 3.9, whereas for Colombia as a whole it was only 1.8 in 1967.

These findings present a case against the transfer pricing policies of multinationals operating in the Andean countries. However, the findings are only as good as the data base which is suspect, since it uses data provided by government agencies, but these data are not available for public review. Vaitsos reports in his Chapter 3 on his methodology in collecting data. He probably did as well as could be expected without having access to the confidential statements of the multinational firms themselves. Another problem is that Vaitsos does not address the issue of whether it is appropriate to use official or market-determined foreign exchange rates when calculating international costs and prices. Nor does he consider in any detail the complex issues of multinational tax policy and double taxation agreements.

Mathewson and Quirin (1979) have examined the impact of transfer pricing by U.S. MNEs on the Canadian economy. The authors concede that, in theory, the multinational corporations can use transfer pricing to create such economic problems as resource misallocation, reduction in employment of labor and capital, erosion of the tax base, and potential evasion of foreign exchange controls. This is a moot point. It is argued in this chapter that the MNEs use transfer pricing in response to such market imperfections as international tax rate differentials or exchange controls. Remove the imperfections (by harmonization of taxes or elimination of barriers to capital flows), and the incentive for MNEs to use internal pricing is removed, since they can then take their profits wherever these are generated without prejudice to their corporate performance.

Some empirical work is attempted by Quirin and Mathewson. They do not believe that reliable data are available for such work, since transfer pricing is "conducted under a cloak of secrecy" (p. 3). Instead, they use a "pseudo-empirical" technique (their own words) to generate a range of imaginary numbers over which the MNEs have the potential opportunity to use transfer pricing. "This range is then used to determine the maximum employment-shifting and other effects under the assumption that full advantage is taken of the opportunities thus presented" (p. 4). Since all their results stem from this hypothetical procedure, it would help to have its validity based on more than an assumption. What if not all of the MNEs can take advantage of these "opportunities"? Does this mean there are real gains in resource allocation rather than the assumed real costs? Sadly we cannot know, at least from this study, if there are any offsetting factors to reduce the upward bias of this procedure.

Having chosen a methodology which appears to bias upward the chances of finding transfer pricing, it is of interest to note that Quirin and Mathewson find little evidence of it. On the basis of their research, the authors conclude "that multinationals have a relatively restricted scope for transfer price manipulation" (p. 87). The use of transfer prices appears to be offset by tax and tariff systems which provided the incentives for the use of transfer pricing in the first place. The evidence presented offers no support for transfer price manipulation, even in the resource sector where there exists the greatest opportunity for such manipulation.

TRANSFER PRICING AND INTERNALIZATION

It has been established on theoretical grounds that the MNE has the ability to use transfer prices and that these may increase the overall profit rate of the firm. One of the best demonstrations of this, using a heuristic programming technique, is by Nieckels (1976). He extends the original work of Hirschleifer (1956), Gould (1964), and others, done in a domestic context, to an international dimension and proves that the performance of an MNE is improved by the use of transfer prices. Similar conclusions, using rigorous linear programming or other analytical models, have been reached by Horst (1971, 1977), Copithorne (1971), Booth and Jensen (1977), Eden (1978), and Lessard (1977). Lessard has also recognized that transfer pricing by the MNE takes place in a world of imperfect markets. Here this insight is extended further and an even stronger interpretation is made; namely, that transfer prices are an efficient response by the MNE to exogenous market imperfections.

The MNE has to operate in a world characterized by international tax rate differentials, foreign exchange controls, currency manipulation, multiple exchange rates, governmental regulations, and barriers to investment. Such market imperfections erect high transactions costs for the international firm if it uses regular markets. To avoid these externalities and other excessive costs, it creates an internal market. The MNE then uses administrative fiat to allocate resources, intermediate products, and other factors between its parent division and foreign subsidiaries. In this process of internalization, it is natural that internal (transfer) prices be used. Such prices are set by administrative decision and have to be respected as the prices necessary to make the MNE function efficiently.

Many critics of the MNE point out that transfer prices arise from the power of the MNE to close a market and that transfer prices may well not equal "arm's length" or market prices. There are at least two errors in such criticism. First, the so-called arm's length prices do not exist. When there is no (external) market, there is no market price. Conversely, when there is an internal market created by the MNE within its own organization, then the resulting transfer prices are the correct ones. Without them the internal market might not exist, so the MNE is entitled to charge whatever prices it wishes for intermediate products provided it produces final goods which can be sold openly. The ultimate control over transfer pricing comes in the market for the final product of the MNE, since an inefficient performance due to incorrect transfer pricing, will lead eventually to the demise of the MNE. Second, the transfer prices are created by the MNE in response to market imperfections. If governments regard transfer pricing as a potential abuse of the power of MNEs, then there is a ready solution at hand. This is to harmonize international tax rates, and eliminate exchange controls and other barriers to capital flows imposed by governments. Such a first best solution will remove the incentive for transfer pricing of MNEs.

The empirical work of Vaitsos (1974), Lall (1973), and others has found evidence of transfer pricing, mainly in the pharmaceuticals industry in Colombia. They also find that the profits of subsidiaries in Latin America are "squeezed" by the parent MNEs. In this chapter and elsewhere (Rugman 1980b), I find no evidence of transfer pricing as reflected in the earnings performance between the parents and subsidiaries of U.S. MNEs active in the Canadian mineral resource industry. While some subsidiaries have low profits, and others higher profits, there is no significant difference after adjusting for risk of earnings.

This ambiguity in the empirical work is in sharp contrast to the theoretical work reviewed earlier which finds that MNEs can use transfer pricing. It appears that, in practice, transfer pricing is hard to find so its abuse by the MNEs must be left in question. Further, the MNE must find it difficult to set a price for intangibles such as knowledge generation, technological advantage, and managerial skills, so there are probably no "correct" transfer prices anyhow. Thus, the theory of internalization reveals that the internal pricing of knowledge advantages by the MNE is merely a response to the lack of a market. It is not a suspicious action but a rational one by an efficient business organization, the MNE.

The use of transfer pricing for tangible goods which can be priced in a recognized external market would be defensible if the MNE responds to an exogenous market imperfection, such as differentials in national tax rates. The tax policies of governments are not uniform, so the MNE is presented with an opportunity to minimize its tax bill by using transfer prices in its intracompany accounting. If tax rates are equalized internationally, then there is no incentive for transfer pricing by the MNE (assuming that no other capital market imperfections exist).

Turning attention to the pricing of an intermediate good such as knowledge or information, as embodied in the products of an MNE, let a transfer price be defined as a nonmarket price set internally by an MNE. If a proper market existed for information, there could be an arm's length price, but since there is no market, the MNE determines the price of information by use of its internal pricing.

The need for an internal market always remains in the valuation of information, and transfer prices for this intermediate product are justified. In this context, transfer prices probably follow a random walk; that is, they respond in a weakly efficient manner to random shocks in the generation of new knowledge and information. In this view, the internal prices used by the organization of the MNE are set by administrative fiat and incorporate all relevant information about exogenous economic and financial conditions. Therefore, transfer prices are not arbitrary numbers, but are the correct internal administrative prices required to make internalization function.

It is meaningless to examine transfer prices on their own, or to attempt to compare them to nonexistent arm's length prices. Instead, the MNE should be allowed to use whatever transfer prices it cares to. Only its performance in producing final goods is of interest to consumer and governments. Thus, the overall profits of MNEs should be analyzed rather than partial aspects of the firms, such as transfer pricing.

In a synthesis of the recent literature on transfer pricing, Plasschaert (1979) makes a clear and definitive statement of the transfer pricing practices of multinational corporations within the context of the theory of internalization. Consistent with internalization theory Plasschaert emphasises the point that transfer pricing is a response of the MNE to exogenous market imperfections such as tariffs, international tax rate differentials, exchange controls and tax havens. Such government imposed market imperfections complement natural externalities in the areas of knowledge and technology. These international externalities act as inducements to the multinational corporation to create and use its own market, in which transfer prices are merely the internal prices required to make this market work efficiently. As a result the MNE needs to have centralized financial management which uses internal pricing to ensure that the joint costs of ongoing, indivisible, research and development are charged to all divisions of the MNE, rather than being borne by the parent alone. Being one of the first authors to apply the Reading theory to the emotional issue of transfer pricing, Plasschaert is able to make valuable criticisms of the existing empirical studies, which have neglected internalization theory. He is also critical of much of the existing public policy in this area and suggests that transfer pricing be viewed in less pejorative terms by governments. His analysis and policy conclusions are very similar to those developed in this chapter.

METHODS OF TESTING FOR TRANSFER PRICING

It is basically an empirical question as to whether or not multinational firms engage in transfer pricing. Unfortunately, little or no data are available on the internal pricing policies of individual firms. Therefore, the independent researcher is faced with a difficult task in attempting to measure any alleged divergence between the theoretically appropriate market price for a product or input and the actual price charged in intrafirm accounting. However, there are ways to overcome the problem of lack of data on transfer pricing.

First, it may be possible to engage in several individual firm case studies, using figures disclosed by firms on personal request. This is not a very practical method, however, unless corporations are willing to set aside the time and resources to answer survey questionnaires, and to prepare detailed accounts.

Second, it is possible to study the world prices of intermediate products at industry level using import and export data. With the use of concentration ratios, the leading firms in an industry group can be identified and the revealed world price can be applied to actual industry level prices charged by the divisions of the MNE. The foreign trade prices of intermediate inputs can be compared to the world price, with the difference being taken as a proxy measure of the distortion caused by transfer pricing. In this manner, dominant corporations in subsectors of the mining industry can be tested for transfer pricing activities. In this approach, it is important to allow for price divergences caused by exchange rate fluctuations, the influence of government barriers to trade (such as tariffs), and other factors outside the control of an individual corporation.

Third, it is possible to use published data on firm and industry profits to indirectly test the effect (or noneffect) of transfer pricing. For example, profit figures for a Canadian subsidiary can be compared with profits of the parent firm. In the absence of transfer pricing it would be expected that profit rates for subsidiary and parent would be approximately equal, given similar patterns of factor costs and government taxation policies. If transfer pricing does exist, then it would be hypothesized that the parent firm's rate of profit would exceed the profit rate of its subsidiary — since the subsidiary must either be underpaid for sales of resources to the parent, or forced to pay too much for purchases from the parent firm.

In this study the third method is pursued, not because it is theoretically superior to the other two, but due to data availability. Given the paucity of objective research on the emotional subject of transfer pricing, such a pioneering approach is necessary as a first step toward a more complete empirical analysis. In the next section, details of the actual research procedure are given and several tables are used to illustrate the performance of mining MNEs and their subsidiaries. It is found that the subsidiaries with high returns also experience high levels of (total) risk. Therefore, a simple mean-variance version of portfolio theory appears to explain the profits of these MNEs. No evidence is found of transfer pricing.

RESULTS

This project extends an earlier study by Rugman (1977), in which the fifteen largest multinational corporations active in the Canadian mining industry were identified and their performance analyzed. The profit rates of consolidated MNEs were found; but here, using annual reports and 10-Ks it is possible to assemble new information on the performance of major divisions and lines of business of the mining MNEs. Although it was difficult to develop a long time series for all of the firms, it was possible to trace back the disaggregated profits for eight of the major firms. Rates of return on revenue, on assets, and a shareholders' equity were then calculated. The profit rates of individual subsidiaries and of the parent are examined for significant differences.

The mean profit rate over time and the standard deviation (S.D.) of the profit stream are found and used to represent expected return and total risk respectively. The resulting means and S.D.'s can be graphed in risk-return space, although space limitations prevent the reproduction here of such diagrams. Instead, Tables 7–1 to 7–3 summarize these data.

The details of the performance measured for earnings on revenue, by division, are reported in Table 7-1 for AMAX (1968-1977), Falconbridge (1971-1977), INCO (1974-1977), IMC (1971-1977), Noranda (1970-1977), Patino (1971-1977), JMC (1971-1975), and Rio Algom (1963-1977). The

TABLE 7-1.   Rate of return on revenues

Firm	Division/Subsidiary	Mean	S.D.
AMAX	(1968–1977)		
	Base metals	5.95	3.24
	Fuels	10.41	7.26
	Molybdenum, nickel etc.	22.28	6.40
	Chemicals	24.36	14.43
	Iron ore	45.79	13.00
	Consolidated	12.2	1.3
FALCONBRIDGE	(1971–1977)		
	Indusmin	7.55	2.23
	Domininia	8.29	4.67
	Oamites	8.56	9.73
	Copper	13.64	11.22
	Integrated nickel	1.13	9.50
	Wesfrob	− 8.00	21.03
	Total	5.47	6.86
INCO	(1974–1977)		
	Subsidiaries	3.54	0.78
	Parent	15.56	6.31
	Total	10.88	5.22
IMC	(1971–1977)		
	Industry	1.67	2.12
	Chemicals (1974–1977)	6.55	3.56
	Agriculture	12.37	4.1
	Consolidated	7.1	3.6
	Foreign subsidiaries 1974–1977	9.22	1.94
NORANDA	(by subsidiary) (1966–1972)		
	Pamour Porcupine	19.39	8.74
	Empresa Minera	20.09	8.68
	Orchan Mines	25.61	4.42
	Kerr Addison	30.86	5.63
	Empresa Fluorspar	67.51	30.63
	Consolidated	12.81	1.41
	(by industrial division) (1970–1977)		
	Manufacturing	3.86	1.78
	Forest products	4.22	1.83
	Other mining	15.26	8.93

TABLE 7–1.   Continued

Firm	Division/Subsidiary	Mean	S.D.
	Total mining	15.76	6.17
	Copper mining, smelting, refining	15.91	3.86
	Consolidated	9.82	4.63
PATINO	(1971–1977)		
	Metals and ore	0.13	0.51
	Tin smelting	2.21	1.28
	Steel	3.11	8.22
	Other activities	11.44	9.18
	Mineral sales	15.96	16.49
	Consolidated	1.3	0.9
RIO ALGOM	(1963–1977)		
	Steel	5.4	3.8
	Mining	33.6	9.9
	Consolidated	12.4	6.7
JMC	(1971–1975)		
	Industrial	4.63	3.53
	General building products	5.47	2.63
	Pipe systems	6.34	5.46
	Thermal insulators	9.26	2.99
	Roofing products	11.45	0.92
	Mining and minerals	19.14	3.30
	Consolidated	9.05	1.97

TABLE 7–2.   Rate of return on assets

Firm	Division/Subsidiary	Mean	S.D.
AMAX	(1968–1977)		
	Fuels	4.6	4.1
	Base metals	8.3	5.8
	Molybdenum, nickel etc.	13.4	9.5
	Iron ore	15.6	4.5
	Chemicals	36.7	29.9
	Consolidated	6.2	1.6

(*Note:* the mean for Consolidated is less than the average of the means of the divisions since unallocated corporate expenses are included in it.)

TABLE 7-2.   Continued

Firm	Division/Subsidiary	Mean	S.D.
FALCONBRIDGE	(1971–1977)		
	Integrated nickel	1.54	3.57
	Dominicane	3.55	2.16
	Indusmin	6.84	2.25
	Oamites	10.50	13.18
	Copper	17.45	14.99
	Wesfrob	–4.45	13.23
	Total	3.13	3.98
INCO	(1974–1977)		
	Subsidiaries	3.1	1.0
	Parent	9.6	8.7
	Total	6.2	3.4
RIO ALGOM	(1973–1977)		
	Steel	10.56	6.10
	Mining-copper	19.06	10.37
	Uranium	36.32	5.24
	Lornex (1972–1977)	7.17	7.66
IMC	(1974–1977)		
	Foreign subsidiaries	8.62	0.12

TABLE 7-3.   Rate of return on equity

Firm	Division/Subsidiary	Mean	S.D.
INCO	(1974–1977)		
	Parent	10.43	4.17
	Subsidiaries	12.92	2.0
	Total	12.87	6.48
IMC	(1973–1977)		
	Industry	12.74	7.65
	Chemicals	13.45	8.28
	Agriculture	17.24	7.08
	Consolidated	14.0	5.6

rates of return on assets and equity give a similar picture, but are not as complete as the return on revenue figures. These are reported in Tables 7-2 and 7-3 respectively. More details appear in Rugman (1980b).

It can be observed that there is typically a wide deviation in profit rates between the divisions of the MNE. Some subsidiaries earn very high profits while others have much less than the firm average. Is this evidence of transfer pricing? To examine the disparity in profit rates further, a simple portfolio theory approach is used. This risk of earning is proxied by funding the standard deviation (S.D.) of profits over time.

It is striking to observe the positive relationship between risk and return for all of the MNEs. Thus, the highly profitable divisions experience the greatest risk, while the less profitable ones have low risk. This is consistent with the implications of portfolio theory and indicates that the subdivisions of the mining MNEs examined are not engaged in any unusual economic activities. Indeed, the internal performance of the MNEs is entirely consistent with portfolio theory, and this may lead to the implication that these MNEs are efficient. These tests, therefore, do not provide any support for transfer pricing among the divisions since transfer pricing is a symptom of market inefficiency.

It is also apparent that the parent (total) firm has a risk-return relationship which is the average of its divisions. Thus, the parent is not able to squeeze its subsidiaries in order to realize an excessive profit rate for any level of risk. In conclusion, no evidence is found of transfer pricing in this examination of the performance of major subsidiaries and divisions of MNEs active in Canadian mining.

CONCLUSIONS

Further empirical work is required before a definite conclusion can be drawn about the lack of transfer pricing by these MNEs. In this chapter an interesting new approach has been suggested; one which allows the independent researcher to overcome the lack of data on internal pricing by the MNE. It should be noted that governments have greater research facilities and that their internal revenue services have access to company information on intracorporate pricing. Therefore, the nation state is in a strong position to observe and regulate the profits of the MNE, if it is engaging in transfer pricing. The tentative conclusion from this research is that transfer pricing is not reflected in the profit performance of the MNE and its subsidiaries.

8 THE ECONOMIC IMPACT OF MULTINATIONALS IN CANADA

INTRODUCTION

This chapter is concerned with the economic impact of U.S.-owned multinationals on the growth and development of Canada. Special attention is directed toward the mining industry and an analysis of its contribution to the Canadian economy is reviewed. The role of the MNE as an agent for the transfer of technology is discussed. Regional aspects of the MNEs in Canada are examined with reference to the Economic Council of Canada study on regional disparities.

The remainder of the chapter deals with issues of Canadian nationalism, the tariff, and the relationship of MNEs to Canadian energy policy. Since Canada has relied upon tariff (and lately nontariff) barriers to protect its industry, since the nation was founded in 1867, it is not surprising that a sophisticated model of nationalism has been developed by some members of the Canadian intellectual elite to defend protection not only of industry but also of oil and other energy resources. This quasi-economic, but mainly political, theory is shown to be one based on distributional considerations, rather than ones of efficiency, which are at the forefront of this book

THE IMPACT OF THE MINING INDUSTRIES
ON THE CANADIAN ECONOMY

Boadway and Treddenick (1977) have undertaken a valuable analysis of the economic impact of the (largely foreign owned) mining industry on resource allocation in Canada. They construct a fairly conventional general equilibrium model which permits an evaluation of the effects on other sectors when the mining sector is suddenly removed from the Canadian economy. While this method of comparative static analysis is familiar to economists, some general readers may wonder what is going on in such a counterfactual experiment. The authors anticipate this problem by explaining that the true economic impact of mining can be found by measuring the changes in output and employment in other sectors if mining is assumed to shut down, or be expanded, or be changed in another dramatic fashion. This approach shows the opportunity cost of investment in mining, and it is a useful method of testing public policies toward mining in an analytical manner.

The results of this approach are, of course, dependent on the quality of the model. The authors use 1966 input-output data with both fixed and variable coefficients and they attempt to examine substitution effects. Once the model is set up to equal actual 1966 values, then the main results of removing the mining industry are, on a disaggregated basis, to expand other manufacturing industries but to contrast service sectors, and, on an aggregative basis, to create a depreciation of the Canadian dollar by up to 5 percent.

These results are interrelated since the model shows that a contraction of a major capital-intensive industry like mining will release capital to other sectors. With the marginal product of labor assumed constant this lowers the wage-rental ratio. In turn, other sectors use capital released from mining to expand production, and to sell their goods at lower prices than would otherwise have prevailed. This stimulates export sales, other things being equal, and the model suggests this expansion in production in other manufacturing sectors almost fully offsets the decline in mining. Such a disaggregated adjustment, in which capital-intensive and tradeable sectors respond most to the lower wage-rental ratio, is forced by the aggregative nature of a model which requires constant full employment of all factors. Thus, the authors can ignore adjustment costs and disequilibrium solutions and have all sectors responding to changes in relative factor prices instantly.

The welfare costs of removal of mining are found, naturally, to be negligible — only one-tenth of one percent when capital is released for use elsewhere, up to a maximum cost of 2.3 percent when capital is removed completely (as it would be in reality, since foreign investment would cease, or at least would never have occurred, if there were no mining sector). The welfare costs are low since the model permits instantaneous full employment adjustment throughout the economy in response to a removal of mining. In practice, the model substitutes expansion of trade for the contraction of mining — a result which is, indeed, possible in an open economy such as Canada, but only in the long run.

Another problem with the welfare cost result is that it is assumed that the mining sector is large enough to alter the wage-rental ratio. It is doubtful that this would occur if the mining sector were removed in stages, such that over time, substitution would take place with the sectors gradually absorbing factors released from mining. The model thus serves to dramatize the effects of removal of mining, and also to play down the underlying adjustment mechanism.

The methodology used by Boadway and Treddenick is questionable in some respects. A major problem is that the mechanical model underlying the econometric simulations assumes instantaneous full employment adjustment and a constant income. Some of the implications for empirical work of the theoretical property of general equilibrium were explored when the fixed coefficient's nature of the input-output model was questioned. Such a constraint in the model tends to bias upward the results, since no substitution is allowed in response to changes in relative prices. With substitution, the impact of mining removed would be reduced, or at least smoothed out.

The budget constraint being constant constrains total income and GNP to remain the same after mining is removed. In fact, there will be adjustment costs over a long period of time, and during this transition period income would fall. Even in the long run, removal of mining would reduce GNP from what it would have been, since foreign investment and capital formation is foregone. Once income is allowed to fall, most of the experiments are complicated. For example, the exchange rate depreciation may be less than the authors find if imports are permitted to fall once income falls. Similarly, if GNP falls, demand for other goods is constrained and unemployment may result in nonmining sectors. What this modification reveals is the powerful role of mining in the economy. If anything, the technique used by Boadway and Treddenick understates the value of mining. By assuming instantaneous and full employment adjustment, they bias downward the time costs of removal of mining. This probably offsets the upward bias caught by using the input-output model.

The comments made here are also relevant to other experiments undertaken in the Boadway and Treddenick study, since the common adjustment mechanism in the model is the change in relative factor prices. For example, in Boadway and Treddenick's Chapter 5, an exogenous increase in mining exports is assumed, which leads to an increase in the price of capital (assuming full employment of both factors) and a fall in the wage-rental ratio. The extra exports cause the price of foreign exchange to fall, presumably due to a net trade surplus. The change in factor prices generates adjustments of output in the other sectors, such that the findings are approximately the reverse of those found for a contraction of mining. In a similar manner, the authors examine the effects of further processing of mining products, changes in commodity and capital taxes, and removal of tariffs.

The foreign-owned mining sector is, in practice, a vital part of the Canadian economy; nobody can entertain serious doubts as to its useful contribution to growth and welfare. Where there is room for some disagreement is over the appropriate mining tax policies for both federal and provincial governments. Boadway and Treddenick imply that these taxes should not be increased to such an extent that mining production is deterred. A fall in mining output would have profound effects throughout the economy, even under the most favorable assumptions that can be made, including one that ignores the adjustment costs of the cessation of mining. In short, mining has net benefits for Canada.

THE MNE AS AN AGENT FOR
TECHNOLOGY TRANSFER

The transfer of technology from advanced to less developed nations raises many interesting questions for economic analysis. The basic premise of authors such as Thomas (1976)[1] is that the transfer of technology is embodied in the multinational enterprise, and that it is the duty of the MNE to ensure that it operates as a satisfactory engine for the development of host nations. Unfortunately, but not surprisingly, it is found that the MNE has devoted more effort toward profit maximization than to the promotion of world economic development. For example, the MNE in Africa has tended to use capital-intensive instead of labor-intensive techniques of production and has often installed obsolete equipment. In addition, the MNE uses expatriate management and research skills instead of promoting the establishment of indigenous educational centers which would improve the volume of human capital in the host nation. To solve these problems, it is recommended that the government of a host nation engage in bargaining with the MNE in order to arrange contractual codes of operation whereby foreign direct investment by the MNE will have greater spillover benefits for the host nation's development objectives.

There are several problems with this argument. First, it is not at all clear that it is the duty of a MNE to promote development, or to transfer technology by itself. These are the planning goals of the host nation and are the responsibility of the local government, which logically may proceed to tax away any monopoly profits of the MNE, but cannot expect it to operate as a development agency.

Second, it ignores the modern theory of FDI, which finds that the MNE expands abroad to extend the market for a monopoly advantage it has achieved in an area of knowledge, research, technology, or management. The market imperfections approach assumes that the MNE responds to an externality in one of these areas, and that the monopoly advantage is firm specific. In this case, no transfer of technology is to be expected since it is in the interest of the MNE to protect its advantage. However, there is a solution to this problem: the government of a host nation should provide a direct subsidy to local industry in order to overcome the original imperfection in the market. Similarly, the government should subsidize education and training services in the hope of realizing external benefits, rather than prompting the MNE to help this sector in an indirect manner.

Third, it is necessary to distinguish between efficiency and distributional objectives. As just shown, the MNE cannot be as efficient as a host government in technology transfer, since it is a second best vehicle. While the MNE can be taxed on distributional grounds (with the funds being used for the subsidies just suggested), it is incorrect to expect the MNE to transfer technology, and inappropriate to criticize it for failing to do something which it has never attempted in the first place.

MULTINATIONALS AND REGIONAL DISPARITIES

In the same way that the multinational enterprise is not a development agency, neither is it responsible for the satisfaction of other government economic policies, such as the elimination of regional disparities. In Canada, differences in real income per capita have been observed for many years. These disparities seem to persist despite major expenditures by the federal government to support industry and development projects in the (relatively) poor regions. They persist despite equalization payments and other fiscal devices.

In the face of these historical regional disparities, it is asking too much of multinationals to help solve what is clearly not an efficiency problem, although such suggestions have been made by nationalists and other writers on Canadian regional economic policy. The multinationals should not be expected to be constrained on efficiency grounds for what is essentially a distributional problem; that is, one which assumes equity in income per capita for each province. To understand why the issue of regional disparities is purely a problem of using taxes and subsidies to redistribute income from the richer to poorer provinces, I now proceed to evaluate the influential study on regional disparities by the Economic Council of Canada. Although the study does not deal with the role of multinationals in regional development, it is important to understand the internal inconsistencies of the regional disparities issue before we can finally accept the elimination of multinationals as either development or regional agencies.

An influential report on regional disparities has been written by a committee of experts at the Economic Council of Canada (1977). Like most committee reports, the final document does not do justice to the original ideas and research effort undertaken by individual members of the team. This is due partly to the problem that arises when attempts are made to reconcile conflicting theories of regional development. It simply may not be possible to build a general economic theory of regional disparities. The reason for the lack of academic respectability for the report is its failure to reconcile the neoclassical and Keynesian models of development. This leads to frequent internal inconsistencies in the report, a lack of logical explanation of many parts of the analysis, and inconsequential policy recommendations.

In some sections of the report, such as its Chapter 6 where regional fiscal policy is advocated, a Keynesian model is being used. At other times, especially in the first part of Chapter 9, and in much of Chapter 5, a neoclassical model is the basis for the analysis. This is a fundamental problem with the report and makes it difficult to follow. Possibly the trouble stems from the poor summary of economic theory in its Chapter 3. Here five models are listed and the authors use each of them when the opportunity arises. This is a methodological error. It is incorrect to back all five horses since they often run in opposite directions. It is necessary to use one theory in a consistent manner; and I suggest that the greatest mileage comes from the neoclassical approach.

The key issue in the study of regional disparities is the degree of mobility of labor. If labor is highly mobile — that is, responsive to wage differentials — then a neoclassical solution to regional disparities is the correct one. The market mechanism can be left alone and basic economic incentives will serve to move labor from low wage peripheral regions of Canada to the high wage central, and mainly urban, areas of the nation. By responding to wage incentives, displaced workers and their families are indicating by their actions that economic considerations dominate social and historical ties to their birthplace.

If labor is observed to be fairly immobile, then we must search elsewhere for an explanation. It is not sufficient to allege immobility and move immediately toward a recommendation for policy intervention, such as the Council made in its Chapter 9. In that section, there is an improper test of migration theory. There it is stated that during the period 1951 to 1971 the average unemployment rate in the Atlantic provinces was about 3 percent above the Canadian average of 5 percent. During these twenty years there was net out migration of some 15 percent of the population, which was "sufficient to close the unemployment gap of 3 percent five times over" (p. 179). The error in this conclusion is that the example ignores the growth of labor supply over time, which is itself likely to have been about 3 percent per annum. Therefore, the opposite conclusion can be reached to that of the Council — out migration has been sufficient to prevent an increase in the unemployment rate of the maritime provinces.

A fundamental conceptual mistake is to measure the success of regional policy by taking equalization of income levels as the main criterion. The provincial league tables — on personal and family income, wage rates, unemployment rates, and social indicators — are interpreted by the Council as evidence of disparities. The conclusion is that "regional disparities in incomes and job opportunities are indeed substantial and remarkably persistent in spite of the amount of labor migration that has taken place over the years" (p. 60).

Several comments are in order before this interpretation of the data is accepted. First, it is not only the mean regional income per capita that should be examined, but also some measure of statistical variability in the time series (1926–1975), such as standard deviation or coefficient of variation. In the unlikely event that the standard deviations of these indicators are similar for all regions, then we have some extra information which may allow us to focus on mean levels, since there is minimal bias. However, if there is considerable variation in the value of standard deviation for any regional series, as is likely, then the mean income levels must be interpreted with more caution. Some of the regions may have lower mean income, but it may be more stable than regions with high mean income. The benefit of stable income and the disutility of variability in income per capita should not be ignored. There should be no difficulty in adding data on such standard deviations, since these are readily available from the computer printout of the calculated means from original data.

A second problem deals with the economic theory interpretation of average income. Why should it be expected that equalization of absolute income levels by province is possible? This is a sensible target only if Canada is assumed to be a homogeneous nation. Yet one of the basic characteristics of Canada is its diversity. Ignoring for the moment considerations of geography, culture, and social differences, it is clear that the structure of the Canadian economy is heterogeneous. There are considerable variations by province in the endowment of factors of production such as land, resources, capital, and labor. Elementary microeconomic principles indicate that these differences in factor endowments lead to variations in factor prices. Therefore, the rewards to owners of resources, labor, and capital are not expected to be the same across Canada.

Another consideration is that knowledge and technical information used in manufacturing industry will itself explain some part of the average wage and income levels. Such knowledge and technology is not available in equal proportions for each province. Thus, the higher average incomes observed in a more capital-intensive manufacturing province such as Ontario would be partly explained on the grounds of technology. Another problem with the concept of seeking the average income is that real world barriers prevent the equalization of factor prices, especially wage rates. This is most apparent in the case of Quebec, where the language barrier and cultural preferences serve to segment the internal labor market (especially for unskilled labor) from that of other provinces. Only the truly bilingual minority group, and others in possession of human capital, are mobile enough to engage in interprovincial (or, for that matter, international) migration.

These insights of economic theory are valuable even in the present-day environment when elimination of regional disparities seems to have become accepted as another unquestionable goal of Canadian policy. To the traditional macroeconomic policy, targets of full employment, price stability, growth, and a satisfactory balance of payments has been added the distributional goal of elimination of regional income differences. In its Chapter 2, the Council downplays the theorems in economics that demonstrate that governments need to have as many policy instruments as there are targets, if there is to be any hope of success in meeting such conflicting objectives. Yet the addition of regional disparities to our laundry list of targets has not been matched by the introduction of any new policy instruments, except in the Council's Chapter 6 where regional fiscal policy is advocated.

In this respect, the perennial conflict between distributional and efficiency goals needs to be remembered. If fiscal policy is used regionally on distributional grounds, to help reduce disparities, then this vital tool of macroeconomic policy is no longer available to help in the efficiency areas of price stability, full employment, growth, and the balance of payments. For example, if Quebec and the Maritimes expand their budget deficits to stimulate regional demand in a period of national inflation, then there will be adverse effects on the national inflation rate, growth, and the balance of payments, while even employment objectives may be hindered. Constitutional limitation on the use of regional monetary policy (which makes sense only if each region has its own currency area and exchange rate) only serves to illustrate the practical difficulties of an effective regional stabilization policy.

The conflict between efficiency and distributional goals is basic to economics, and is not peculiar to the subject of regional disparities. However, it is regrettable that the authors of the report on regional disparities appear to have forgotten some basic economic theory in the face of Ottawa policy constraints. This failing appears to be a common experience for economists once they move from the shelter of academia into positions as advisors to governments, since it is tempting to assume the parameters of government policy, even when these contain internal economic inconsistencies. In fact, it is hard to find many economists employed in public service who still believe in the proper use of economic theory; that is, in the paramount importance of efficiency. The lack of success in our economic management on both a regional and national level may not be unrelated to such constraints on the use of sound economic theory.

A solution for regional disparities is suggested by economic theory, but it has been ignored by most regional economists (especially government ones). It is to tax the richer provinces and give direct cash subsidies to the poor ones. The latter subsidies can be thought of as Confederation Bounty. This procedure redistributes income per capita, and if taken far enough, it will average out income by province. The simplicity of this approach, coupled with its practical difficulties, may not commend itself to bureaucrats or politicians, but the point remains that existing policies, such as DREE, which attempt to influence job creation, are not successful. The underlying philosophy of the Department of Regional Economic Expansion (DREE) is incorrect since subsidies to firms (even multinational firms) merely distort the efficient allocation of capital and other resources without solving the distribution issue. DREE is attempting to use efficiency tools to tackle a distributional problem. Viewed in this light, the failure of conventional regional policy is not too surprising. Until there is a change in the fundamental conception of the issue of regional disparities, there is unlikely to be a much greater degree of success in reducing them.

By way of summary, some qualifications are in order, given the negative nature of these comments. It has been suggested that in formulating potential economic solutions to the problem of Canadian regional disparities normative statements should not masquerade as scientific analysis. The price of social nostalgia is economic inefficiency. The report by the Economic Council attempts to reach the general social scientist. This laudable objective can, on occasions such as this, lead to superficial writing which may not do justice to the quality of the background research. It also subjects the Council to criticism for its failure to make known the details of individual models or empirical work which might support its approach. In this particular case, it is especially necessary to substantiate the claim that "no truly general theory of disparities has yet emerged" (p. 215). The resulting eclectic approach favored by the Council leads to inconsistent policy recommendations, some of which are mainly neoclassical (recommendations 1-6, 11-14) while others appear to be Keynesian (recommendations 7-10, 15, 16) in spirit. These two sets of policies are likely to conflict with each other, to the detriment of both the problem of regional disparities and economists charged with the task of providing answers for its solution.

A genuine alternative approach to the issue of regional disparities is available. It suggests that elimination of regional disparities is an equity goal, which can be achieved by a purely distributional policy of income equalization plus a market solution favoring labor migration. This is the type of policy that might be labeled as neoclassical socialism. It recognizes that regional disparities have social and political elements that can be treated by a policy of income redistribution, the essence of socialism. Yet it reserves economic instruments for improvement of the efficiency of market forces, rather than imposing controls as constraints on the economy, as does much Keynesian policy. The neoclassical paradigm alone has a narrow focus on efficiency. It ignores distributional issues as such, but reveals how the goal of (regional) income redistribution can be achieved efficiently. It is a benchmark that economists ignore at their peril.

NATIONALISM IN CANADA

Many nationalists and left-wing writers have argued that, in effect, Canada is run by certain corporate, financial, and academic élite groups, all operating with a common interest in promoting Canadian growth and development with the aid of foreign investment. These groups foster their own interests at the expense of the majority of Canadians living on lower incomes.

A new twist of the conspiracy theory has been given by an anti-nationalist. Heisey's[2] version is that the Canadian media have influenced public opinion in Canada to the extent that the political leadership in all three major parties has adopted a nationalistic viewpoint. He is particularly sorry that the Progressive Conservative party has fallen into this error and suggests some "fresher options" for that party and anyone else interested in listening. Most of these suggestions for reform of his party can be classified as libertarian, in particular his repeated emphasis on the need for unfettered foreign investment. He argues for a North American customs union in his Chapters 6 and 16, and makes a reasonable summary of the economic advantages of such a free-trade option. He believes that economic integration will inevitably be followed by political integration, but, somewhat paradoxically, argues that Canada has in fact a strong negotiating position due to the unique character of Canadians and the strength of demand for Canadian resources. In this connection, he refers with approval to the entry of Britain into the European Economic Community, and he argues that Canadian incomes will be higher if there is "some new form of economic and political community in North America."

Heisey is in favor of unrestricted investment, and he attributes the current moves by political leaders of all three federal parties to control foreign investment to the inspiration of the media, especially the beguiling influence of Walter Gordon of the *Toronto Star*. Lack of leadership shown by the Southam papers and other potential leaders of public opinion is criticized, and he hopes that the chartered banks (which have been protected from foreign ownership) may argue in favor of removal of such protection as they can now compete in a North American market. Heisey will not help to stop the stampede to economic nationalism with this poorly written book. Heisey's is an intensely personal account of his feelings about the emerging nationalist consensus in Canada.

In his polemic, Heisey does not attempt to evaluate the economic issues at any other level than gossip. For example, his argument in favor of a customs union for North America is mistakenly confused with an argument for free trade. These are not the same. On the one hand, it can be demonstrated that multilateral foreign trade is beneficial to all nations as they may then trade according to their comparative advantage; on the other hand, it is well known that a customs union does not involve free trade, since a common external tariff barrier is erected in addition to the removal of internal tariffs. Second, most of Canada's trade is with the United States, and if Canada wishes to end protection by removing tariffs and other barriers of trade she should probably attempt to diversify markets if a policy of free trade is implemented. Third, a point not recognized by Heisey is that the tariff itself has encouraged foreign investment in Canada as multinational firms have set up branch plants in order to sell similar goods in the local Canadian market.

One of the most thoughtful critiques of the neoclassical position on multinational corporations is to be found in Mel Watkins' paper (1978) presented to the Harry G. Johnson Memorial Symposium. He uses a Marxist nationalist viewpoint to reject Johnson's writings on foreign investment in Canada. I believe that Watkin's detailed criticisms can all be refuted, but that he is correct in his main point when stating that proponents of either the liberal continentalist free-trade position or the Marxist nationalist position cannot reconcile their different views of the world. As he suggests, their paradigms are self-contained and mutually exclusive. Naturally, I consider that the neoclassical paradigm is of sufficient validity, with its emphasis on efficiency only, to operate as an independent and internally consistent model. Efficiency is what economists know about, and it is what they should confine their attention to.

The neoclassical model also explicitly ignores distributional issues, not because these are regarded as unimportant, but due to the necessity to restrict economic analysis to one problem (that of efficiency) at a time. It is better to have something correct to say about this one problem, than to mix up efficiency and distributional issues, as is done by many political economists and all Marxists. I believe that once an economist surrenders his or her unique concern for efficiency, then there is nothing left to distinguish the economist's policy advice from that of any other citizen. Yet the input that an economist makes into policy decisions, with the emphasis on efficiency, is unlikely to be duplicated by any other group of professionals, since other disciplines ignore this concept, or at least do not have it as the central principle.

In a recent article, Cohen and Krashinsky (1976) (hereafter C-K) argue for a Crown Corporation in the mineral resources sector. This is necessary, they suggest, due to the excessive profits, or rents, made by firms active in this sector. For example they say:-

> Canadians do not earn a "fair" return on their natural resources (p. 411).
> . . . there is still a feeling that many firms in the resources sector earn excessive profits (p. 414).
> . . . We agree that excess profits exist in the resources sector (p. 422).

These are strong statements, basic to the thesis of their paper. As social scientists, it is incumbent upon C-K to provide some evidence of such excessive profitability. However, no such figures are presented except by reference to the discredited study of Eric Kierans. Yet an analysis by Hedlin Menzies showed that Kierans used out-of-date statistics, ignored the changes of the Income Tax Act of 1970, which prevented mining firms claiming deferred taxes, and was inaccurate in the calculation of profits, even on his own inappropriate definitions.

C-K address themselves to some of the conceptual problems of definition of profits, but are content to conclude that "measurement problems" and lack of data prevent quantitative estimates. This is an inappropriate procedure since there are data readily available on profits in the resources sector, both at industry and firm level. These have been analyzed elsewhere and examination of some of the relevant figures there fails to provide any evidence of excessive profits. Thus, I am forced to conclude that the argument

TABLE 8-1. Annual rate of profit (*E*) on stockholders' equity (*K*), percent

| Year | Canadian | | U.S. |
	Total Manufacturing Industry (1)	Petroleum and Coal (2)	All Manufacturing Corporations (3)
1975	13.43	14.49	11.10
1974	16.69	17.53	14.90
1973	14.07	15.30	13.05
1972	11.03	11.50	10.06
1971	9.52	10.42	9.68
1970	7.38	8.82	9.30
1969	10.23	8.62	11.48
1968	9.95	9.39	12.08
1967	9.18	8.63	11.73
1966	11.03	8.84	13.45
1965	11.12	8.16	12.98
1964	11.03	7.52	11.60
1963	10.15	6.56	10.25
1962	9.04	6.94	9.78
Mean	10.99	10.19	11.53

E = net income after taxes; or net profit; or net earnings
K = sum of capital stock, retained earnings (dividends), surplus.
Sources: Canadian (*E/K*): Statistics Canada, *Industrial Corporations: Financial Statistics,* Ottawa. Catalogue No. 61-003 Quarterly.
U.S. (*E/K*): Federal Trade Commission, *Quarterly Financial Report for Manufacturing Corporations.*

for a Crown Corporation is unjustified. Table 8-1 confirms that the profit rates in the Canadian manufacturing and oil industries are not excessive, and indeed they are less than in U.S. manufacturing.

APPLICATIONS OF A MODEL OF NATIONALISM[3]

There are three contributions in a recent essay on Canadian commercial and science policy by Daly and Globerman (1976). First, there is a good survey of the ever growing literature on the costs of the Canadian tariff. This goes beyond the usual aggregative proposition that the tariff serves to reduce the level of national income per capita by incorporating a discussion of its distributional and regional impacts. The distributional issue is taken up at length by a clever twist of the Stolper-Samuelson theorem. The authors assume that management is the scarce factor of production in Canada, relative to labor and other factors. This leads to the prediction that owners of knowledge and management skills gain from protection relative to workers and owners of capital and resources. Several interesting explanations of nationalism in Canada and implications for tariff and science policy follow from this insight. Third, there is a good critical review of Canadian science policy. Here it is shown that present research expenditures on basic innovations would be better directed toward support of methods which speed up the diffusion of existing technology.

The three sections are integrated by constant reference to the Albert Breton-Harry Johnson model of economic nationalism. The authors state that this model predicts that the Canadian tariff reduces real national income, increases prices of goods to consumers and workers, but leads to extra payments for owners of the scarce factor. In Canada the scarce factor is human capital, especially management and research skills. This assumption is central to the basic theme of the book, which is that highly educated managers, bureaucrats, and research scientists are able to earn higher relative incomes than would be possible under a system of free trade with its competition from outside rivals. This argument, best developed in Daly and Globerman's Chapter 3, goes a long way in explaining the history of Canadian nationalism as it has manifested itself in commercial, science, and immigration policies. These are all tinged by the self-interest of small groups of individuals, members of the Canadian intelligentsia, who articulate a rationale for nationalism. The impact of this trade theory insight by Daly and Globerman is that it provides a link between conventional economic theory and work on the Canadian elite by other social scientists such as Clement. It shows that even very neoclassical economists can develop a radical critique of the conventional politics of the Canadian establishment.

Condemnation of nationalism is continued by the authors in their Chapters 4 and 5, this time in the context of science policy. Expenditures under present policy are said to favor basic research and innovations of new technology. This work is fostered by members of the science and research profession to increase their prestige and job responsibility. The authors favor a change in science policy, one which places much more emphasis on the economic efficiency of technology. They suggest that such a new policy would favor adaption of existing techniques rather than invention of new ones. More attention should be devoted to the diffusion of technology in Canada, since it is allegedly slower than in the United States. In support of their new science policy, Daly and Globerman provide some rather anecdotal evidence. Three examples of slow diffusion are reported: innovations in numerical control for machine tools, the introduction of special presses for paper making, and the use of tufted carpets in the textile industry. The last example is used to advance a further point. Canadian manufacturers are often risk averse and are unwilling to adopt new technology since they are able to continue with inefficient production behind the tariff barrier.

Perhaps the main contribution of Daly and Globerman is to highlight the adverse impact of the tariff on the apparently unrelated area of science policy. The inefficiency of protection is felt throughout the Canadian economy with unexpected distributional consequences for managers and researchers. The formulation of science policy cannot escape from the vested interests of leaders in that field. These are challenging conjectures for national policy makers, although they will not surprise very many trade economists. The distributional aspects of the tariff can be extended to regional issues. The West and other areas peripheral to central Canada are often recognized as suffering net losses from the tariff since they buy manufactured goods at inefficient protected prices yet sell resources at world prices. When such adverse distributional effects of the tariff are added to its well known welfare losses for the nation as a whole, as confirmed by Young and the Wonnacotts, then the use of protection to foster Canadian independence is called into question. The virtue of this study is that it confronts the nationalist with some of the logical implications of tariff policy. Daly and Globerman have raised a valid issue and their work should stimulate further empirical research on this important topic.

POLITICAL ASPECTS OF A FREE-TRADE POLICY[4]

A short monograph by Lyon (1975) examines the political consequences for Canada of forming a free-trade area with the United States. It is one of the background studies commissioned by the Economic Council of Canada to help in the preparation of its recently published report on free trade, entitled "Looking Outward: A New Trade Strategy for Canada." A free-trade area between Canada and the United States (which Lyon labels a "CUFTA") is only one of several possible free-trade options considered by the Economic Council. However, it appears to have a greater probability of being adopted than options such as: multilateral free trade; free trade with Europe, Japan, and the United States; or various combinations of the latter. A study of the politics of a free-trade area is a useful supplement to the predominantly economic issues considered in the other background papers for the Economic Council.

Professor Lyon, of Carleton University, engages in a sweeping review of the literature on political and economic integration. In this review, he finds no support for the common Canadian fear that formation of a free trade area will eventually lead to political integration of the United States and Canada. There are no historical examples of such a trend, and Lyon advances many arguments to show that Canadian independence will be greater than it is now once a free-trade area is formed.

Prominent among these is the argument that Canadian independence is constrained at the present time by the large amount of foreign ownership in manufacturing and resource industries. Such foreign direct investment is attracted by the Canadian tariff as U.S. firms attempt to make sales by subsidiaries in Canada rather than by exports from home. Lyon has picked up the suggestion that elimination of the tariff will reduce U.S. direct investment in Canada and replace it with increased trade in goods and/or factors of production. With less foreign investment, it is assumed that there can be more independence. To me it seems that independence comes from trade diversification rather than greater concentration in one market.

Associated with this viewpoint is the belief that a free-trade area will increase real per capita income, and that with a larger GNP, Canadians will be able to achieve more independence — a view which believes that independence is a luxury good. Lyon adds a new twist to this rather materialistic conception of human motivation by linking the increased income argument to anticipated cultural benefits stemming from the Canada-United States association being a "disparate dyad." This dyad is like an economist's small country assumption. It says that Canada is too insignificant for the larger United States to bother to influence, and that local Canadian concern for cultural "disparities" can flourish in an atmosphere of indifference by the larger partner. Lyon refers with approval to the free-trade area between the Irish Republic and the United Kingdom, which he alleges has not reduced Irish independence. He seems to imply that Canada would be happy to be in a similar position to the Irish — a somewhat unfortunate example.

While the main theme of Professor Lyon's paper should be taken seriously, many of his points are inadequately developed or are purely speculative. (See Lyon's pp. 26–29.) His Chapter 3 is poorly conceived since he attempts to imitate economic jargon when unnecessary. His use of abbreviations is unfortunate. For example, NAFTA is used for the New Zealand-Australian free-trade area rather than the North Atlantic free-trade area advocated by Harry Johnson and others in a large and well known literature. Also, CUFTA might lead the casual reader into the mistaken notion that a customs union is under consideration rather than a free-trade area. An appendix by C. C. Pentland argues that free trade will eventually lead to political integration, although the writer seems to have a customs union model in mind rather than the free-trade area option studied by Lyon.

In conclusion, I did not find that Lyon's study made acceptable justifications for his assertion that there are no negative political costs to a free-trade area. It is probably more difficult to model the political side of the question than the economic side. Consequently, it would be advisable to leave the political debate open. The economic rationale for a free-trade area is so strong that it should be considered on its own merits by those engaged in public policy.

OIL PRICES AND SELF-SUFFICIENCY

In the last few years there has been extensive discussion of the political and economic aspects of the energy crisis, and especially of the impact of the short-run 1973–1974 Arab oil embargo and the effects of longer-run increase in the world price of oil by the OPEC countries. One important consideration is insufficiently emphasized; namely, that the future world price of oil is uncertain and is unrelated to purely economic costs. Its price is determined by a monopoly and economic rents are earned. Here it is argued that the price of oil must be predicted as accurately as possible in order to provide a basis for sensible policy alternatives. If the price of oil is recognized as being variable downward as well as up, then current policies of self-sufficiency need to be rethought.

At the simplest level, two possibilities may be considered. Either the world price of oil will stay at the present high level over the next few years, or the world price will fall considerably below this — at the extreme to about $2 a barrel, the price that prevailed until 1973. Most of the policy advisers and government officials in North America assume that the world price of oil will continue indefinitely at the present high level. A few economists, such as Adelman, Houthakker, Waverman, and Erickson,[5] have predicted that the world price of oil will fall within a few years. Their predictions follow from an argument that the increase in the world price of oil in 1973–1974 was facilitated by temporary economic and political factors, which are unlikely to be repeated in the same combination in the future. The present high price is almost entirely due to monopoly elements and the underlying supply and demand price is well under $2 a barrel.

At the time of the 1973–1974 energy crisis, there was a situation of implicit excess demand in North America due to a series of government policy actions which interfered with underlying market forces. For example, in the

United States, the price of natural gas was held down at an artificially low level throughout the 1960s. The multinational oil firms had been successful in using their political influence to avoid payment of normal business taxes, which resulted in an artificially low price for oil products, as well as excess profits for their corporations. On an international level, the multinational corporations had historically gained access to the oil fields of Arab countries on very favorable terms, again leading to a tendency for excessive production at low prices.

Until 1971, there was no evidence that the producing nations would be able to form an effective cartel, but in that year and the next, the consuming nations indicated a preference for stability of supplies over any concern for the level of oil prices. The events of late 1973 lead to a short-run adjustment problem. Consumers were faced with higher production costs due to both a redistribution of economic rents away from the multinational firms and toward the producing nation states, and the simultaneous collapse of domestic government policies which had protected the energy consumer. However, the higher price of oil is likely to produce substitution effects within a few years, whereby consumption will be more realistically related to the long-run opportunity costs of production.

Political factors were of great importance in the energy crisis. The 1973 Arab oil embargo and the associated increase in the world price of oil by the OPEC countries can be regarded as a unique event, unlikely to be repeated in the future. The special conditions prevailing in 1973 made the western nations dependent on the Arab oil-producing countries, and also left them unprepared for an interruption of oil supplies. The shock value of the 1973 measures is unlikely to be as strong if similar policies are repeated in the future since the industrialized countries are developing alternative sources of supply, and are also now including in their calculations the possibility of interruptions in oil supply. This implies that the OPEC cartel is likely to break up eventually.

This possibility is strengthened by the public reaction against multinational oil companies. The oil companies served to reinforce the OPEC (production) cartel by acting as a second cartel (in distribution). The oil firms were able to act as intermediaries for OPEC, simply passing on to consumers the full increase in costs. Now national governments of consuming nations are attempting to bargain directly with the oil producers and the two-stage oil cartel will face extra pressures as a result.

Today there is a mistaken emphasis on policies of self-sufficiency in energy. Such policies are unjustified on economic grounds because of the excessive costs involved in home production when compared to feasible alternatives such as free trade and stockpiling of reserves in case of future embargos. Instead of making excessive expenditures to become self-sufficient in energy, both the United States and Canada should instead estimate the probabilities of future interruptions in oil and other energy supplies. Using calculated probabilities, the nations should formulate optimal energy policies designed to build up stocks of oil and other resources as required. It is likely that a policy of trade plus reserve holding of oil will be much cheaper than investment in expensive tar sands or oil shales.

The optimal energy policy to be followed depends on an integrated analysis of complex economic and political factors. By the imaginative use of economic theory, in which opportunity costs are always considered, it will be possible to generate policy prescriptions which are efficient and superior to the misguided policies currently being pursued. To do this, at a minimum, it is necessary to forecast the future world price of oil to consider the possibility that it may even fall if OPEC shows signs of breaking up. In addition, policies of self-sufficiency in oil should be avoided whenever there are more efficient solutions.

A NATIONAL ENERGY POLICY?

Philip Sykes[6] has made a persuasive plea for the development and implementation of an independent Canadian energy policy. Such a policy would include evaluation of the full social costs and benefits of resource and energy projects, and would not necessarily discriminate against foreign investment. However, as Sykes attributes many of Canada's past failures and present problems in the energy field to the multinational oil firms and corporate American influence, it is implied that an independent Canadian energy policy would involve greater taxation of foreign private developers and domestic development through crown corporations.

Sykes gives a carefully documented account of previous energy and resource failures. These begin with the classic example of the Columbia River Treaty under which Premier Bennett, with the acquiescence of the federal government, sold out control of the flows of the Columbia and Kootenay rivers for a total payment of about $455 million. The benefits to the United States amount to many billions of dollars, and the new Libby Dam in Montana is a potential keystone in the development of a North American water and power alliance, under which the benefits to the United States will be even greater. This scheme aims to reverse the flow of Canadian rivers flowing to the Arctic and divert them for American use. Sykes points out that Premier Bennett enjoyed a short-term advantage in requiring the Americans to finance development of the Peace River Dam project, but the development of secondary manufacturing industry in British Columbia was retarded and much valuable farmland lost when upper valleys of the Columbia river system were flooded. Furthermore, the development of the two rivers neglected a consideration of environmental effects, such as the virtual destruction of the way of life of the native peoples of the Peace-Athabasca delta. The same type of inadequate cost-benefit analysis characterized the proposed dam in southern Alberta which, in Sykes' view, was fortunately cancelled after the election of Premier Lougheed.

The author is extremely critical of the hydro development of the Churchill and Nelson rivers in Northern Manitoba, and of the James Bay project in Quebec. In both projects no evaluation was made of the full social costs and benefits; specifically, the impact on the native peoples in the two areas was ignored since the studies used by the respective governments emphasized engineering requirements more than economic and ecological questions. For example, the loss of recreational facilities was not included as a social cost. Besides these questions about supply of energy, Sykes also questions the demand projections of the hydro engineers. He argues that the projections of increased demand for energy reflect unacceptable preferences for more energy intensive consumption goods. He believes that a change of consumer tastes is possible whereby demand from energy will no longer continue to increase at such a rapid rate in the next twenty years. It is also suggested that the peak demand for energy need no longer be covered as it has been in the past. The price mechanism can be used to reduce peak demand.

The price of energy products is not dependent on supply and demand conditions alone. Another important determinant is monopoly influence. Sykes argued correctly (in 1973) that an international cartel of oil producers had managed to keep up the price to the consumer of oil and gas in the early seventies, although the costs of production of these multinational oil companies had actually been falling considering the worldwide scale of their operations. The market power of the oil companies was, of course, challenged by the national governments in the Middle East. This example of the nation state exerting a countervailing influence over the multinational enterprise is a new twist and is not recognized by Sykes, although it tends to reinforce his point about production costs being influenced by monopoly elements. The impact of these factors on Canada is that the multinational oil corporations control the price of oil and gas in Canada, as they maximize their profits on their world operations.

One implication of this point is that Canada must retain control of its energy sources — oil, gas, and water power — by means of a comprehensive national policy. Sykes therefore hints at public ownership of the energy companies and the use of crown corporations to finance future resource development. A second policy is to charge a higher tax; for example, on the operations of the petroleum industry in Canada, over 90 percent of which is American owned. Sykes does not discuss the difficult nature of establishing an optimal tax that will remove the excess profits made by the corporations and yet allow them to continue research and development of risky new projects. He strongly advocates the Kierans approach, which emphasizes that Canadians have not been receiving a sufficient rate of return when renting the use of their provincially owned natural resources to foreign companies.

There is a fundamental difference between these two policies. The option of increased taxation allows the multinational firm to develop Canadian resources within the context of the market system and free trade as subject to government regulation. The other option of nationalization and use of crown corporations to develop natural resources is a self-reliant policy with the aim of retaining control over Canadian resources. The latter approach requires a stronger political argument for independence, as it is not sufficient in economic terms alone.

The economic argument for independence is really an argument about income distribution. It suggests that with more control of resources and industry, Canadians will be able to internalize the potential profits instead of losing them to the multinational enterprises. Such income redistribution can be achieved by a comprehensive tax-subsidy scheme, whereby any gainers from trade are taxed to compensate the losers. Such a tax-subsidy system, coupled with free trade, is superior to protection in efficiency terms. Therefore, the benefits of a nationalist policy must be justified on political grounds in order to overcome the economic costs of independence.

ENDNOTES

1. Babatunde Thomas, *Importing Technology into Africa. Foreign Investment and the Supply of Technological Innovations,* Praeger Special Studies in International Economics and Development (New York: Praeger, 1976), p. 202.
2. Alan Heisey, *The Great Canadian Stampede: The Rush to Economic Nationalism* (Toronto: Griffin House, 1973).
3. This section first appeared in *The Canadian Journal of Economics* 11 (August 1978). Reprinted with permission.
4. This section first appeared in *Canadian Public Policy: Analyse de Politiques* 2 (Winter 1976). Reprinted with permission.
5. See their essays in Erickson and Waverman (1974).
6. Philip Sykes, *Sellout: The Giveaway of Canada's Energy Resources* (Edmonton: Hurtig Publishers, 1973).

III PUBLIC POLICY TOWARDS MULTINATIONALS

9 THE FOREIGN OWNERSHIP DEBATE IN CANADA*

THE WATKINS, WAHN, AND GRAY REPORTS

Recent reports (Watkins 1968, Wahn 1970 and Gray 1972)[1] have examined the impact of foreign investment on the Canadian economy and its implications for American-Canadian political and economic relations. Official reports have considered only direct investment as a problem and portfolio capital has been ignored. There is substantial foreign ownership (mostly American) in the Canadian manufacturing, resources, and mining sectors.

All three reports found it convenient to separate direct investment from portfolio investment, as the former is defined to involve control; for example, by foreigners owning over 50 percent of the shares issued in a company.[2] While all statistics on direct investment involve the 50-percent control, many have argued that effective control is achieved with a holding of fewer shares. Many individuals therefore consider this as evidence of even more foreign involvement. Writers generally ignore portfolio investment as there is no question of foreign ownership involved.

*From *Journal of World Trade Law* 10 (March, April 1976): 171–176. Reprinted with permission.

In general, all three reports have expressed concern over:

1. the amount of foreign investment, which is now over $33 billion,
2. the growth of the share of U.S. direct investment to over 80 percent of the total,
3. the concentration of U.S. direct investment in key industrial sectors,
4. the apparent lack of investment opportunities for abundant Canadian savings,
5. the apparent financing of the majority of direct investment from Canadian sources; for example, retained earnings of foreign subsidiaries, and
6. the implied political dependence of Canada on the United States.

These topics of concern have led to policy recommendations which may be distilled as follows:

1. Restriction of unlimited capital inflows, especially for "key sectors," in which it is vital to prevent foreign control. This has been adopted in the past for transportation, communications, the financial industry, and utilities. There is some possibility that this key sector approach may be extended to Canadian resources, although this is not discussed in these reports.
2. Subsidization of domestic research and development (R&D), education, and management training. This is required in order to overcome the research advantage of large American multinational enterprises.
3. Establishment of a Canadian Development Corporation to channel domestic savings into productive use. It has been argued that the outflow of Canadian funds to U.S. financial markets could be prevented if better opportunities were available to Canada, and to some extent a Canadian Development Corporation might serve to diversify and reduce risk.
4. The establishment of a screening agency to evaluate foreign investment and to prevent foreign takeovers and mergers which are not in the national interest.
5. The end of extraterritoriality and the establishment of Canadian sovereignty over political decisions.
6. The recognition that probably a new industrial strategy is required to overcome the many problems of foreign ownership, such as truncation.

It is worthwhile noting that the reports did not recommend measures such as the establishment of capital controls, the buying back of foreign-owned industries, or the nationalization of existing subsidiaries.[3]

These three reports on foreign investment in Canada represent an impressive collection of statistics and analysis by professional economists of all political viewpoints. The reports have generated a great amount of public debate in Canada in recent years, and the general level of understanding and awareness of the economics of the issue has increased substantially. Legislation has proceeded at a much slower pace than academic research.

LEGISLATION FOR THE CONTROL OF FOREIGN INVESTMENT

A major effort was made by Finance Minister Walter Gordon in his budget of 1963, to restrict foreign investment. There was strong political objection to his tax proposals, and the Liberal government chose to withdraw the more controversial foreign investment provisions from the budget. While not commanding the immediate support of his party, Gordon's influence was felt in subsequent government-sponsored research of foreign investment. Legislation had previously been enacted to prevent foreign ownership of "key sectors" in the Canadian economy. Such key sectors were transportation, communications, utilities, and the finance industry. In the 1960s, more legislation was enacted to preserve Canadian content in magazines and in the Canadian broadcasting industry.

The Watkins Report of 1968 had little immediate impact on policy. In the report there was an emphasis on the industry context of foreign investment and an attempt to evaluate its costs and benefits. This involved an evaluation of Canada's tariff, competition, and tax policies. One of its recommendations was to establish a Canadian development corporation to channel domestic savings into Canadian-owned projects. A small scale version of this corporation was established in 1970. The Wahn Report was mainly concerned with political questions, and is not discussed here.

The official version of the Gray Report was delayed in publication until mid-1972, but a draft of the Report was leaked to the *Canadian Forum* and published in late 1971. Both versions of the Report refer to the increasing power of multinational enterprises and to the potential conflict between them and nation states. The latter have responsibility for stabilization policy, but multinational enterprises are not so concerned with employment, inflation, and balance of payments problems.

The Gray Report shows awareness of the modern theory of foreign investment as it emphasizes industrial determinants. Foreign investment is specific to each industry sector and is determined by micro rather than aggregate factors.[4] It occurs, for example, when the investor has the ability to exploit an advantage in the host economy market. The vehicles of such monopoly exploitation may be by licensing, trade, or foreign investment. Much of the Report is concerned with wider economic issues, including an appropriate industrial, scientific, and technological strategy for Canada, and with broad political questions such as extraterritoriality.[5]

A basic premise of the Gray Report is that the multinational enterprise has different interests from the government of Canada. The latter is charged with safeguarding the political, cultural, and economic independence of the nation and will seek to maximize taxation from the multinational enterprise. The former will wish to maximize profits and will rationally attempt to avoid taxation, for example, by one of the three following devices.

First, the multinational enterprise can engage in transfer pricing policies under which costs of supplies from the parent subsidiaries are artificially increased to reduce the profits and taxable income of the host country subsidiary. Second, the subsidiary can be thinly capitalized such that debt capital is issued instead of equity capital, which allows the subsidiary to deduct interest charges from its taxable income. Third, as no tax is paid on loans of under one year, the subsidiaries may borrow in Canada on the short run and channel the funds back to the parent company at low interest rates.

The main recommendation of the Gray Report is to establish a screening agency to review new investments in Canada when such investments are likely to lead to a substantial proportion of foreign ownership. The aims of the screening agency are to prevent monopoly foreign ownership and to act as a bargaining agent with the powerful multinational enterprise. Such a screening agency could operate flexibly such that changing policy objectives over time were appropriately weighted in the overall decision as to whether or not new foreign investment should be permitted. For example, greater weights could be given to foreign investment projects which promoted more employment or reduced regional inequalities. Each project financed by foreign investment would require a cost-benefit analysis with "suitable" weights given to the various parameters. If the Canadian interest were not served by proposed foreign investment, then the agency would have the power to block such foreign investment. Recently, an embryonic foreign investment review agency (FIRA) has been set up, with its initial concern only being to review foreign takeovers and mergers.[6]

CANADIAN ATTITUDES TOWARD
FOREIGN INVESTMENT

The political atmosphere in Canada is becoming perceptibly more nationalistic, with all three federal parties being opposed to foreign ownership in various degrees. This probably reflects the changing social and political attitudes of Canadians toward foreign investment. It is reported in every opinion poll that there has been a hardening of public opinion against American direct investment. According to Gallup polls, between 1964 and 1972 the number of Canadians stating that there is enough U.S. capital invested in Canada has increased from 46 percent to 67 percent; while in the same period the number of those wanting more U.S. capital has fallen from 33 percent to 22 percent.

In a study conducted by a team from the University of Windsor headed by Professor Alex Murray, a series of cross-sectional surveys has been conducted in which the same questions are asked in successive years, a so-called longitudinal analysis. To the question, "Is the U.S. ownership of Canadian companies good or bad for our economy?", 34 percent answered bad in 1969 and 43 percent answered good. By 1972, 47 percent answered bad and only 38 percent answered good. These are national figures and vary somewhat according to region, income level, party membership, and other factors.

While there is this growing trend of opinion against foreign investment, Canadians do not rank it (in opinion polls) as such an important issue as unemployment, inflation, and other economic problems. A Gallup poll in January 1974 found that the great majority of Canadians were in favor of restrictions on foreign investment. The question asked was, "Would you favor or oppose legislation which would significantly restrict and control foreign investment in Canada?" In favor were 52 percent, partially in favor were 17 percent, opposed were 18 percent, and don't knows were 13 percent. At about the same time as the poll was taken, the federal government introduced measures to restrict foreign takeovers and to set up a screening mechanism which would permit foreign investment only if it contributed to the public interest, with the latter including noneconomic factors.

These surveys should be interpreted with some caution as the response seems to depend on the type of question asked. For example, when people were asked a more critical economic question in the Murray survey there was less of a majority for independence. The question asked was whether the respondent was prepared to accept "a lower standard of living for more control over the Canadian economy by reducing or abolishing U.S. investment." Indicating a complete division of opinion, 44 percent answered yes, while 46.6 percent said no.

It appears that while Canadians are increasingly concerned about the extent of foreign control over the economy and are in favor of restricting further foreign investment, they are not so certain that their standard of living should be reduced in order to achieve this end. It is up to the advocates of a nationalist policy to convince at least half the public that they will not be poorer if American investment is restricted. The other half of the public are already willing to trade off a lower level of income in return for more independence.

A frequent argument made in the public policy debate is that foreign ownership increases the degree of monopoly in the Canadian economy, or at least that firms subject to foreign control tend to be larger than domestic firms. In an earlier piece of research, Safarian[7] raised the question of whether foreign-owned subsidiaries are about the same size as domestic firms. He concluded that "in broadly comparable circumstances the two sets of firms do not diverge markedly in most cases in terms of size".[8] In a more recent piece of research by Rosenbluth,[9] this was not found to be the case because foreign-owned subsidiaries are larger than most home firms. First, foreign firms are up to two-and-one-half times as large as domestic firms in the same industry. Second, foreign firms are concentrated in industries which themselves have a large average size.

Rosenbluth found that the level of concentration was not related to the level of foreign control, and that there had not been a trend toward increasing concentration in the ten years of his study from 1954 to 1964. Most foreign control was in industries with a "medium high" concentration ratio.[10] There was high foreign control (over 90 percent) in concentrated industries such as automobiles, tobacco, and aircraft; but a low proportion of foreign control in similarly highly concentrated industries such as beverages, cotton, iron and steel, transportation, telephones, and banks. (It might be noted that the last three industries mentioned are "key sectors.") It is unfortunate that Rosenbluth's data only cover until 1964 because there may have been an increase in foreign-owned oligopolies since then.

On the related question of mergers, Rosenbluth did not find any evidence to suggest that foreign-controlled firms are involved in more mergers than domestic ones. He did find that foreign-owned firms engage in horizontal, conglomerate, and forward linkage mergers; whereas domestic firms engage in backward integration. This indicates that for the period studied, U.S. firms were not engaged in buying up Canadian resources at least through vertical integration.

Recent policy provision to regulate mergers and foreign ownership suggest that there is a gap between published research and its acceptance by officials and the general public. Indeed, there are many high quality studies on Canadian trade and investment, frequently published in professional journals, which are virtually ignored. Instead of theoretically sound models which have been rigorously tested, it is more common for the average Canadian intellectual to read Levitt, Rotstein, Sykes, and Laxer on the one hand, or Fayerweather and Heisey on the other.[11] None of these studies presents a rational economic analysis of the foreign-ownership issue. Perhaps it has become too controversial a political question to lend itself to scholarly study any more.

In conclusion, it has been shown that public policy in Canada has been motivated by concern over the extent of foreign ownership and the influence of multinational enterprises on the Canadian government and economy. Legislation has lagged behind academic research, and the latter has to some extent brought forth ambiguous policy implications. This analysis of the Canadian debate on foreign ownership is useful as it highlights the conflicting objectives of nation states and multinational enterprises, especially as perceived by the general public.

EPILOGUE[12]

The information reprinted above was first written in 1973 and published in early 1976. Since then, the Foreign Investment Review Agency (FIRA) has been established and has now been operating for five years. Despite the institutionalization of the foreign investment review process in FIRA, much of the previous analysis remains relevant. The underlying issues in the foreign-ownership debates were not solved by the establishment of FIRA and they remain alive today.

The Act which established FIRA was a compromise measure forced upon the minority Liberal government of 1972–1974 by its temporary socialist partner, the New Democratic Party. The terms of the Act establish a screening agency (FIRA) which has the authority to review foreign takeovers and foreign investment in new businesses. FIRA attempts to evaluate the net benefits of such new foreign direct investment. It does not have the authority to review investment for the expansion, replacement, or modernization of existing, foreign-controlled businesses in Canada. This type of foreign investment accounts for a majority of the new direct investment recorded in official statistics of foreign control. Thus, the power of FIRA to control the value of foreign-owned assets in Canada is severely constrained by the very legislation which set it up.

The debate over foreign ownership in Canada has been somewhat less strident following the establishment of FIRA and observation of its neutrality. The reasons for the debate remain unresolved, however, so it is anticipated that there will be further outbreaks of concern at times of provincial and federal elections or on other occasions when the atmosphere in which business (and especially foreign business) operates becomes more charged.

The fundamental conflict between equity and efficiency considerations dominates most economic-based choices, with the tradeoff between independence and foreign investment being one of the more difficult ones. In a simplistic sense, the choice is between political independence plus some economic inefficiency on the one hand, or some constraints on sovereignty in an interdependent world plus growing economic wealth on the other. These issues are explored in more detail in Chapter 10.

Here we have seen that the policy issues that gave rise to the foreign-ownership debate in Canada remain unresolved despite the establishment of FIRA. Indeed, that review agency embodies in itself the schizophrenic attitude of Canadians toward their national identity in general and the foreign-ownership issue in particular. They contrast the perceived economic benefits of foreign direct investment with concern for the independence and political integrity of the nation and expect to postpone the tradeoff involved. Clearly, the debate over foreign ownership in Canada will continue in the future.

ENDNOTES

1. M. Watkins et al., *Foreign Ownership and the Structure of Canadian Industry,* Report of the Task Force on the Structure of Canadian Industry (Ottawa: The Queen's Printer, 1968); Wahn Report, *Eleventh Report of the Standing Committee on Defence and External Affairs Respecting Canada-U.S. Relations* (Ottawa: Queen's Printer, 1970); Government of Canada, *Foreign Direct Investment in Canada* (Ottawa: Information Canada, 1972). (This is often referred to as the Gray Report.) See also "A Citizen's Guide to the Herb Gray Report," *Canadian Forum* (December 1971).

2. The United States adopts a different definition of direct investment, based on a figure of 10 percent. The Canadian data also include cases where less than 50 percent is known to constitute control.

3. This might be contrasted with some of the recommendations in the Kierans Report on the mining industry in Manitoba, which advocates charging a higher rent for foreign use of resources, which under the Canadian Constitution

belong to the Province, and after ten years the replacement of private mining operations by Crown Corporations. See Professor Eric Kierans, *Report on Natural Resources Policy In Manitoba,* Secretariat for the Planning and Priorities Committee of Cabinet, Government of Manitoba, Winnipeg, Manitoba, 1973.

4. For a detailed exposition of the theoretical determinants of foreign investment, see Alan M. Rugman, "Foreign Operations and the Stability of U.S. Corporate Earnings," Unpublished Ph.D. thesis, Simon Fraser University, 1974.

5. Also see Clarence L. Barber, "Presidential Address: A Sense of Proportion," *Canadian Journal of Economics* (November 1973).

6. The Foreign Investment Review Act came into force in April 1974. In its first year, the Foreign Investment Review Agency and the Federal Cabinet considered eighty-two applications by foreign corporations for takeovers of Canadian companies. Of these, fifty-five were approved, eleven rejected, and sixteen were withdrawn. Another forty-four applications were pending. In addition, it has been argued that a number of potential takeovers have been discouraged as they were unlikely to provide "significant benefit" to Canada, as defined by the Review Agency. See Herb Gray, "Good Fences: Controlling Foreign Investment," *The Canadian Forum* 55 (June 1975). The operations of FIRA are explored in more detail in Chapter 10.

7. A. E. Safarian, *Foreign Ownership of Canadian Industry* (Toronto: McGraw-Hill, Canada, 1972).

8. Ibid., p. 267. Note that Safarian excluded very small firms from his comparison.

9. Gideon Rosenbluth, "The Relation Between Foreign Control and Concentration in Canadian Industry," *Canadian Journal of Economics* (February 1970).

10. Ibid., p. 19 and Table II.

11. Kari Levitt, *Silent Surrender: The Multinational Corporation in Canada* (Toronto: Macmillan, 1970).

    Abraham Rotstein and Gary Lax, eds., *Independence: The Canadian Challenge* (Toronto: Committee for an Independent Canada, 1972).

    Philip Sykes, *Sellout* (Edmonton: Hurtig, 1973).

    James Laxer, *The Energy Poker Game* (Toronto: New Press, 1970).

    John Fayerweather, *Foreign Investment in Canada* (Toronto: Oxford University Press, 1974).

    Alan Heisey, *The Great Canadian Stampede* (Toronto: Griffin House, 1973).

12. This Epilogue contains new materials not published in the original version.

10 THE REGULATION OF FOREIGN INVESTMENT IN CANADA*

INTRODUCTION

The economic benefits of foreign investment are being questioned by influential groups of Canadians. This has resulted in political action to mitigate the suspected adverse effects of foreign investment. Since April 1974 the Foreign Investment Review Agency (FIRA) has reviewed all foreign takeovers and mergers, and since October 1975 it has been responsible for screening new types of foreign investment.

This chapter examines the reasons for establishing FIRA, critically reviews the operations of this agency, and considers alternatives to the regulation of foreign investment. Since 80 percent of net direct investment into Canada is from the United States, the chapter also indirectly considers the impact of FIRA on Canadian-American economic relationships.

*From *Journal of World Trade Law* 11 (July, August 1977):322–333. Reprinted with permission.

The major theoretical argument made is that foreign investment provides net benefits to Canada, and that on grounds of efficiency FIRA should not be part of a process which restricts such capital inflows. However, it is recognized that there may be a preference for independence, a noneconomic objective. When this second objective is considered, FIRA is faced with a policy dilemma, since economic efficiency and political independence may have to be traded off. The theoretical implications of this tradeoff are studied with reference to the recommendations made by FIRA. The Agency itself does not have the power to approve or disapprove investment proposals, yet its recommendations (made on economic grounds) must be regarded as the major input into the final (political) decision made by the federal government.

Analysis of the reasons for foreign takeovers and the characteristics of foreign subsidiaries within the Canadian economy has been undertaken by many economists. For example, see Safarian (1973) and Reuber and Roseman (1972). This work is not repeated here since this chapter is concerned solely with an economic analysis of the operations of the Foreign Investment Review Agency. The reasons for the establishment of FIRA have been discussed elsewhere (see Rugman, 1976a).

In recent years, Canada has experienced an increase in public concern over the large amount of foreign control of the resource and manufacturing sectors. This has been accompanied by general expressions of criticism against Canada's traditional continentalist free-trade policy, which may be interpreted here as an increased preference for independence. Although there are questionable and even paradoxical elements in these attitudes, the federal government eventually moved to implement most of the proposals of the Watkins and Gray Reports. The latter recommends establishing a screening agency to review foreign takeovers and new foreign investment in Canada.

The Foreign Investment Review Act was proclaimed in force on April 9th, 1974. It established an agency, FIRA, to screen new foreign direct investments in Canada. The Act does not apply to financial capital flows, or portfolio investment as this is known. The first sections of the Act, Phase I, applied only to takeovers of existing Canadian firms by foreign-owned firms. Phase II of the Act was proclaimed effective October 15th, 1975. This phase completes the powers of FIRA and requires the review of foreign investments which establish new businesses in Canada and of some investments which are financed by funds raised within Canada; for example, when existing foreign controlled firms diversify into new and unrelated businesses.

FIRA — THE RECORD TO DATE

In its first two years of operation, FIRA has approved about 80 percent of the proposed takeovers that it reviewed. The latest figures available at the time of writing are reported in Table 10-1. Of the 240 takeover proposals resolved, only 33 have been rejected, while a further 37 were withdrawn, and the remaining 170 were approved. The attrition rate is slightly higher than these figures indicate since a few applications for FIRA's stamp of approval were withdrawn voluntarily before being reviewed. Presumably there are also examples of takeovers which have been discouraged by the mere presence of FIRA, and which have consequently never been developed into a formal application. However, from these figures it appears that FIRA is willing to approve the great majority of takeovers and is indeed something of a "paper tiger" in terms of its record during the first two years.

TABLE 10-1. Outcome of takeover applications to FIRA

	Fiscal Year April 9th, 1974 to March 31st, 1975	Fiscal Year April 1st, 1975 to March 12, 1976	1974–1976 Total
Applications for takeovers	230	N.A.	N.A.
Withdrawn prior to certification	7	N.A.	N.A.
Returned as non-reviewable	55	N.A.	N.A.
Decision as to reviewability pending at year end	18	N.A.	N.A.
Certified as reviewable	150	139	289
Resolved	92	148	240
Allowed	63	107	170
Disallowed	12	21	33
Withdrawn	17	20	37
Under assessment at year end	58	N.A.	49

Sources: Foreign Investment Review Act, Annual Report (Ottawa: FIRA, October 1975), Table 1, p. 23.
Notes for Remarks by Mr. Gorse Howarth (FIRA, mimeo, March 25th 1976), p. 1–2.

Supplementary information on the outcome of takeover and new business applications is reported in Tables 10–2 and 10–3. The data on these cases were supplied by FIRA. It is apparent from Table 10–2 that FIRA has continued to approve most of the takeover applications. Table 10–3 reveals that FIRA has also recommended approval of virtually every new business investment; in fact, only one has been disallowed (and five withdrawn) of forty-five resolved in the first eighteen months of operation of Phase 2 of the Act.

TABLE 10–2. Summary of reviewable acquisition cases from April 9, 1975, to July 30, 1976

	Fiscal Year 1974/1975	Fiscal Year 1975/1976	April 1/76 to July 30/76
	No. of Cases		
Reviewable cases	150	144	49
Total resolved cases	92	153	48
Allowed cases	63	110	36
Disallowed cases	12	22	9
Withdrawn cases	17	21	3
Under review at end of period	58	49	50

Source: FIRA, private communication to author, August 1976.

TABLE 10–3. Summary of new business cases from October 15, 1975, to July 30, 1976

	October 15, 1975 to March 31, 1976	April 1, 1976 to July 30, 1976
	No. of Cases	
Reviewable cases	26	64
Total resolved cases	6	39
Allowed cases	4	35
Disallowed cases	—	1
Withdrawn cases	2	3
Under review at end of period	20	45

Source: FIRA, private communication to author, August 1976.

The basis for FIRA's decisions is the evaluation of the "significant benefit" provided by a foreign investment. Significant benefit may be obtained if the firm involved has beneficial effects in one or more of the five following areas: (a) economic activity, (b) Canadian participation, (c) efficiency of industry, (d) competition, and (e) federal and provincial economic policies. In the assessment process, the net benefit from all of the criteria relevant to a particular case is established.

Section 2(2) of the Act reads as follows:

> In assessing, for the purpose of this Act, whether any acquisition of control of Canadian business enterprise or the establishment of any new business in Canada is or is likely to be of significant benefit to Canada, the factors to be taken into account are as follows:
>
> (a)   the effect of the acquisition or establishment on the level and nature of economic activity in Canada, including, without limiting the generality of the foregoing, the effect on employment, on resource processing, on the utilization of parts, components and services produced in Canada, and on exports from Canada;
>
> (b)   the degree and significance of participation by Canadians in the business enterprise or new business and in any industry or industries in Canada of which the business enterprise or new business forms or would form a part;
>
> (c)   the effect of the acquisition or establishment on productivity, industrial efficiency, technological development, product innovation and product variety in Canada;
>
> (d)   the effect of the acquisition or establishment on competition within any industry or industries in Canada; and
>
> (e)   the compatibility of the acquisition or establishment with national industrial and economic policies, taking into consideration industrial and economic policy objectives enunciated by the government or legislature of any province likely to be significantly affected by the acquisition or establishment.[1]

It will be observed that these criteria are extremely broad and cover most aspects of economic life. Indeed, any potential foreign investment would be likely to qualify on at least one of these five grounds, if not on several. Presumably most types of foreign investments would satisfy criteria (a) and (c), but each of the other criteria presents opportunity for bargaining between FIRA and the foreign investor. The matrix of benefits is calculated by cost benefit analysis, but no information has been released as to how this is done.

The essence of the administration of the Act appears to be to negotiate greater benefits for Canadians (in one or more of the five areas) than would originally have accrued from the proposed foreign investment. Thus, one dimension of the role of FIRA is to act as a bargaining agent with foreign investors. It seeks increases in the benefits to Canada of proposed takeovers and new foreign investments. The argument has been advanced by the Ontario Economic Council (1976) that FIRA takes part in a bargaining process in order to increase the net benefits to Canada of direct investment. It can withhold approval of a foreign takeover until promises of more jobs, investment, or exports for Canada are given by the multinational firm. While the Agency itself does not claim to have secured such improvements, in practice it is clear that the high success rate of applications reflects the ability of FIRA to negotiate improvements for Canada on an individual case basis. Whether these specific improvements, as defined in the five areas of significant benefit, have significant aggregative benefits for the Canadian economy is another question — one which is examined in the last section of this chapter.

The Canadian business press is far from happy with the activities of FIRA. In its issue of May 20th, 1976, *The Northern Miner* states that ". . . the act's underlying philosophy, to buy Canada back, is thought to be one of the many causes contributing to Canada's less than spectacular recovery." *The Financial Post* has run reports regularly in the first half of 1976 on the complexities of the regulations and the possibility of the extension of FIRA powers. In these reports, the negative decisions of FIRA tend to be highlighted perhaps as part of a more general campaign by the business press against the increasing role of government in regulating business. Despite this, the reports are fairly factual and informative, yet appear to be overly pessimistic. FIRA has not yet shown itself to be a major barrier to foreign investment and it certainly does not have the power nor the intention to buy Canada back.

INTERPRETATION OF FIRA'S ACTIVITIES:
EQUITY VERSUS EFFICIENCY

On an analytical level, it is well known that free trade is Pareto optimal and that tariffs and other barriers to trade, including government controls on capital flows, introduce market imperfections and distortions that produce costs in terms of foregone potential economic welfare. These welfare costs of protection have been evaluated by generations of economists in their studies of the effects of the Canadian tariff and of government actions to promote policies such as eastwest gas and oil pipelines. These studies have been summarized elsewhere (Rugman 1973). Recently, the Economic Council of Canada (1975) has produced a definitive report on the benefits of free trade for Canada, and has further shown that much of the net foreign direct investment into Canada is induced by the tariff.

The tariff has two problems. Not only does it create and protect inefficient industry within Canada, but it also helps to increase the extent of
foreign ownership of the Canadian economy. Now comes a paradox. In
order to help reduce, or at least contain, the high degree of foreign ownership of the resource and manufacturing sectors, the federal government has
introduced another barrier to trade in the form of FIRA. An alternative
policy would have been to remove the original incentive to much foreign investment — namely, the tariff. Instead, Canada now has tariffs plus FIRA.
Presumably this will produce an inefficient industrial sector financed by a
larger proportion of Canadian rather than American funds.

From this brief review of the propensity for governments to implement
trade policies which involve welfare costs, we observe the perennial conflict
between equity and efficiency goals. The reason for tariff policies and for
restrictions on the free inflow of foreign capital is that the Canadian government does not pursue the sole objective of maximizing economic welfare. Instead, it has many other targets, some of which conflict with efficiency. One such noneconomic goal is to foster national independence. For
better or for worse, the government appears to believe that an inefficient
protected domestic industry is necessary for national survival and that
increases in foreign ownership of the industrial sector cannot be tolerated.
The preference of governments for independence, and for increased taxation of the multinational enterprise, is part of the dispute over international
factor shares; that is, it is essentially concerned with income distribution
rather than with efficiency.

Realizing that most of the criticism directed toward foreign investment
by nationalists is concerned with income distribution effects rather than
with considerations of efficiency, it can be asked if such criticism is justified. The answer requires further analysis. It is alleged that an MNE can use
its market power to generate excess profits. For example, it may do this by
maintaining monopoly control over supplies of resources, or over the forward distribution of goods in a national market. Some MNEs achieve both
of these advantages — they enjoy both backward and forward integration.
In addition, horizontal integration will allow a firm to expand a monopoly
advantage achieved in one country into foreign markets. In general, monopoly profits are generated when the firm sets a higher price than would be
possible under competitive conditions. Therefore, one test of monopoly
influence is to examine prices.

With reference to the Canadian situation, it is frequently observed that
prices of goods produced by a MNE are higher in Canada than in the United
States. A frequently quoted example is the price of automobiles. Under the

free-trade auto pact agreement of 1965, Canadian production of autos enjoys economies of scale by selling into the integrated North American market. However, the price to American consumers of automobiles is less than the Canadian price by some 10 percent. If this price difference is not due to scale, government taxes, tariff, or other such exogenous policy problems, then presumably it is due to policies endogenous to the MNE. In fact, the price differential has been exaggerated by the premium on the Canadian dollar in recent years.

Another alleged example of the opportunities available for excess profits through foreign investment is found in the factor market. By producing a good in a foreign economy with low factor costs, for example with a low wage bill due to surplus labor, it is possible to generate excess profits. A low wage cost product can then be sold in the U.S. market at normal prices for that market, but excess profits can be generated because the factor costs were set in the cheaper foreign economy rather than in the domestic one. This argument has to take account of risk problems, but it is possible that such foreign investment in the factor market can generate a higher rate of return than comparable domestic investment. The argument also requires MNE control of the factor market to prevent competition — an unlikely possibility.

The problem with these arguments, and also with transfer pricing, is that they concentrate on one part of the operations of the MNE without looking at the rest of the picture. A distinction must be made between exploitation of a true monopoly advantage in the goods market (which means there is a single producer) and the operations of the MNE as it attempts to exploit temporary advantages due to superior management, technological, or research capabilities. The latter advantages are in the factor market and cannot be maintained for long unless protected by patents or other government licenses. These advantages have been generated within the firm and should be distinguished from a monopoly advantage resulting from control of the product market.

The efficient way to correct any monopoly advantages of a MNE is to remove the patents, or other barriers to entry, that encourage the development of a monopoly. If learning by doing is necessary to promote competition, then appropriate subsidies to new firms are likely to be better than regulatory devices. Actions such as these in the economic field will be more effective in curbing the alleged excessive powers of the MNE than any number of political agreements on codes of conduct. In the host country-MNE zones of conflict, the nation state retains great economic power and it should use this to maximize aggregate social welfare rather than to achieve narrow objectives such restricting foreign investment, particularly when such a partial policy has unforeseen repercussions on the rest of the economy.

Noneconomic goals always conflict with efficiency and have led economists to calculate the welfare costs of such goals, as indicated previously. Here it should be remembered that economists have only one input to make into the matrix of policy decision and that their emphasis on efficiency can be contrasted with other social targets, such as income redistribution, independence, and so on. The most useful contribution to be made by an economist in a policy group is to argue consistently for efficiency since other social scientists will presumably advance the case for noneconomic goals. The economist can also calculate the opportunity cost of the final policy approved, using a general equilibrium model to generate the optimal welfare solution as a hypothetical standard of comparison against which the political policy can be measured.

In the context of foreign investment, it is clear that the Canadian government has made a political decision to review foreign takeovers and new investments in Canada. However, to implement this political policy it has chosen to evaluate the benefits of proposed capital inflows on mainly economic grounds. This rationale for establishing FIRA as a review agency which screens foreign investment on economic grounds should not disguise the political nature of the Act. FIRA makes a recommendation to the Minister (of Industry, Trade, and Commerce), and the decision in each case is ultimately approved or rejected by the federal cabinet. The administration of the Act involves a two-way flow of information, with the officials in FIRA being aware of the thinking of cabinet members, the Prime Minister's office, and the Minister responsible for the Act in particular. On the other hand, the details of each case are unlikely to be fully absorbed by members of cabinet and other departments due to time constraints. Therefore, at present, FIRA can operate with a great amount of discretionary power and can generate policy as it administers an essentially vague, general, and open-ended Act.

The extent to which FIRA is actually restricting foreign investment is another question. While it has the potential powers to significantly reduce capital inflows and Canadian-financed foreign investment, the evidence to date indicates that FIRA does not wish to do so. Indeed, with well over 80 percent of reviewable applications being accepted, it is questionable whether FIRA is operating as a barrier to foreign investment at all. In the statements of senior officials of FIRA, it is made clear that Canada continues to welcome foreign investment with open arms provided that it can "perform." See the remarks by Howarth (1976b), Barrow (1975), and Byleveld (1975) for additional information. By performance is meant the "significant benefit" that the foreign investment can provide for Canada.

FOREIGN INVESTMENT AND THE CANADIAN
BALANCE OF PAYMENTS

The last section discussed the perennial tradeoff problem of a choice between economic efficiency with free trade and no barriers to capital flows, or political independence safeguarded by tariffs and restrictive barriers to flows of goods and factors. It also suggested that although the operations of FIRA may be conducted on economic grounds, with the efficiency effects of proposed foreign investments being determined, in reality it is a political agency. This section assumes that FIRA will continue to operate, but advances arguments in favor of the Agency pursuing a relatively open policy with regard to foreign investment. The major point made is that foreign investment is a significant contributor to economic growth and, for balance of payments reasons, it is necessary to have a capital account surplus to pay off Canada's persistent current account deficit — one which is unlikely to disappear given present trade policies. See the Economic Council of Canada (1975) on free trade for a development of this point.

In the theoretical literature explaining the capital account of the Canadian balance of payments, there is a dichotomy between the real and monetary explanations. According to the monetary explanation, direct investment is to be treated jointly with portfolio investment as a long-term capital flow. Monetary variables, such as interest rate differentials, determine such capital movements. In her classic survey of balance of payments theory, Krueger (1969) follows this traditional viewpoint, and fails to give any explicit attention to the theoretical determinants of direct investment.

The real theory explanation of the capital account makes a distinction between direct investment and portfolio investment with the former being determined by long-term financial variables such as income, scale, tariff, and other such variables. These explanations have been formalized into a general theory of market imperfections (Rugman 1975). According to this approach, direct investment is undertaken by multinational firms in order to exploit abroad a monopoly advantage they have acquired in areas of research, management, and technology. This is more of a microtheory of foreign investment, emphasizing firm specific variables rather than aggregative monetary variables.

There is a need to reformulate the traditional explanation of the capital account to permit a distinction between direct and portfolio investment, in which monetary variables are recognized as determining portfolio investment, while nonfinancial variables determine direct investment. There is some empirical support for such a distinction, as econometricians have tested the many variables thought to be important in the capital account. In general, such studies confirm that both short-term and long-term portfolio investment is responsive to interest rate differentials while direct investment is not affected by this monetary variable. For example, the major study by Caves and Reuber (1971) confirms this, and also finds that variables such as market size and economies of scale explain direct investment into Canada, rather than monetary variables.

One of the major findings of Caves and Reuber was that an inflow of foreign direct investment generates additional domestic investment in the Canadian economy. They find that in the 1951–1962 time period, $1.00 of direct investment was associated with between $1.50 and $3.00 of Canadian capital formation. The lower figure was appropriate in periods when there was a lack of effective aggregate demand, giving some unemployment in the Canadian economy. The upper figure was appropriate in times of full employment. These two boundary figures were also found to be relevant when the model was disaggregated. For example, Canadian capital formation was stimulated by the extra $1.50 amount when foreign investment went into takeovers or into new mining and resource ventures. On the other hand, some $3.00 of Canadian investment was generated for every $1.00 of direct investment in the secondary manufacturing sector.

These empirical findings tend to refute the argument that foreign investment is a substitute for domestic investment. Instead foreign investment in Canada generates substantial associated domestic investment. A more detailed analysis of the relationship between domestic and foreign investment reveals that U.S. direct investment is complementary to Canadian investment in each sector. If the American investment generates Canadian investment (and this direction of causation cannot necessarily be captured in a regression model), then it is providing an external economy to Canada. This should lead to favorable growth of income effects. In summary, if direct investment is a complement to Canadian investment, rather than a substitute for it, then it should foster Canadian economic development.

A striking fact emerges from a study of the Canadian balance of payments statistics in recent years. From Table 10–4 it can be observed that there is a persistent inflow of direct and long-term portfolio investment (column 1), and highly volatile and usually negative short-term portfolio investment (column 2). These items are reported as net amounts; that is, the difference between credit and debit items for each category in the balance of payments statistics. One of the most stable net inflows, until 1973, has been direct investment (column 6), which has averaged about four to five hundred million dollars a year since 1950. Net direct investment has always been positive until the recent net outflows of 1973 to 1975. The reason for this may be associated with the formation of FIRA, but no hard evidence of

TABLE 10-4. Canada's balance of payments, 1967–1975, million dollars

| Year | Capital Movements | | | Total Current Account Balance 4 | Net Official Monetary Movements 5 | Net Direct Investment (part of col. 1) 6 | Net interest and dividends (part of col. 4) 7 |
	Balance in long-term forms 1	Balance in short-term forms 2	Total net capital balance 3				
1967	+1,415	−896	+519	−499	+20	+566	−916
1968	+1,669	−1,223	+446	−97	+349	+365	−906
1969	+2,337	−1,355	+982	−917	+65	+350	−915
1970	+752	−328	+424	+1,106	+1,663	+540	−1,022
1971	+482	−147	+335	+442	+896	+660	−1,141
1972	+1,657	−967	+690	−471	+336	+225	−1,080
1973	+373	−858	−485	+18	−467	−50	−1,265
1974	+1,036	+631	+1,667	−1,643	+24	−90	−1,485
1975	+3,656	+1,014	+4,670	−5,074	−404	−205	−1,957

Source: Statistics Canada. *Quarterly Estimates of the Canadian Balance of International Payments,* vol. 23, no. 4, April 1976 (Information Canada, Ottawa).

causality is available. From column 3 of Table 10–4 it can be observed that there has usually been a surplus on the capital account; the only exception since 1952 being in 1973. This surplus on capital account finances the normal deficit on current account (column 4); the current account having been in surplus since 1952 only in 1970, 1971, and 1973.

These relationships have been discussed at some length by Canadian economists and have been exhaustively analyzed in the study by Caves and Reuber (1971). An additional point frequently overlooked is that the debt servicing of the persistent long-term capital inflow has naturally increased, and now often exceeds the capital account surplus. The interest and dividends (column 7) are recorded as an item in the current account of the Canadian balance of payments. The reason for this is probably due more to a statistical convention than to economic theory. As the interest and dividends due on foreign investment reflect the annual flow of capital required to finance the stock of foreign investment, they should really be in the capital account. Payments on net interests and dividends now exceed the conventionally defined capital account surplus (column 3), therefore net payments of interest and dividends exceed by a large margin net direct investment into Canada on an annual basis. It is clear that Canada has not been paying its way on capital transactions in recent years.

These trends in the Canadian balance of payments can be partly explained by monetary theory. The persistent inflow of long-term capital into Canada is due to either a greater rate of return than is available on similar assets in the foreign economy or is for portfolio diversification reasons. Most long-term capital comes from the United States, due largely to the observed positive differential in the long-term rates of return between Canada and the United States. This is more valid for the long-term portfolio investment component of long-term capital than for direct foreign investment, since the latter is determined by nonmonetary variables as analyzed elsewhere (Rugman 1975).

The volatile short-term portfolio investment item is, in general, determined by the U.S.-Canadian interest rate differential. When there is a positive interest differential for Canada, there is an inflow of short-term American capital and vice versa. The sensitivity of short-term investment to the interest rate differential has been confirmed by Caves and Reuber (1971). An additional point can be made in explaining short-term portfolio investment. The American financial market will embody less risk than the Canadian financial market, simply due to the larger size of the former. Therefore, if investors are risk averse, they will have an incentive to invest in short-term American assets rather than Canadian, if all other things are equal. The outflows of short-term capital have led many nationalist commentators to suggest that Canada is financing its own sellout. Using economic theory, we see that such capital outflows are for rational economic reasons, and it would be inefficient to regulate them.

In general, use of the term structure of interest rates can help in the analysis of the capital account of the Canadian balance of payments. Consider the following relationships:

$$r_{LT}^C \qquad r_{LT}^{U.S.}$$
$$r_{ST}^C \qquad r_{ST}^{U.S.}$$

where r represents the rate of return, ST is short term, LT is long term, C is Canada, and U.S. is the United States.

Given these relationships, there will be an inflow of long-term financial capital into Canada and an outflow of short-term capital. The long-term American rate of return may be lower than the Canadian due to a larger stock of capital. This leads to a lower marginal productivity of capital in the United States when compared to Canada. The American demand for long-term assets will spill over into the Canadian market, and until capital movements equalize the rates of return, there will be a continuous inflow of long-term capital. While direct investment is motivated by factors other than the long-term interest rate differential, the ultimate factor common to all determinants is profit maximization; American direct investment in Canada takes place because the marginal investment in Canada offers a better yield than a domestic investment. These underlying market forces can be offset by barriers to trade in capital, such as FIRA, but there is an economic cost in doing so; and one which serves to reduce social welfare.

CONCLUSIONS

On the basis of information available in the public domain, it appears to me that FIRA operates in a very favorable manner toward proposed foreign direct investments. While it has the potential to block foreign takeovers and to restrict new foreign investment, it has not administered the Act in a restrictive manner. Therefore, it is concluded that FIRA does not offer a substantial barrier to trade in capital and that Canada continues to enjoy the benefits of international capital flows. It is suggested, furthermore, that this is a fortunate outcome since both economic theory and the history of the Canadian balance of payments accounts reveal the need for foreign investment if economic growth is to be sustained. A partial policy, such as FIRA, imposed to sustain political goals of national independence will inevitably lead to economic costs in terms of foregone aggregate social welfare.

EPILOGUE[2]

Since the work for this chapter was completed in the summer of 1976, new data have become available from FIRA. These are summarized in Tables 10-5 and 10-6.

It is probably a fair summary of them to suggest that these data, for five years of FIRA operations, support the analysis made above, an analysis based on data for only the first year or so of operations. Thus, we can observe that the percentage of allowed takeovers (acquisitions in Table 10-5) has always been high, ranging between 66 percent of the incomplete first year of 1974 to a high of 91 percent in 1977. The number of resolved acquisition cases in 1978 was double that of the first full year of review, studied above. Similarly, Table 10-6 reveals approval of between 80 and 89 percent of the reviewable new business cases which have been resolved in any year. Of the 1,650 separate FIRA cases reviewed, only 130 have been disallowed and about 150 were withdrawn, the rest being approved. Safarian (1978) suggests that this is a high rejection rate by international standards.

TABLE 10-5.　Reviewable new acquisition cases, outcome of status

	1974*	1975	1976	1977	1978
Reviewable new cases	102	166	171	261	360
Carryover from previous period	—	52	54	65	73
Total of above	102	218	225	326	433
Total resolved	50	164	160	253	327
Allowed	33	116	124	231	282
Disallowed	8	21	19	12	28
Withdrawn	9	27	17	10	17
Carried over to next period	52	54	65	73	106
Allowed cases as per cent of resolved (%)	66	71	78	91	86
Value of assets, all cases ($000,000)	479	1,070	1,069	1,145	4,491

*Provisions for review of new businesses came into force October 15, 1975.
Source: Foreign Investment *Review,* Spring 1979.

Tables 10–7 and 10–8 report the breakdown of takeover or new business cases by country. Most takeovers are by U.S. firms, but there is a growing amount of European involvement in Canada. This now accounts for nearly one-third of the cases, although these are often for smaller size investments than the average American one. Tables 10–9 and 10–10 report the breakdown by industry sector. The largest number of cases are in the construction and services sector, followed closely by manufacturing.

These tables, along with the earlier ones in this chapter, point up the inadequate nature of the data supplied by FIRA. It is, of course, limited by the Act in revealing individual case details or the confidential nature of firm specific financial data. Yet there is little economic value in only having data on the number of cases. These need to be adjusted for size of firm, profitability, financial ratios, and so on, before any meaningful analysis can be undertaken about the economics of foreign investment in Canada. Then we could begin to test hypotheses about the relative performance of foreign-controlled versus domestic enterprises and their relative economic impact on Canada (and other nations.) Until such data are forthcoming, either

TABLE 10–6. Reviewable new business cases, outcome of status

	1975	1976	1977	1978
Reviewable new cases	6	196	328	331
Carryover from previous period	—	6	58	52
Total of above	6	202	386	383
Total resolved	—	144	334	319
Allowed	—	115	297	273
Disallowed	—	9	12	21
Withdrawn	—	20	25	25
Carried over to next period	6	58	52	64
Allowed cases as per cent of resolved (%)	—	80	89	86
Planned investment, all cases ($000,000)	5	324	803	323

Source: Foreign Investment Review, Spring 1979.

TABLE 10-7. Reviewable new acquisition cases, country of control

	1974*	1975	1976	1977	1978
Total	102	166	161	261	360
United States	61	116	109	171	243
United Kingdom	21	15	23	40	47
Other Europe	15	27	34	41	52
Belgium	1	2	1	2	1
Denmark	—	—	—	2	1
France	3	6	6	6	5
Germany, West	5	2	10	15	17
Italy	—	2	1	3	1
Liechtenstein	2	2	—	—	1
Luxembourg	—	—	3	—	1
Netherlands	—	5	—	4	8
Norway	—	1	—	—	1
Sweden	—	2	9	2	7
Switzerland	4	5	4	7	9
All other	5	8	5	9	18
Australia	2	1	—	1	—
Bermuda	—	2	1	—	—
Japan	2	2	3	3	7
Others	1	3	1	5	11
Allowed cases as percent of resolved	%	%	%	%	%
United States	65	77	73	91	87
United Kingdom	70	79	82	95	78
Other Europe	71	50	86	90	89
All other	50	30	100	80	80

*Provision for review of acquisitions came into force April 9, 1974.
Source: Foreign Investment Review, Spring 1979.

from FIRA or other sources, further empirical analysis of these cases is severely limited.

Given the inadequacy of the data made available by FIRA, I have chosen
in this book to pursue an alternative approach in measuring the relative performances and economic impacts of multinational versus domestic firms.
As explained in Part II, I focus on individual multinational firms, or groups
of firms, and evaluate their profits, risk, and economic effects using published information in annual company reports and government bulletins. It
is possible to travel a long way making analytical use of these published
data; perhaps as far as is feasible at the present time.

TABLE 10-8.   Reviewable new business cases, country of control

	1975	1976	1977	1978
Total	6	196	328	331
United States	4	90	184	193
United Kingdom	—	22	30	26
Other Europe	1	63	85	79
Austria	—	—	—	3
Belgium	—	1	—	1
Denmark	—	5	6	4
Finland	—	1	1	1
France	—	9	17	16
Germany, West	—	22	26	18
Greece	—	—	1	1
Ireland	—	—	—	1
Italy	1	9	10	10
Liechtenstein	—	2	—	—
Luxembourg	—	—	—	1
Monaco	—	—	1	—
Netherlands	—	2	3	1
Norway	—	—	3	3
Spain	—	1	—	2
Sweden	—	3	9	5
Switzerland	—	8	8	12
All Other	1	21	29	33
Australia	—	2	3	3
Hong Kong	—	3	3	3
India	—	3	1	1
Japan	—	4	10	6
Others	1	9	12	20
Allowed cases as per-cent of resolved	%	%	%	%
United States	—	73	88	86
United Kingdom	—	93	82	85
Other Europe	—	80	95	87
All other	—	91	81	79

Source: Foreign Investment *Review,* Spring 1979.

TABLE 10-9. Reviewable new acquisition cases, industrial sector

	1974*	1975	1976	1977	1978
Total	102	166	171	261	360
Primary	15	18	15	20	30
Agriculture, fishing, and trapping	2	1	2	4	5
Forestry	3	1	—	1	1
Mines, quarries, oil wells	10	16	13	15	24
Manufacturing	47	82	93	108	161
Food, beverage, and tobacco	6	11	9	15	15
Rubber, plastic, and leather	3	3	4	6	12
Textiles, knitting, and clothing	3	3	3	5	4
Wood, furniture, and paper	6	10	7	12	14
Printing, publishing, and allied	—	3	1	2	4
Primary metal and metal fabrication	2	9	19	12	20
Machinery and transport equipment	13	17	7	14	27
Electrical products	1	9	11	12	16
Nonmetalic mineral products	8	3	9	5	8
Petroleum and coal products	—	—	2	1	1
Chemical	3	11	15	10	22
Miscellaneous	2	3	6	14	18
Construction and services	40	66	63	133	169
Construction	2	2	2	3	1
Transportation, communication, utilities	6	6	9	10	11
Trade	18	37	38	72	102
Finance, insurance, real estate	10	14	8	15	19
Community, business personal services	4	7	6	33	36

*Provision for review of acquisitions came into force April 9, 1974.
Source: Foreign Investment Review, Spring 1979.

TABLE 10-10.   Reviewable new business cases, industrial sector

	1975	1976	1977	1978
Total	6	196	328	331
Primary	—	12	22	27
Agriculture, fishing, and trapping	—	2	6	2
Forestry	—	—	2	2
Mines, quarries, oil wells	—	10	14	23
Manufacturing	2	67	94	99
Food, beverage, and tobacco	—	3	7	6
Rubber, plastic, and leather	—	4	5	5
Textiles, knitting, and	—	4	9	5
clothing	1	5	5	6
Wood, furniture, and paper				
Printing, publishing, and allied	—	—	—	4
Primary metal and metal fabrication	1	15	19	12
Machinery and	—	6	19	19
transportation	—	7	5	7
equipment	—	3	5	6
Electrical products	—	—	—	—
Nonmetalic mineral products	—	6	3	6
Petroleum and coal products	—	14	17	23
Chemical	4	117	212	205
Miscellaneous	—	4	4	14
Construction and services				
Construction	1	10	5	11
Transportation, communication, utilities	1	68	133	102
Trade	1	10	16	11
Finance, insurance, real estate	1	25	54	67
Community, business, personal services				

Source: Foreign Investment Review, Spring 1979.

ENDNOTES

1. Canada Foreign Investment Review Act, House of Commons, 21–22 Elizabeth II, Chapter 46, p. 620.
2. This Epilogue consists of new materials not published in the original version.

11 TARIFF AND TRADE EFFECTS OF MULTINATIONALS IN CANADA

INTRODUCTION

One of the great paradoxes of Canadian economic history is that foreign direct investment has been attracted by the Canadian tariff. The large amount of foreign ownership of Canada's manufacturing sector was encouraged by the tariff. The aim of the tariff was to protect and build up indigenous industry, yet the subsidiaries of U.S. multinationals entered instead. As we have seen earlier, much of the motivation for such multinational activity is explained by the theory of internalization. Yet, as a policy device, the tariff has been a disaster.

This chapter explores the costs of the tariff and reviews the economic aspects of Canadian commercial policy. It is found that the tariff is inefficient on both theoretical and empirical grounds. A large academic literature has grown up to evaluate these inefficiencies, and the results of these studies are surprisingly unambiguous for economists. All of them find evidence of welfare costs caused by the tariff and other protectionist devices. In this climate of Canadian inefficiency and misguided public policy, the multinational enterprise has grown in importance and, indeed, has performed frequently in a superior manner to domestic Canadian enterprise.

CANADIAN COMMERCIAL POLICY

The state of thinking (by the Canadian economics establishment, at least) on Canadian commercial policy was revealed with the publication of a summary volume of the Canada in the Atlantic Economy series called *Canada in a Wider Economic Community*. (See English et al. 1972.) The three distinguished academic authors provide a good review of the dozen or so research studies in the series, and also report the results of a study of free-trade options for Canada in the changing world of the seventies. Due to the importance of this series, the vital nature of trade in an open economy such as Canada and the interrelationships between tariffs and FDI, this section presents a fairly detailed analysis of the major points raised in the study. The statements reviewed here may be compared usefully to those made in the studies on Canadian commercial policy published by the Economic Council of Canada (1975).

Professor Wilkinson restates the well known analysis that historically Canada has relied on exports of resource intensive goods to finance imports of highly manufactured products. There have been successive export staples, such as fish, fur, timber products, grains, metals, oil, and gas. Trade in these primary products has encouraged some development of the Canadian economy through linkages and other external effects, but such development has been confined to resource-intensive products, and not manufactured goods. Indeed, manufacturing industry grew under tariff protection, and such protection has generated, in general, an inefficient industrial base. One notable exception to the traditional inefficiencies of protected industry is the pulp and paper industry, which became an efficient producer within Canada and eventually generated substantial exports.

There are three special features of Canadian trade. First, Wilkinson says there is "enormous reliance upon the United States" (p. 31). This is due to the fact that over 70 percent of exports and imports are with the United States, and this percentage is increasing. Agreements such as the 1965 U.S.-Canadian auto pact resulted in even closer connections between the two economies. An objective of future Canadian trade policy should be to diversify trading partners as much as possible.

A second feature of Canadian trade is its commodity composition. Most of Canada's exports are resource intensive, while imports are of manufactured goods. It is necessary to increase exports of manufactured goods, and this may well be achieved by a movement toward free trade which permits Canadian industry to engage in rationalization in order to achieve the benefits of large-scale production. With free trade there will be a larger market than is available in the protected Canadian economy. In addition, it is desirable in the future to achieve more processing of energy and other natural resources within Canada prior to exporting. In turn, this will generate a larger domestic industrial sector with more employment opportunities. The traditional lack of management skills in Canada may also be overcome due to the incentives resulting from a movement toward free trade and the consequent development of Canadian industry.

The third feature of Canadian trade is the large amount of foreign ownership in the mining and manufacturing sectors. About 80 percent of net direct investment into Canada comes from the United States. American firms control most of the mining and many of the manufacturing industries of Canada. This leads to trade between the subsidiaries and parent companies in multinational corporations. In fact, it has been estimated that one-half of the total of Canadian trade is such intracorporate transfers. Wilkinson says that the objective of Canadian trade policy in this area should be to encourage Canadian financing and to promote a domestic capital market.

Wilkinson also reports the results of some original research into the potential benefits to Canada from joining one of five alternative free-trade associations. His methodology is based on customs union theory and involves a static measure of the short-run gains and losses resulting from the removal of tariff barriers. This approach takes the existing trade patterns by country and by commodity group as given, and calculates the effects of a removal of tariffs. The longer-run dynamic changes cannot be captured in this approach since they involve changes in such trade patterns, as well as structural changes within the economy.

Based on the in the institutions of the early 1970s, such as the European Free Trade Area (EFTA), the five alternative free-trade associations proposed are:

1. Canada and the United States
2. Canada, United States, and EFTA
3. Canada, United States, and the Pacific (Japan, Australia, New Zealand)
4. Canada and the Pacific countries
5. Canada, United States, EFTA, EEC, and the Pacific.

The research was undertaken before Britain voted to join the EEC in January 1973. Therefore, option 2 is no longer a viable alternative since the EFTA grouping has effectively been eliminated.

Wilkinson's findings from the static trade creation and trade diversion analysis are somewhat surprising. Four of the five free-trade alternatives involve net losses for Canada, with the greatest loss being for option 5, followed by options 2, 3, and 1. Under one method of calculation, a free-trade association with the United States provided some net benefits. The only free-trade association providing an unambiguous benefit to Canada is option 4, with the Pacific countries. However, trade with these countries at present accounts for only about 5 percent of imports and exports, leading to the implication that such a free-trade association is trivial.

The gains to Canada from these free-trade associations are negative due to the present structure of tariffs. Most Canadian imports are of highly manufactured goods on which there are high tariffs. Once these are removed in a free-trade association, Canada's import bill will increase. There is not an offsetting gain in revenue from exports since most Canadian exports are of primary and resource-intensive goods, on which there are already low tariffs, partly due to previous General Agreement on Tariffs and Trade (GATT) rounds. As long as this general pattern of trade prevails for Canada there will be few static gains from free trade.

The potential dynamic benefits may be considerable, but due to their uncertain nature they cannot be readily measured. If the pattern of Canadian trade changes such that export of manufactured goods increases, with less reliance being placed on primary and resource intensive goods, and if imports of manufactured goods can be replaced by domestic production, then free trade may result in future benefits to Canada. The structural change required in domestic industry may well occur if scale economies are available under free trade. Similarly, advances in research, technology, and management skills may well be greater under free trade.

In short, the present structure of the Canadian economy reflects many inefficiencies due to the protection of domestic industry by the tariff. Only in the long run can these inefficiencies be overcome and yield overall benefits to the Canadian economy. Larger-scale production will be required, and rationalization of industry is therefore associated with any movement toward free trade.

In a summary chapter on the industry studies commissioned for Canada in the Atlantic Economy series, Edward English emphasizes the latter point. As Canada moves toward free trade, there will be opportunities for sales of goods in a larger (world) market. Therefore, Canadian industries and other producers will be able to enjoy economies of scale that often do not exist under the present structure of tariff protection. In nearly all of the studies summarized by English, it was found that rationalization would be required if the industry was to be competitive under free trade. The diverse and inefficient small producers must be replaced by large-scale producing firms which can generate management, research, and technological advances of their own.

Another example used by Professor English to support his argument for free trade is that central Canada enjoys a locational advantage as it is close to the major American markets of the midwest and northeastern coast. Indeed, this Canadian manufacturing region enjoys a greater locational advantage than nearly all of the American regions. Therefore, under free trade, or even a free-trade association between Canada and the United States, the scale advantages would be available for a Canadian industrial center which also has a locational advantage. These points have been examined previously by Wonnacott and Wonnacott (1967) and others.

English suggests that the regional impacts of free trade are likely to differ depending on the time horizon considered. In the short run, the major benefits will accrue to Western Canada and the Atlantic provinces. At present, these areas have to purchase Canadian industrial goods produced in central Canada and sold at a higher price than the world free-trade price. In the long run, Ontario and Quebec will benefit from free trade once their industries start to rationalize and thereby become efficient producers, able to compete in world markets.

The concentration of industry, and the resulting scale economies, depend on the degree of factor substitution possible in the Canadian economy. Given enough time, factor substitution will occur, but in the adjustment period some special government subsidies may be required for declining industries and areas. Such a government adjustment policy should be confined to the transition period, and once unemployment, relocation, and other distortions have been minimized, any such subsidies should be removed.

Use is made of the conventional explanation of Canada's balance of payments accounts that the persistent deficit on current account is financed by a surplus on capital account. The latter surplus is mostly in the form of long-term portfolio capital and net direct investment. These long-term capital inflows are motivated by greater rates of return available in Canada, and by the opportunities available to multinational firms to expand their markets. On the other hand, short-term capital flows are responsive to interest rate differentials. The theory also suggests that under a fixed exchange rate system it is difficult to operate an independent monetary policy due to the sensitivity of such short-term capital to changes in interest rates. Under a flexible exchange rate, monetary policy can affect the internal balance, since then the movement in the exchange rate tends to reflect capital flows.

A simplistic growth theory model is implicit in the summary of international capital movements by English. Any inflow of capital is regarded as beneficial since it will increase domestic gross national product. In turn, greater Canadian productivity will allow Canadians to pay off the initial capital loans. This argument should be formally modeled and needs to be thought out in much greater detail. Included in this analysis should be a mechanism that reconciles the interest and dividends payable on debt capital with his optimistic supposition that such payments are less than the increase in productivity generated by foreign investment. It is not clear that this is the case. When the data on capital flows are studied, it can be noticed that the interest and dividends payable each year by Canada exceed the net capital inflow by a large amount. This flow of debt will continue for many years as the stock of foreign capital is large and constantly increasing.

The development of domestic capital markets in Canada has been constrained by the inflow of foreign capital, and it is not clear that this pattern will change in the future, especially when attention is given to the risk dimension. The larger American financial market permits greater risk diversification than does the smaller more specific Canadian market. Therefore, Canadians (both individuals and governments) may continue to purchase American assets if they are risk averse. The long-run solution to this problem is for Canadians to seek the promotion of efficient domestic financial intermediation, which, in the short run, may require some government subsidization.

In Chapter 6 of English et al. (1972) there is an inadequate discussion of some of these points, in a review of literature on the capital account. This topic has been dealt with more thoroughly in the book by Caves and Reuber (1971). The two major points advanced here are correct, but hardly surprising. First, a system of flexible exchange rates is required in order to operate an independent domestic monetary policy, as has been theoretically explained by Mundell and others. Second, it is suggested that the adjustment problem that arises with a movement toward free trade can be avoided by moving slowly toward such an objective. This permits substitution and more factor mobility over time, a neoclassical point which is undoubtedly correct in theory but lacking in practice.

Chapter 7 of English et al. (1972) is on tax harmonization policy. It is shown by Professor Eastman that the world economies are interdependent and that national tariff, tax, regional subsidization, and other policies will spill over into other economies. If a system of flexible exchange rates is adopted, there needs to be less harmonization of policies since there can be more independence, but in a world of managed flexibility the need for policy harmonization is greater. Chapter 7 of English et al. does not distinguish sufficiently between efficiency and equity questions. Eastman discusses the topic mostly in terms of efficiency and suggests that harmonization of government policies is required to approximate the advantages of free trade. However, most of the government policies he discusses have been introduced for income redistribution reasons. Such policies are frequently in conflict with efficiency objectives at the national level, let alone at the international level.

The definitive work on Canadian trade, industry, and foreign investment is by Eastman and Stykolt (1967). In their empirical chapters they find persistent evidence of a lack of scale economies in several tariff protected Canadian industries. The Canadian market alone appears to be of insufficient size to support the minimum size of plant required to exploit economies of scale. In turn, this lack of efficient industrial production is related to the low productivity of Canadian manufacturing industry. The seminal work of Eastman and Stykolt has led to further study by economists of the interrelationships between industrial inefficiency, low productivity, and the lack of scale economies in Canada. The reason for these problems can be traced back to the original historical policy decision to base Canada's industrial strategy on the tariff rather than on free trade. The problems of industrial inefficiency are also compounded by the large amount of foreign control, since the theory of internalization predicts that little research, innovation, and knowledge generation will occur in Canadian branch plants.

THE COSTS OF INDEPENDENCE

The objectives of this section of the chapter are limited to a consideration of the economic costs of Canadian independence. There is a survey of empirical work undertaken by Canadian economists in which the costs of the tariff and other protective trade devices are measured. Attention is restricted to the international trade implications of independence.

The benefits of Canadian independence are not considered in this section. This is not because they are believed to be trivial or unimportant, but because the benefits are mostly of a political nature. It might be assumed that the majority of Canadians will have a preference for independence, if all other things are equal. However, I have found that all other things are *not* equal, and that there are, in fact, substantial economic costs for independence in Canada.

There are many aspects of independence, of which social, political, and cultural factors are of concern. Here only the economic aspects are examined, especially the effect on income when protective measures are implemented to foster domestic production of goods and services at the expense of foreign imports. The main protective device considered is the tariff, which has been with us since Confederation. Other devices, such as transportation (freight rates), are ignored at this stage, as are monetary and exchange rate problems. The analysis is of the real sector alone in this section. Later, monetary problems and foreign investment are considered.

The analysis is focused on the tariff, but the implications drawn are similar to those which would result from a study of nontariff barriers to trade, which are increasing rapidly as tariffs themselves are being reduced by GATT and other agreements.

If Canada were to open its economy to free trade with the United States, it would be able to increase the scale of production of its industries. Production runs would be longer and costs lower. There is a fundamental difference in size of the U.S.-Canadian economies, with the Canadian market being too small. Canada presently exports 70 percent of its goods to the United States, and with free trade, this percentage might increase — but with a gain in efficiency. Other advantages to Canada of free trade would be increased competition, better management, and a greater rate of technological innovation and economic growth.

The Wonnacott's (1967) study found that Canadian wages are 25 percent less than American wages paid in comparable industries due to a lack of production economies of scale. See also Wilkinson (1972, p. 10). In the seventies, differentials in factor prices, especially wage differentials, narrowed, but not sufficiently to invalidate Canada's comparative advantage in resources and labor compared to the U.S. advantage in technology and capital. With free trade, central Canadian industry would be favorably located for sale to the large U.S. markets, as the Toronto-Montreal area lies close to the U.S. East Coast and Midwest marketing areas. The Wonnacotts (1967) found the latter manufacturing region to be the most favorably located one in North America, based on thirteen U.S. and five Canadian regions. The central Canadian region is located closest to this leading region. English et. al. (1972, p. 79) confirm this point.

For these reasons, free trade, or a move toward trade liberalization, will improve the efficiency of Canadian manufacturing and processing industries. This will mean lower prices and higher per capita incomes for all Canadians. Proceeding in a Johnsonian manner it can be assumed that, with the nation as a whole better off under free trade, specific income distribution questions can be ignored. If they were to be considered, it could be shown (in theory) that a costless tax-subsidy scheme would serve to redistribute income from the owners of the abundant factor to the owners of the scarce factor. From the Heckscher-Ohlin theorem, or its variants, we know that the incomes of the owners of the abundant factor would increase in absolute and relative terms with more production of the export good under free trade, and that incomes of the owners of the scarce factor are reduced with a movement from isolation to free trade.

Canada has historically relied on tariffs to protect domestic industry. The tariff raises the price of imported good(s) and permits industies to produce that which could not survive at competitive world prices. The tariff, therefore, fosters inefficiency. The tariff, and also a fairly open immigration policy, have permitted Canada to acquire a greater total GNP, but a lower per capita GNP than would have probably occurred under free trade as shown by Dales (1966) in his Chapters 2 and 6.

The main causes of the costs of the tariff are inefficiencies in production and consumption due to the relatively small scale of the Canadian economy. Tariff protection to foster infant industries in Canada has resulted in inefficient import substitution. The doyen of Canadian economists, Harry Johnson, argued that even the infant industry argument is an invalid argument for a tariff. See Johnson (1971). In fact, he demonstrates that all arguments for a tariff are invalid except for the optimum tariff argument which applies when the country has monopoly power in trade — an unlikely case in today's interdependent economy. In the case of infant industries, not only must the John Stuart Mill test be passed (that is, the price of the protected good must fall and eventually equal the world price), but also a more difficult test must be passed — the Bastable Test. This says that the higher price of the protected good must be discounted over time such that the price of the good falls below the world price, and is sufficient to compensate previous foregone alternative uses of the funds spent on higher prices for the protected good.

Free trade, therefore, is better than protection on the grounds of efficiency. Free trade is Pareto optimal (first best), whereas a tariff imposes a distortion by creating a divergence between the foreign rate of transformation and the domestic marginal rate of transformation. A domestic tax-subsidy scheme is superior to a tariff since it will prevent this distortion, yet in turn is still inferior to free trade. Production of goods can be encouraged by direct subsidies, while these subsidies can be financed by taxes on consumption which will shift the demand curves downward. As Canada has historically had a tariff there will be economic benefits if it is removed. We might note in passing that the protective effect of the tariff reflects the way in which customs duties are administered as well as the rates and levels of the duties themselves. See Blake (1957).

EMPIRICAL WORK ON THE COSTS OF THE TARIFF

We now turn to a survey of empirical work measuring the costs of the Canadian tariff. The first study was undertaken by John Young. In his monograph, *Canadian Commercial Policy,* published in 1957, he estimated the cash cost of the tariff as between 3.5 and 4.5 percent of GNP per annum. This was based on 1954 dollar values, and was a measure of the consumption costs only. This aggregated to about one billion dollars, out of the 1954 GNP of about twenty-five billion dollars. The costs of the tariff on the expenditure side mostly reflect higher domestic prices due to protection, when compared with lower world prices. World prices are lower because of greater efficiency from producing and selling with economies of scale in a larger world market. The cash costs of some industries were as follows, again all in 1965 dollars:

Industry	$million
Machinery	150
Clothing	110
Furnishings	110
Construction	105
Food	95
Tobacco	35
Gas	11
Alcoholic beverages	11

It should be noted in the Young estimate that the cost of the tariff (about 4 percent of the GNP) is only a measure of the consumption cost. The other half of the costs of the tariff is the production cost. Assuming the production and consumption costs are about the same, the total cost of the tariff based on the Young study would add up to 8 percent of GNP per annum.

There are other major studies of the costs of the tariff. In their book on U.S.-Canadian free trade, published in 1967, Ronald and Paul Wonnacott estimated the costs of the tariff to be at least 10 percent of GNP per annum. Wonnacott (1975) confirms the 10-percent estimate using more recent data. In a separate study, Eastman (1964) calculated the cost of the tariff to be about 12 percent of GNP. Dauphin (1978) generates lower numbers but Williams (1978) provides additional evidence of the high cost of the tariff.

In terms of productivity, Canadian manufacturing is much less efficient than comparable American industry. See Eastman and Stykolt (1967). Studies sponsored by the Economic Council of Canada have documented the extent of this productivity gap. In 1960, the level of net national product per employee in Canada was 21 percent lower than in the United States, and this estimate may be somewhat on the low side. In another study, Daly, Keys, and Spence (1968) found that Canadian net output is about one-third below that of comparable industry in the United States. Their study confirmed earlier work done in the 1950s which found that "net output is no less than 35 to 40 percent below that in the same sector of the American economy" (1968, p. 9).

The reasons for this relative lack of productivity, according to these studies, are due more to organizational difficulties than to a problem with factor inputs themselves. There is relatively less management training and education in Canada, with a resulting inadequate use of factors of production. Low productivity of Canadian industry is due to a lack of specialization, coupled with too small a scale of production. These two factors are due, in turn, to the historic reliance on the tariff to protect industry which otherwise would not be able to compete at world prices. In Canadian manufacturing, there is an excessive range of products produced and too diverse a set of markets. Production runs are too short due to the lack of volume in sales in the small internal Canadian market. Wages in Canada (at the time of these studies) were only about 80 percent of those in the United States, and, assuming that the wage is determined by the marginal product of labor, this implies that Canadian labor is less productive than its American counterpart. On the other hand, prices of capital and machinery are about 125 percent of the American cost. These two facts will make Canadian manufacturing industry more labor intensive, and therefore more inefficient than American industry.

Costs are also higher to finance industrial and commercial expansion. This is allegedly due to greater risk in the thin Canadian capital market, which leads to a persistent outflow of short-term capital to the New York finance market where more diversification and financial intermediation take place. Offsetting this is a persistent inflow of net long-term portfolio and direct investment into Canada, the latter giving, of course, the problem of foreign ownership.

Related to the low relative productivity of Canadian industry are the higher prices of Canadian goods. In the Daly study (1968), based on interviews with thirty manufacturing industries using 1963 data, it was found that only five industries had lower costs of production than their American counterparts. These were: wringer washer, pole, boiler, tank, and ACSR wire. Over one-half of the industries had costs which were some 20 percent higher, and one-quarter of the industries had costs which were 35 percent higher. Motor electrical equipment was found to be 267 percent of the cost of similar United States products, with other high cost items being lamps, automatic washers, BX wire, synthetic textiles, aluminum clips, gas pumps, and meters. All of them were over 130 percent of the American cost.

In another study, West (1971) confirmed that net output per employee in Canada is some one-third lower than in the United States. Labor productivity is, on average, 28 percent below the U.S. level. The average price of Canadian manufactured goods is 18 percent higher, but this is partly offset by lower costs in some sectors, especially service industries. The productivity differential and the higher costs are mostly explained by a scale variable. There is a lack of internal economies on the economy-wide level. There is an observed lack of competition in the thirty industries studied, with the level of market power being associated with higher prices. In the West study, it was found "that efficiency levels for labor and capital in Canadian manufacturing were more than 20 percent lower than in the United States, and for materials and fuel some 12 percent lower."

It should be noted that these empirical studies observe Canadian manufacturing industry as it is; that is, the studies are based on data which incorporate distortions due to tariff protection. The resulting inefficiencies in production are compared with industries operating in the larger American market. Therefore, these studies are only a guide to the costs of the tariff. They present some evidence to show the problems facing protected Canadian industry. The remedy is more difficult than the diagnosis. Perhaps the solutions are to move toward free trade with multilateral tariff reduction; to adopt a continentalist trading policy with the United States alone; and to attempt trade diversification by opening up markets with new trade partners. All of these options are considered in the Economic Council of Canada study (1975).

FREE TRADE AND CANADIAN INDEPENDENCE[1]

The Economic Council of Canada (1975) has taken an unequivocal position in favor of free trade. The theme of their recent report, and of most of the associated background studies, is that free trade is efficient and justified on economic grounds. Such an argument is traditional, yet the economic rationale for free trade has usually been constrained by the presumed adverse political and social costs which will result from removal of tariffs and other protective devices. The Economic Council met this objection head-on by challenging the alleged political and social costs of tariff removal. It is argued that independence has not been fostered by the tariff, since today there is both a large degree of foreign ownership and a concentration of trade with the United States. The Economic Council advocates a strategy of free trade and suggests that the short-run costs of adjustment can be financed by temporary government subsidies in view of the long-run benefits to industrial productivity and growth which will result from greater specialization under free trade.

This study by the Economic Council of Canada was released in July, 1975, after being in the works for several years. The initial public reception was less than overwhelming and the report seems doomed for the bookshelves of libraries and academic economists. This is a pity since the report is well worth reading, is an excellent piece of literature, and should be used as a reference work in any future debates on the issue of free trade for Canada.

The themes of the study are as follows:

1. Canada needs to adopt a new trade policy as she is being excluded from major trading blocs and her competitive position in world trade is being eroded by low productivity.

2. The latter is due to a lack of human capital, research, management skills, and entrepreneurial ability — all of which have been retarded by the historical reliance on tariff protection for domestic industry.

3. The tariff raises the price of imports and allows domestic production to occur that would not exist under free trade. By definition, such production is inefficient and several studies have estimated the cost of this inefficiency to be at least 5 percent of GNP per annum.

4. Associated with the tariff has been a persistent inflow of foreign direct investment, mostly from the United States. Today there is a large amount of foreign ownership of the Canadian economy, especially in the resource and manufacturing sectors. It is thought by many Canadians that such foreign ownership acts to constrain independence. To answer this charge, the Council argues that foreign investment was initially attracted into Canada to avoid the protective tariff. It is suggested that foreign subsidiaries of multinational firms will have less incentive to be set up if there is no tariff.

5. The Council recommends a move to a free-trade area (that is, removal of tariffs), but it does not suggest formation of a customs union. The most likely trading partner in a free-trade area will be the United States; trade with Europe and the Pacific Rim nations is very small. The Council does not feel that the free-trade area option is a form of continentalism, since significant economic efficiencies will result in an increase of Canada's wealth, and lead to greater political independence rather than less. The Council is very careful to advocate a free-trade area rather than a customs union. The latter would involve some political integration as well as economic, and the divisive debate in recent years over Britain joining the EEC suggests that a full customs union is much harder to sell than a purely free-trade agreement.

6. There will be adjustment costs in moving toward complete free trade; for example, some unemployment in previously protected industries and in some regions. To overcome such costs, the Council

recommends special selective subsidiaries during the transition period, which may last up to ten years. It is also suggested that the agriculture and energy sectors be excluded from a free-trade policy as they are special cases. (The reasons given for excluding these sectors appear to have more to do with political log-rolling than logical economic theory.)

7. Finally, there are some econometric estimates of the impact of various trade strategies, using the Candide model. These are of limited value, but they do serve to illustrate that during the transition period government subsidies are likely to be of considerable magnitude, and that only after several years will the full benefits of free trade begin to help the economy.

Questions can be raised about several key propositions in the report. On the economic side these relate to the small size of market/low productivity link, and on the political side to the high tariff/high foreign investment argument. There are other related points which fit into these two major headings.

Despite reference to a large literature which purports to demonstrate that the Canadian market alone is too small for scale economies to exist, I am disappointed in the lack of statistical evidence advanced by the Economic Council in support of this key proposition. In the report, the Council tends to assert that the home market is too small rather than to prove the point. Further, an examination of the background studies and other references on this topic gives me the impression that much work remains to be done to establish this point. In the studies, there is little or no attempt to measure the long-run average cost curves of individual firms or industries to test the extent of the decline in costs as output expands. There are no estimates of the "optimal" amount of production which minimizes costs. Instead, most of the studies simply assume that the cost curve keeps falling and the more output the better. This may be true for auto production, but for how many other industries is it relevant? The Economic Council suggests that a few industries in manufacturing will benefit, such as heavy engineering, steel, snowmobiles, and some others. There are no data reported to support such claims. Presumably, the large market concept does not apply outside of manufacturing — for example, to services. But this weakens the case for free trade, as services account for more employment than manufacturing industry. Related to the large market proposition for goods is the assumption that productivity will be improved with free trade. This leaps from an industry-specific to an aggregate level, and necessitates the belief that the tariff is to blame for all of the ills of the Canadian economy.

The second area in which the report is weak is in its treatment of political issues. In the past, economists have been content to demonstrate that free trade is efficient, and they have accepted outside constraints imposed by government decisions, such as the National Policy. It has still been in order to calculate, for example, the welfare costs of the tariff or of the east-west gas pipeline and to advise that these are some of the costs of independence. Now the Economic Council challenges past political decisions in favor of independence and argues that measures such as tariffs have not worked in Canada's favor, but have even increased dependence on the United States. Yet a free trade area with the United States, as advocated by the Economic Council, will presumably increase the amount of Canadian trade with the United States (which is already over 70 percent of the total). How can such an option increase independence? Instead of concentration of trade on one market, it is necessary to diversify trade, although such diversification may be difficult. We must move to associate with the EEC, and to develop trade with Pacific Rim nations. In practice, this means that Canada should always argue for multilateral free trade. As a small nation, Canada is not able to be self-sufficient and therefore stands to gain from free trade — if it is diversified.

The Economic Council is also rather provocative in arguing that removal of the tariff will decrease foreign investment. While it is correct to notice that with the tariff there has been an ever-increasing amount of foreign investment, it is not shown definitively that the tariff was a causal factor. Indeed, the literature on the determinants of foreign investment suggests that the tariff is only one of several variables to be examined as a motivating factor. It is likely that the decision in setting up a foreign subsidiary is made in the home country (United States) in the hope of exploiting market imperfections. Policy in the host nation (Canada) is possibly less important than the decisions made by multinational firms as they seek to maximize profits and minimize risk.

In conclusion, the Economic Council of Canada has put forward a very strong case for free trade on economic but not on political grounds. A free-trade area (even with the United States alone) will expand Canada's market, and this should indeed encourage specialization and lower per unit costs. In addition, there may be beneficial effects on productivity, but this probably requires further policies to stimulate competition and to provide a better macroeconomic environment for industry. Free trade may also promote more research and improve management skills, but then again it may not. The removal of the tariff may reduce the amount of foreign investment and thereby increase Canadian independence. It is here that the Economic Council's case is open to question. They are not convincing when arguing that free trade is a viable political policy at the present time. However, their report, and the excellent technical studies being published along with it, should help to improve the standard of public debate on the issue of free trade. If the intellectual case for free trade is correct, then, over time, it will presumably gain enough converts to eventually become a truly viable policy for Canada.

MORE RECENT STUDIES ON THE TARIFF

The definitive empirical study of the costs of the Canadian-U.S. tariff presented by an expert international trade economist, Professor James Williams of McMaster University, was published in 1978. The study has been in circulation since 1973 as an obscure discussion paper unavailable to most students of international economics. The findings of this study are already being quoted in the academic literature on Canadian commercial policy and it is essential to have available the abstract general equilibrium model from which they are derived.

There are two major findings in the study. First, the tariff has not served to develop Canadian manufacturing industry as much as it should have. Indeed, the tariff has led to most of our industry being concentrated in the earlier stages of processing rather than in production of end products. Only in textiles, chemicals, food, and agriculture has the tariff performed as anticipated to increase end product output. In all other sectors, the tariff has failed and is inefficient.

The second finding is that the cost of the tariff is high in terms of foregone welfare and national output. By elimination of both Canadian and U.S. tariffs, there would be at least 4 percent more of consumption goods or (measured in another manner) 9 percent more of investment goods for Canadians. These estimates of costs of the tariff are "exceptionally conservative" according to Williams. They are derived from a static linear programming model which does not capture important dynamic elements such as potentially large-scale economies, greater specialization, and increased competitiveness. Once these benefits are added, the case for free trade becomes very strong.

Caves (1975) reports some empirical work on the effect of the limited size of the Canadian market on the scale of production for firms. He shows that in contrast to U.S. firms in similar industries, the Canadian firms are less specialized in production. Further, Canadian firms produce a greater variety of goods than U.S. firms of similar size. These two findings imply that Canadian firms are not as efficient as U.S. ones, and that there will be greater costs in Canada as a result. In addition, it would be argued (by others) that such small-scale, diversified, and inefficient production is due to the tariff that limits the size of the market for many protected Canadian manufacturers. The tests reported by Caves are not very satisfactory due to the difficulty of separating out the interrelated components of industrial production. His work is a step in the right direction, but much more research is required on the subject of industrial diversification.

Turning to specific case studies, we may look at the examples of natural gas and the Autopact agreement. Waverman (1972) found that the cost to Canada of its national gas policy was some $200 million. He also found that the price of gas to the average Canadian consumer was 20 to 30 percent higher than under free trade. Third, he found that the only beneficiaries of the national gas policy were the producers, based in the oil- and gas-abundant province of Alberta. As most of the oil and gas industry is foreign owned, the profits were, therefore, going to Americans.

Waverman undertook a linear programming analysis of optimal gas flows from sources of supply to regions of demand based on 1966 data. The major cost determinant is transportation costs. The east-west pipeline in Canada is expensive because of the difficulty in building it across the pre-Cambrian shield of northwest Ontario. In his optimal free-trade solution, Waverman found that much of the Eastern Canadian demand for natural gas would be supplied from southeastern United States. Under the national policy for gas, the eastern Canadian market is supplied with Albertan gas at a higher price, as all Canadians pay for this inefficiency. The group of consumers who actually gain from the Canadian east-west pipeline are those in the Chicago area. These consumers pay a lower price for gas due to the Canadian gas policy than they would have to if eastern Canadians were competing with them for the southeastern U.S. supply of gas. This gain to American consumers is about twelve million dollars in total.

This analysis must be modified in the light of recent events. When Waverman undertook his study, based on 1966 data, the United States Federal Prices Commission was keeping the price of U.S. gas artificially low and therefore the eastern Canadian consumers were paying more for inefficient Alberta gas, in the sense of higher transportation costs. Now there is an energy crisis in the United States and Canada. The price of American gas has increased beyond the Canadian price and the federal government in the mid-seventies wished to maintain a two-tier price system for gas under which the export price (to the United States) is greater than the domestic price. It is not our purpose to analyze this policy here, and it need only be reemphasized that the Canadian price in any case reflected the inefficiency of east-west transportation.

Wilton (1972) finds that the advantages of free trade in automobiles to Canada are of four types. The price of automobiles is reduced by 10 percent. There is a larger automobile industry, its size being 68 percent greater than under protection. Employment is greater by 32 percent; that is, an extra 9,000 new jobs result from free trade in automobiles. Finally, there are beneficial effects on the Canadian balance of payments because Canadian exports of automobiles and parts exceeded imports between 1968 and 1972. More recently, of course, the auto trade balance has been reversed, mainly due to large net imports of parts.

In a study of the regional impacts of free trade, Shearer and his colleagues (1971) found the potential gains to British Columbia from free trade were some 6.6 percent of British Columbia personal income. This was based on 1963 figures. It was also found that 1 percent of the labor force in British Columbia would be unemployed with a move to free trade, and their retraining in other programs would increase factor substitutions.

In conclusion, we have established that there are substantial economic costs of the tariff. Historically, arguments have been advanced in favor of protection, with the tariff being one of the planks of Confederation. The costs of Canada's national policy have been high. On the other hand, the politicians and people of Canada have clearly favored the commitment to east-west trade lines, and the protection of industry in central Canada. Now let us briefly consider some monetary factors, as they affect independence.

FOREIGN INVESTMENT AND MONETARY POLICY

One of the most ironic results of the use of the tariff is that it has encouraged more foreign investment in Canada. Subsidiary branch plants are set up in order to avoid the tariff on imports. Nowadays, Canadians are much concerned with the level and extent of foreign ownership, especially as over 80 percent of foreign investment comes from one country — the United States.

As discussed in Chapter 6, Grubel (1974) and Jenkins (1973a,b), have shown that there is a social benefit to Canada from foreign investment, due to the double taxation agreement. The foreign corporations pay taxes to the Canadian government, but do not have to pay them again to the American government. This involves a social benefit to Canada of some 2 percent of GNP per annum, according to Jenkins. Grubel found that the net social rate of return to America of U.S. direct investment was negative 10 percent. Canada appears to be doubly unfortunate in that the tariff is inefficient, having a cost of nearly 10 percent of GNP, plus a national dislike of the resulting American foreign investment. If there had not been tariffs in Canada, there would have been less incentive for foreign investment and the two unfortunate effects might have been avoided.

Further, the economic costs of independence may be analyzed in terms of freedom to use domestic stabilization instruments in order to achieve nationally defined targets. Here the major difficulty lies in the use of monetary policy, as it has been demonstrated on both theoretical and empirical grounds (Mundell 1968; Wonnacott 1972) that a small open economy such as Canada is only able to use monetary policy as a stabilization instrument if there is a flexible foreign exchange rate. If there is a fixed exchange rate, as there was in Canada between 1962 and 1970, then monetary policy is relegated to the defence of the exchange rate.

For three reasons it is unlikely that, in the very long run, the Canadian dollar value will be greatly different from the American dollar. These reasons are: the large size of the U.S. economy relative to Canada; the reliance of Canada on trade with the United States with over 70 percent of exports and imports being with the United States; and the reliance on American direct investment in Canada, which accounts for 80 percent of total net direct investment. The resulting dominating effect of the U.S. economy makes it difficult for Canada to insulate itself from the state of the American economy. In fact, Canadian and U.S. business cycles are almost identical, with at most there being a slight lag of the Canadian peaks and troughs behind the American ones (Bonomo and Tanner, 1972). To the extent that Canada is able to preserve an independent economic policy, it must adopt a flexible exchange rate, and thereby give itself one extra degree of freedom — that is, the use of its own monetary policy. Fiscal policy is an independent policy instrument, and its use is not as much affected by the exchange rate issue.

WHY CANADA CANNOT HAVE AN INDEPENDENT ECONOMIC POLICY

In many ways the Canadian economy is dominated by the U.S. economy. Concern for Canada's sovereignty has increased in direct proportion to the amount of foreign ownership of Canadian industry and resources. In postwar years, the source of about 80 percent of net direct investment into Canada has been the United States. The costs and benefits of foreign ownership have been debated extensively, but the debate has frequently neglected any consideration of portfolio capital; that is, financial capital flows between the United States and Canada. The volatile nature of these short-term capital flows presents an extra difficulty for Canada over and above those thought to be presented by multinationals.

One of the problems facing an open economy such as Canada is the difficulty of operating an independent monetary policy under a system of fixed foreign exchange rates, such as Canada experienced from 1962 to 1970. Recently, this problem has increased due to the high degree of integration of the world's money markets. Short-term financial capital flows are extremely responsive to slight differences in interest rates between the countries of Europe and North America. For example, the Canadian government attempted to reduce the rate of inflation from 1968 to 1970. This policy necessitated a slowing down in the rate of increase of the money supply, and led to a rise in interest rates. The widening Canada-U.S. interest rate differential attracted American short-term funds into Canada leading to upward pressures on the foreign exchange rate. The central bank had to buy up the incoming foreign currency in order to preserve the exchange rate. The anti-inflationary policy was frustrated. Therefore, in June, 1970, the Bank of Canada was instructed by the Canadian government to allow the exchange rate to float. This led to an upward reevaluation of the Canadian exchange rate and, in time, choked off the excessive inflow of foreign currency.

. As a result of the floating of the dollar for the last six months of 1970, the rising trend of prices in Canada was halted. But since 1971 (and until 1976), the floating exchange rate has not been a truly flexible one in that it has not been fully responsive to market forces. A dirty float has been manipulated by the Bank of Canada, perhaps to prevent too rapid an appreciation of the dollar, or to attempt to preserve a psychological parity with the American dollar, or to help keep unemployment down. The high unemployment of the early seventies was itself a result of the anti-inflationary policies pursued from 1968 to 1970, which were suddenly allowed to bite in June, 1970, when the exchange rate was floated.[2] Probably other structural factors have been important in explaining the recent situation of inflation and unemployment together, but Canada's experience in the early seventies presents some evidence of a continuing tradeoff between the two evils.

If Canada maintained a truly flexible exchange rate, its domestic stabilization policy would be easier to achieve. The choice of the appropriate objective for the government to follow is not an economic but a political decision with the major parties laying different emphasis on the importance of preventing unemployment. In general, the Canadian economy is less susceptible to foreign financial influences under a flexible exchange rate.

The open nature of the Canadian economy is also apparent when attention is turned from the capital account to the current account. Of all the final goods and services measured in Canada's GNP, about one-quarter are in the form of exports or imports; however, when intermediate products are considered, the influence of the tradable sector is considerably increased.

When it is remembered that over 70 percent of Canada's trade is with the United States, the great influence of that economy becomes apparent. If there is inflation in the United States, its effects are sure to be felt in Canada, and this also holds for unemployment. These close trading connections with the United States make it difficult for Canada to pursue independent domestic policies aimed at stabilizing aggregate demand.

The interdependence of the two economies will remain even if Canada adopts a truly flexible foreign exchange rate system. Some recent statistical studies have indicated that the Canadian trade cycle is almost identical to the American trade cycle.[3] To insulate itself from any adverse effects of the American economy, Canada must attempt to diversify its trading patterns. This may become more difficult since Britain joined the European Common Market since it is to be expected that the 7 percent of Canada's trade with the United Kingdom will be even further diminished. To some extent, it may be possible to increase the percentage of Canada's trade with Pacific Rim countries, but most of the world's trade is in an east-west direction between the wealthy advanced nations of Europe and North America, and Canada is being increasingly cut out of most of these markets.

In summary, the close ties of Canada to the U.S. economy are apparent once there is an examination of the factors determining the capital and current accounts. To achieve a fully independent economic policy is probably impossible for Canada, but a more effective domestic monetary policy can be operated under a truly flexible exchange rate. A more diversified trading pattern will help to insulate the Canadian economy from the adverse effects of the American trade cycle. Given these underlying economic facts of life, the interdependence of the United States and Canada is unlikely to be affected very much by the presence, or possible absence, of American multinationals in Canada. Their role is essentially neutral when compared to the logic of geography, location, cultural affinity, and economic forces.

ENDNOTES

1. This section first appeared in *Canadian Public Administration* 19 (Summer 1976):308–311. Reprinted with permission.
2. For more evidence on this point, see Paul Wonnacott, *The Floating Canadian Dollar: Exchange Flexibility and Monetary Independence* (Washington, D.C.: American Enterprise Institute, 1972); and Robert M. Dunn, Jr., *Canada's Experience with Fixed and Flexible Exchange Rates in a North American Capital Market* (Montreal: Canadian-American Committee, 1971).
3. See Richard E. Caves and Grant L. Reuber, *Capital Transfers and Economic Policy: Canada 1951–1952* (Cambridge, Mass.: Harvard University Press, 1971).

12 CONCLUSIONS

The objectives of this book were to introduce recent developments in the theory of trade and foreign investment to a wider audience and to relate this literature to the Canadian debate on foreign ownership and regulation of multinationals.

The traditional theory of international economics demonstrates that free trade is efficient since greater net production and consumption can occur once countries specialize according to their comparative advantage. Many studies have shown that the historical Canadian reliance on the tariff to protect domestic manufacturing industry has imposed welfare costs as high as 10 percent of GNP per annum. In general, economists have argued for the removal of the tariff and other nontariff barriers to trade in order to eliminate these purely economic costs of independence. Such an approach to commercial policy is appropriate only in a world characterized by competition and reasonably free markets that clear to set equilibrium prices of factors and goods. These neoclassical-type markets probably hold in the long run, but this approach needs to be revised if these conditions do not hold in the short run.

The increasing importance of the multinational enterprise illustrates the need to revise the traditional approach to international economics. This is especially true for Canada since much of its trade is restricted to transfers between the subsidiaries of an MNE firm. Some writers have argued that in the 1970s the majority of Canadian trade was restricted to such intracorporate transfers. In addition, it has been shown that MNEs engage in transfer pricing in order to maximize profits on a global scale. They also influence the taxation policies of governments in both the home and host countries.

Against this background, the book developed two innovative points on the theory of foreign investment. A distinction was made between direct investment, over which the investor retains control, and portfolio investment, which is a financial investment involving no control. The motivation of these two types of foreign investment is explained by two distinctive theories. Basically, portfolio investment depends on monetary variables, such as interest rate differentials; whereas direct investment is better explained by the theory of internalization, a development of Hymer's theory of industrial organization. The MNE embodies in itself specific advantages in research, knowledge, management, and technology. These advantages cannot be sold on a market and are protected by the MNE through its decisions to set up foreign subsidiaries that produce the same type of product as in the home country. This allows the MNE to maximize its level of profits. It was also shown that foreign operations give an additional advantage to the MNE in that the risk of its profits can be reduced through international diversification of sales, provided that the economies of nations in which such sales are made are not perfectly positively correlated, as occurs when they are operating at different stages of their trade cycles.

A separate theme in the book described the impact of the United States on the Canadian economy. Today, about 70 percent of Canadian trade in both exports and imports is with the United States, and this percentage is increasing. Furthermore, over 80 percent of net direct investment into Canada is from the United States, and interests in that country have large holdings in the Canadian oil, mining, and manufacturing sectors. The dominance of the U.S. economy in economic stabilization policy was illustrated, especially in connection with the difficulty of operating an independent monetary policy under a fixed exchange rate system. The problems of trade diversification and of insulating the Canadian economy from any adverse effects of the U.S. economy were investigated.

Using this theoretical basis, attention turned toward an analysis of recent Canadian public policy toward trade and foreign investment. The federal reports on direct investment and foreign ownership were summarized with the major emphasis given again to economic arguments rather than political or social ones. Both the federal and provincial responses were studied, and use was made of public opinion polls testing the public's attitude toward independence. The new regulations on foreign investment were reported and some assessment made of their impact.

The book developed the policy section by giving special attention to trade and regional disparities bearing on regulation of the MNE. The use of foreign or domestic capital was discussed with reference to the development of Canadian energy and resources. In general, arguments on economic efficiency grounds were compared and constrasted with political arguments for sovereignty and independence.

In the empirical chapters no evidence was found of excessive profits being earned by MNEs active in Canada. Even in the petroleum and mineral resource industries, where the opportunities to earn economic rents are apparent, no such indication of rents could be found in an objective evaluation of the earnings of the major MNEs. Does this mean that the tests were invalid or misconceived? It does not, for the following reasons.

Since the performance of any firm is the ultimate test of its cost-effective operations, management ability, and capital-raising skills, it is of relevance here to examine the profitability of the parent firm of the MNE. The parent firm consolidates all the net earnings of its subsidiaries, and it thereby acts to absorb in its own profit rate all the performances of individual sections of the MNE. The appropriate indicator of the performance of the MNE as a whole is the profit rate of the parent.

The generally accepted measure of profit rate is net income after taxes divided by the value of shareholders' equity. While other profit measures can be utilized and advanced for various theoretical or pragmatic reasons, the earnings on equity measure adopted here serves to minimize size bias and it acts as a useful nonvariable standard of profit performance for the time periods studied. In any case, on the occasions in Part II when return on assets, or even return on revenue, are used to supplement the basic data of return on equity, no differences of any magnitude are found in the three measures of profitability.

It takes a curious turn of mind to suggest that profit rate is *not* a valid measure of performance. The level of profits and their variation over time are the most important determinants of the value of shares of the MNE, since these pieces of information are summary indicators of the success of the firm. It is impossible for firms to persistently disguise or manipulate their profits over time. Efforts to do so will be detected by investors since information on all aspects of the performance of MNEs, including their production and marketing activities, is widely available.

The nature of the competitive system makes it difficult for even large and powerful firms to persist as monopolists, even if some firms are successful in securing a closed market in the short run. In the case of MNEs active in

Canada, there are few examples that can be detected of genuine monopolists earning excess profits. Instead, many subsidiaries of U.S. MNEs appear to enjoy temporary advantages in the production of some sort of technologically advanced goods developed by their parent firms. The parents attempt desperately to protect their knowledge advantage, but it is in danger of being constantly eroded. The MNEs therefore engage in continuing expenditures on research and development to generate new knowledge advantages before the existing ones are dissipated. This is a costly and difficult process, due to the threat of competition, so the normal profit rate observed for MNEs in Canada is not too surprising.

The process of internalization discussed in Part I explains why the MNEs use transfer pricing to administer their closed internal markets, but it also suggests the limitations on the power of firms. The MNE is able to benefit from internalization only as a response to exogenous market imperfections. The imperfect markets for knowledge and technology motivate the MNE. But internalization costs the MNE something. It is the price paid for the creation and maintenance of an organizational structure within the MNE to replace the missing external market. If there had been perfect markets in the first place, the MNE would never have developed.

As Adam Smith was the first to show, the great advantage of a regular market (when firms are fortunate enough to use it) is that the open market performs its remarkable functions of allocation and distribution in a costless manner. Yet, in reality, the MNEs cannot benefit from the implicit subsidy of such a regular market. Instead, the MNEs themselves have to bear all the costs of organizing internal markets.

Why are MNEs denied regular markets? The answer lies in imperfect markets, in government regulations themselves, and in concerns for sovereignty by nation states. Such regulations, controls, and tariffs are imposed for reasons of national self-interest and equity rather than for reasons of efficiency. They serve to reinforce the natural externalities that confront the firm attempting to service foreign markets. Both the government regulations and the natural externalities motivate the process of internalization by the MNE.

My final comment is both a qualification and a warning. The subject of the MNE is a vast and growing one. I could never attempt to discuss all aspects of the MNE and its effect on the Canadian economy. Realizing this, I have been deliberately selective in my choice of topics and in my treatment of them. I have chosen to highlight the pure economics of foreign direct investment rather than the broader and more emotional issues of political economy, which interest writers such as Levitt (1970) or Marchak (1979). This choice should not reduce the value of this book, nor limit its relevance.

Instead, it demonstrates some surprising and interesting propositions about the lack of excess profits but the overall efficiency of MNEs in Canada.

I have attempted to push economic theory and neoclassical methodology as far as it could reasonably go in this analysis of the MNE. Some readers may think I have pushed economic theory too far; others not far enough. In any case, the policy implications should speak for themselves, given the explicit premises of the work. The relevance of this research depends on a careful interpretation of the assumptions and predictive nature of the theoretical and empirical results by those wishing to make use of these findings. While the literature on the MNE and Canadian public policy continues to expand rapidly, I believe that the basic analysis of this book will remain valid in future years. If is does not, I shall always be happy to learn something new about both multinationals and Canada.

SELECTED BIBLIOGRAPHY

Additional references may be found in the endnotes. This bibliography lists all items from the main body of the text, plus additional important references.

Agmon, Tamir, and Kindleberger, Charles P. *Multinationals from Small Countries.* Cambridge, Mass.: M.I.T. Press, 1977.

Aliber, Robert Z. "A Theory of Direct Foreign Investment." In *The International Corporation,* edited by Charles P. Kindleberger. Cambridge, Mass.: M.I.T. Press, 1970.

———. "The Integration of National Financial Markets: A Review of Theory and Findings." *Welwirtschaftliches Archiv* 114 (September 1978): 448–479.

———. *Exchange Risk and Corporate International Finance.* London and Basingstoke: Macmillan, 1978.

Bandera, V. N., and White, J. T. "U.S. Direct Investment and Domestic Markets in Europe." *Economia Internazionale* 21 (February 1968): 117–133.

Barber, Clarence L. "Presidential Address: A Sense of Proportion." *Canadian Journal of Economics* 6 (November 1973): 467–482.

———. "The Customs Union Issue." In *Options.* Toronto: University of Toronto, 1978, pp. 213–232.

Barnet, Richard J., and Muller, Ronald E. *Global Reach: The Power of the Multinational Corporations.* New York: Simon and Schuster, 1974.

Barrow, B. G. "Notes for an Address to the Frankfurt, West Germany, Conseil Général de l'Industrie of Quebec." 1975.

Bergsten, C. Fred; Horst, Thomas; and Moran, Theodore H. *American Multinationals and American Interests.* Washington, D.C.: The Brookings Institution, 1978.

Blake, Gordon. *Customs Administration in Canada: An Essay in Tariff Technology.* Toronto: University of Toronto Press, 1957.

Boadway, R. W., and Treddenick, J. M. *The Impact of the Mining Industries on the Canadian Economy.* Kingston, Ontario: Centre for Resource Studies, Queen's University, 1977.

Bonomo, V., and Tanner, E. J. "Canadian Sensitivity to Economic Cycles in the United States." *Review of Economics and Statistics* (February 1972): 1–8.

Booth, E. J. R., and Jensen, O. W. "Transfer Prices in the Global Corporation under Internal and External Constraints." *Canadian Journal of Economics* 10 (August 1977): 434–446.

Branson, William H. *Financial Capital Flows in the U. S. Balance of Payments.* Amsterdam: North-Holland, 1968.

Brown, W. R. "Islands of Conscious Power: MNCs in the Theory of the Firm." *MSU Business Topics* (Summer 1976): 37–54.

Bruck, Nicholas K., and Lees, Francis A. "Foreign Investment, Capital Controls and the Balance of Payments." *The Bulletin,* New York University Graduate School of Business Administration Institute of Finance, No. 48–49 (April 1968).

Buckley, Peter, and Casson, Mark. *The Future of the Multinational Enterprise.* Basingstoke and London: Macmillan, 1976.

Burns, R. M. *Conflict and Its Resolution in the Administration of Mineral Resources in Canada.* Kingston, Ontario: Centre for Resource Studies, Queen's University, 1977.

Byleveld, Herbert C. "Foreign Investment Review Act: Now Fully Hatched." *The Canadian Banker* 82 (November-December 1975): 25–29.

Cairns, R. D. "Ricardian Rent and Manitoba's Mining Royalty." *Canadian Tax Journal* 25 (September-October 1977): 558–567.

Canadian Forum. "A Citizen's Guide to the Herb Gray Report." December 1971.

Casson, Mark. "A Theory of International Entrepreneurship." Mimeographed. University of Reading, Department of Economics, 1978.

_____. *Alternatives to the Multinational Enterprise.* London: Macmillan, 1979.

Caves, Richard E. "International Corporations: The Industrial Economics of Foreign Investment." *Economica* 38 (February 1971): 1–27.

_____. *Diversification, Foreign Investment and Scale in North American Manufacturing Industries.* Ottawa: Information Canada, 1975.

Caves, Richard E., and Reuber, Grant L. *Capital Transfers and Economic Policy: Canada 1951-1962.* Cambridge, Mass.: Harvard University Press, 1971.

Chambers, Winston G. "Transfer Pricing, The Multinational Enterprise and Economic Development." Mimeograph, Department of Energy, Mines and Resources, Ottawa, 1975.

Clement, Wallace. *The Canadian Corporate Elite: An Analysis of Economic Power.* Toronto: McClelland and Stewart, 1975.

_____. *Continental Corporate Power.* Toronto: McLelland and Stewart, 1977.

Coase, Ronald H. "The Nature of the Firm." *Economica* (1937): 386–405.
Cohen, Benjamin I. "Foreign Investment by U. S. Corporations as a Way of Reducing Risk." Mimeographed, Yale University, Economic Growth Center Discussion Paper. No. 151, September 1972.
_____. *Multinational Firms and Asian Exports*. New Haven, Conn.: Yale University Press, 1975.
Cohen, John, and Krashinsky, Michael. "Capturing the Rents on Resource Land for the Public Landowner: The Case for a Crown Corporation." *Canadian Public Policy-Analyse de Politiques* 2 (Summer 1976): 411–423.
Copithorne, L. W. "International Corporate Transfer Prices and Government Policy." *The Canadian Journal of Economics* 4 (August 1971): 324–341.
Corden, Max. *Trade Policy and Economic Welfare*. Oxford: Oxford University Press, 1974.
Dales, John H. *The Protective Tariff in Canada's Development*. Toronto: University of Toronto Press, 1966.
Daly, D. J., and Globerman, S. *Tariff and Science Policies: Applications of a Model of Nationalism*. Toronto: University of Toronto Press, 1976.
Daly, D. J.; Keys, B. A.; and Spence, E. J. *Scale and Specialization in Canadian Manufacturing*. Staff Study No. 2, Economic Council of Canada, Ottawa, 1968.
Dauphin, Roma. *The Impact of Free Trade in Canada*. Ottawa: Supply and Services, Canada, 1978.
Dow, Alexander. "International Minerals Policy Should be Adopted by Canada." *International Perspectives* (November-December 1977): 19–25.
Dunning, John H. *American Investment in British Manufacturing Industry*. London: Allen and Unwin, 1958.
_____, ed. *The Multinational Enterprise*. London: Allen and Unwin, 1971.
_____. "The Determinants of International Production." *Oxford Economic Papers* 25 (November 1973): 289–336.
_____. "Trade, Location of Economic Activity and the MNE: A Search for an Eclectic Approach." In *The International Allocation of Economic Activity*, edited by Bertil Ohlin et al. Proceedings of a Nobel Symposium held at Stockholm. London: Macmillan Press, 1977.
Eastman, H. C. "The Canadian Tariff and the Efficiency of the Canadian Tariff." *American Economic Review* 54 (May 1964).
Eastman, H. C., and Stykolt, S. *The Tariff and Competition in Canada*. Toronto: Macmillan, 1967.
Economic Council of Canada. *Looking Outward: A New Trade Strategy*. Ottawa: Information Canada, 1975.
_____. *Living Together: A Study of Regional Disparities*. Ottawa: Supply and Services Canada, 1977.
Eden, Lorraine. "Vertically Integrated Multinationals: A Microeconomic Analysis." *Canadian Journal of Economics* 11 (August 1978): 534–546.
English, Edward H.; Wilkinson, Bruce W.; and Eastman, H. C. *Canada in a Wider Economic Community*. Toronto: University of Toronto Press, 1972.

Erickson, Edward W., and Waverman, Leonard. *The Energy Question.* Toronto: University of Toronto Press, 1974.

Fayerweather, John. *Foreign Investment in Canada.* Toronto: Oxford University Press, 1974.

Floyd, John E. "International Capital Movements and Monetary Equilibrium." *American Economic Review* 59 (September 1969): 472-493.

_____. "Monetary and Fiscal Policy in a World of Capital Mobility." *Review of Economic Studies* 36 (October 1969): 503-517.

Foreign Investment Review Agency. *Annual Report 1974-1975.* Ottawa: Information Canada, October 1975.

Gagne, Wallace. *Nationalism, Technology and the Future of Canada.* Toronto: Macmillan, 1976.

Giddy, Ian H. "Devaluations, Revaluations and Stock Market Prices." Unpublished doctoral dissertation, University of Michigan, 1974.

_____. "The Cost of Capital in the International Firm." Columbia University, Graduate School of Business Research Working Paper (August 1977).

_____. "The Demise of the Product Cycle Model in International Business Theory." *Columbia Journal of World Business* 13 (Spring 1978): 90-97.

Giddy, Ian H., and Rugman, Alan M. "A Model of Trade, Foreign Direct Investment and Licensing." Mimeographed, Graduate School of Business, Columbia University, 1979.

Gould, J. "Internal Pricing in Firms where There are Costs of Using an Outside Market." *Journal of Business* 37 (1964): 61-67.

Government of Canada. *Foreign Direct Investment in Canada.* Ottawa: Information Canada, 1972.

Grubel, Herbert G. "Internationally Diversified Portfolios: Welfare Gains and Capital Flows." *American Economic Review* 58 (December 1968): 1299-1314.

_____. "The Private and Social Rates of Return from U.S. Asset Holdings Abroad." *Journal of Political Economy* 82 (May-June, 1974): 469-488.

Grubel, Herbert G., and Sam Sydneysmith. "The Taxation of Windfall Gains on Stocks of Natural Resources." *Canadian Public Policy* 1 (Winter 1975): 13-29.

Heisey, Alan. *The Great Canadian Stampede.* Toronto: Griffin House, 1973.

Hirsch, Seev. "An International Trade and Investment Theory of the Firm." *Oxford Economic Papers* 28 (July 1976): 258-270.

Hirschleifer, J. "On The Economics of Transfer Pricing." *Journal of Business* 29 (1956): 172-184.

Holland, Daniel M., and Myers, Stewart, C. "Trends in Corporate Profitability and Capital Costs." Mimeographed, Working Paper No. 937-77, Sloan School of Management, M.I.T., 1977.

Hood, Neil, and Stephen Young. *The Economics of Multinational Enterprise.* London: Longman, 1979.

Horst, Thomas. "The Theory of the Multinational Firm: Optimal Behaviors Under Different Tariff and Tax Rates." *Journal of Political Economy* 79 (1971): 1059-1072.

———. "The Industrial Composition of U.S. Exports and Subsidiary Sales to the Canadian Market." *American Economic Review* 62 (March 1972): 37–45.

——— "Theory of the Firm." In *Economic Analysis and the Multinational Enterprise,* edited by John H. Dunning. London: Allen and Unwin, 1974.

———. "American Taxation of Multinational Corporations." *American Economic Review* 67 (June 1977): 376–389.

Howarth, George. "Foreign Investment Review Act Not Material Change in Attitude." *The American Banker* (March 12, 1976a).

——— Notes for Remarks to the Committee on Finance, Trade and Economic Affairs, March 25, 1976b.

Hufbauer, Gary C. "The Multinational Corporation and Direct Investment." In *International Trade and Finance,* edited by Peter B. Kenen. New York: Cambridge University Press, 1975, pp. 253–320.

Hymer, Stephen H. *The International Operations of National Firms: A Study of Direct Foreign Investment.* Cambridge, Mass.: M.I.T. Press, 1976.

Jenkins, Glenn P. "The Measurements of Rates of Return and Taxation from Private Capital in Canada." Mimeographed, Harvard University Institute of Economic Research Discussion Paper No. 282, 1973a.

———. "Measurement of the Gains and Losses from Foreign Investment." Mimeographed, Harvard University Institute of Economic Research Discussion Paper No. 283, 1973b.

Johnson, Harry G. *The Canadian Quandary: Economic Problems and Policies.* Toronto: McGraw-Hill, 1963.

———. "The Efficiency and Welfare Implications of the International Corporation." In *The International Corporation,* edited by Charles P. Kindleberger. Cambridge, Mass.: M.I.T. Press, 1970, pp. 35–56.

———. *Aspects of the Theory of Tariffs.* London: Allen and Unwin, 1971.

———. *Technology and Economic Interdependence.* London: Macmillan, 1975.

Kierans, Eric. *Report on Natural Resources Policy in Manitoba.* Winnipeg, Manitoba: Secretariat for the Planning and Priorities Committee of Cabinet, Government of Manitoba, 1973.

Kindleberger, Charles P. *American Business Abroad: Six Lectures on Direct Investment.* New Haven, Conn., and London: Yale University Press, 1969.

Knickerbocker, Frederick T. *Oligopolistic Reaction and Multinational Enterprise.* Cambridge, Mass.: Harvard University Press, 1973.

Kojima, Kiyoshi. *Direct Foreign Investment: A Japanese Model of Multinational Business Operations.* London: Croom Helm, 1978.

Krueger, Anne O. "Balance of Payments Theory." *Journal of Economic Literature* 7 (March 1969): 1–26.

Lall, Sanjaya. "Transfer Pricing by Multinational Manufacturing Firms." *Oxford Bulletin of Economics and Statistics* 35 (August 1973): 173–195.

Lamfalussy, Alexandre. *Investment and Growth in Mature Economies.* Oxford: Basil Blackwell and Mott, 1961.

Laxer, James. *Canada's Energy Crisis.* Edmonton: Hurtig, 1972.

Lee, C. H. "A Stock Adjustment Analysis of Capital Movements: The U.S.-Canadian Case." *Journal of Political Economy* 77 (July 1969): 512–523.

Leff, Nathaniel H. "Industrial Organization and Entrepreneurship in the Developing Countries: The Economic Groups." *Economic Development and Cultural Change* 26 (July 1978): 661–675.

Lessard, Donald R. "Transfer Prices, Taxes and Financial Markets: Implications of Internal Financial Transfers within the Multinational Firm." Mimeographed, M.I.T. Working Paper No. 919–977, April, 1977.

Levitt, Kari. *Silent Surrender: The Multinational Corporation in Canada.* Toronto: Macmillan, 1970.

Litvak, I. A.; Maule, C. J.; and Robinson, R. D. *Dual Loyalty: Canadian-U.S. Business Arrangements.* Toronto: McGraw-Hill, 1971.

Logue, Dennis E.; Salant, Michael A.; and Sweeney, Richard James. "International Integration of Financial Markets: Survey, Synthesis, and Results." In *Eurocurrencies and the International Monetary System,* edited by Carl H. Stem; John H. Makin; and Dennis E. Logue. Washington, D.C.: American Enterprise Institute for Public Policy Research, 1976, pp. 91–137.

Lyon, Peyton V. *Canada-United States Free Trade and Canadian Independence.* Ottawa: Information Canada, 1975.

MacDougall, G. D. A. "The Benefits and Costs of Private Investment from Abroad: A Theoretical Approach." *Economic Record* 36 (1960): 13–35.

Machlup, Fritz; Salant, Walter S.; and Tarshis, Lorie. *International Mobility and Movement of Capital.* New York: Columbia University Press, 1972.

MacKenzie, Brian W. "Economic Characteristics of Base Metal Investment in Canada and the Effect of Mining Taxation Systems." Mimeographed, Kingston, Ontario: Centre for Resource Studies, Queen's University, 1977.

Magee, Stephen P. "Multinational Corporations, the Industry Technology Cycle and Development." *Journal of World Trade Law* 11 (July–August 1977): 297–321.

_____. "Information and the Multinational Corporation: An Appropriability Theory of Direct Foreign Investment," in *The New International Economic Order,* edited by J. N. Bhagwati. Cambridge Mass.: M.I.T. Press, 1977, pp. 317–340.

Marchak, Patricia. *In Whose Interests?* Toronto: McClelland and Stewart, 1979.

Mathewson, G. F., and Quirin, G. D. *Fiscal Transfer Pricing in Multinational Corporations.* Toronto: University of Toronto Press, 1979.

McFetridge, D. G. *Government Support of Scientific Research and Development: An Economic Analysis.* Toronto: University of Toronto Press, 1977.

McKern, R. B. *Multinational Enterprise and Natural Resources.* Sydney: McGraw-Hill, 1976.

McManus, John. "The Theory of the International Firm." In *The Multinational Firm and the Nation State,* edited by Gilles Paquet. Toronto: Collier-Macmillan, 1972, pp. 66–93.

Melvin, J. R. "Increasing Returns to Scale as a Determinant of Trade." *Canadian Journal of Economics* 2 (November 1969): 389–402.

_____. "Commodity Taxation on a Determinant of Trade." *Canadian Journal of Economics* 3 (February 1970): 62–78.

Mundell, Robert A. *International Economics.* New York: Macmillan, 1968.

Musgrave, Peggy B. *United States Taxation of Foreign Investment Income: Issues and Arguments.* Cambridge, Mass.: Harvard Law School International Program, 1969.

Nieckels, Lars. *Transfer Pricing in Multinational Firms.* Stockholm: Almqvist and Wiksell, 1976.

Norrie, K. H. "Some Comments on Prairie Economic Alienation." *Canadian Public Policy* 2 (Spring 1976): 211–224.

Ontario Economic Council. *National Independence.* Toronto: University of Toronto Press, 1976.

Paquet, Gilles. *The Multinational Firm and the Nation State.* Don Mills, Ontario: Macmillan, 1972.

Parry, Thomas G. "The International Firm and National Economic Policy: A Survey of Some Issues." *The Economic Journal* 83 (December 1973): 1201–1221.

Pattison, J. C. *Financial Markets and Foreign Ownership.* Toronto: Ontario Economic Council, 1978.

Penner, R. G. "Policy Reactions and the Benefit of Foreign Investment." *Canadian Journal of Economics* 3 (May 1970): 213–222.

Perlmutter, H. "The Tortuous Evolution of the Multinational Corporation." *Columbia Journal of World Business* 4 (January-February 1969): 9–18.

Plasschaert, Sylvain R. F. *Transfer Pricing and Multinational Corporations.* Farnborough: Saxon House, 1979.

Porter, Michael G. "International Interest Rate Differentials Interpreted as Behavior Towards Exchange Rate Expectations." International Monetary Fund *Staff Papers* 8 (November 1971): 613–645.

Ray, Edward John. "The Choice Between Licensing and Foreign Direct Investment." Mimeographed, Ohio State University, April 1977.

Reuber, Grant L., and Roseman, Frank. "International Capital Flows and the Take-over of Domestic Companies by Foreign Firms: Canada 1945-1961." In *International Mobility and Movement of Capital,* edited by Fritz Machlup; Walter Salant; and Lorie Tarshis. New York: Columbia University Press, 1972.

Robbins, Sidney M., and Stobaugh, Robert B. *Money in the Multinational Enterprise.* New York: Basic Books, 1973.

Robinson, Richard D. *National Control of Foreign Business Entry: A Survey of Fifteen Countries.* New York: Praeger, 1976.

Robock, S. H.; Simmonds, K.; and Zwick, J. *International Business and Multinational Enterprises.* Homewood, Illinois: Irwin, 1977.

Ronstadt, Robert. *Research and Development Abroad by U.S. Multinationals.* New York: Praeger, 1977.

Rosenbluth, Gideon. "The Relation Between Foreign Control and Concentration in Canadian Industry." *Canadian Journal of Economics* 3 (February 1970): 14–38.

Rotstein, Abraham, and Lax, Gary, eds. *Independence: The Canadian Challenge.* Toronto: McClelland and Stewart, 1972.

Rugman, Alan M. "The Costs of Independence." Mimeographed, University of Winnipeg, November 1973.

_____ . "Motives for Foreign Investment: The Market Imperfections and Risk Diversification Hypotheses." *Journal of World Trade Law* 9 (September-October 1975): 567-573.

_____ . "The Foreign Ownership Debate in Canada." *Journal of World Trade Law* 10 (March-April 1976*a*): 171-176.

_____ . "Free Trade and Canadian Independence." *Canadian Public Administration* 19 (Summer 1976*b*): 308-311.

_____ . "Risk Reduction by International Diversification." *Journal of International Business Studies* 7 (Fall 1976*c*): 75-80.

_____ . "The Regulation of Foreign Investment in Canada." *Journal of World Trade Law* 11 (July-August 1977*a*): 322-333.

_____ . "Risk, Direct Investment and International Diversification." *Weltwirtschaftliches Archiv* 113 (September 1977*b*): 485-500.

_____ . "International Diversification by Financial and Direct Investment." *Journal of Economics and Business* 30 (October 1977*c*): 31-37.

_____ . "Risk and Return in the Canadian Mining Industry." Working Paper No. 2. Kingston, Ontario: Centre for Resource Studies, Queen's University, 1977*d*.

_____ . *International Diversification and the Multinational Enterprise.* Lexington: D. C. Heath, 1979.

_____ . "Internalization as a General Theory of Foreign Direct Investment." Graduate School of Business, Columbia University. Research Working Paper No. 218A, April 1979. Forthcoming in *Welwirtschaftliches Archiv* (Review of World Economics) 1980*a*.

_____ . "Transfer Pricing Problems of Multinational Corporations." In *Functioning of The Multinational Corporation,* edited by Anant R. Negandhi. New York: Pergamon, 1980*b*.

Safarian, A. E. *Foreign Ownership of Canadian Industry.* Toronto: McGraw-Hill, 1966. 2nd. edition, University of Toronto Press, 1973.

_____ . "Policy on Multinational Enterprises in Developed Countries." *Canadian Journal of Economics* 11 (November 1978): 642-655.

_____ . "Foreign Ownership and Industrial Behaviour: A Comment on 'The Weakest Link.' " *Canadian Public Policy* 5 (Summer 1979): 318-335.

Scaperlanda, Anthony E., and Mauer, Lawrence Jay. "The Determinants of U.S. Direct Investment in the E.E.C." *American Economic Review* 59 (September 1969): 558-568.

Shapiro, Alan. "Financial Structure and The Cost of Capital in the Multinational Corporation." *Journal of Financial and Quantitative Analysis* 13 (June 1978): 211-226.

Shearer, Ronald A.; Young, John H.; and Munro, Gordon R. *Trade Liberalization and a Regional Economy: Studies on The Impact of Free Trade on British Columbia.* Toronto: University of Toronto Press, 1971.

Sykes, Philip. *Sellout.* Edmonton: Hurtig, 1973.

Teece, David J. *The Multinational Corporation and The Resource Cost of International Technology Transfer.* Cambridge, Mass.: Ballinger, 1976.

Thomas, D. Babatunde. *Importing Technology into Africa: Foreign Investment and The Supply of Technological Innovations.* New York: Praeger, 1976.

Vaitsos, Constantine. *Intercountry Income Distribution and Transnational Enterprise.* Oxford: Oxford University Press, 1974.

Vernon, Raymond. "International Investment and International Trade in the Product Cycle." *Quarterly Journal of Economics* 30 (May 1966): 190–207.

_____. *Sovereignty at Bay: The Multinational Spread of United States Enterprises.* New York: Basic Books, 1971.

_____. *Storm over the Multinationals: The Real Issues.* London and Basingstoke: Macmillan, 1977.

Viner, Jacob. *Canada's Balance of International Indebtedness, 1900–1913.* Toronto: McLelland and Stewart, 1975.

Wahn Report. Eleventh Report of The Standing Committee on Defence and External Affairs Respecting Canada-U.S. Relations. Ottawa: Queen's Printer, 1970.

Watkins, M. et al. *Foreign Ownership and The Structure of Canadian Industry.* Report of the Task Force on The Structure of Canadian Industry. Ottawa: The Queen's Printer, 1968.

_____. "The Economics of Nationalism and The Nationality of Economics: A Critique of Neo-Classical Theorizing." *Canadian Journal of Economics* 11 (November 1978).

Waverman, L. "National Policy and Natural Gas: The Costs of a Border." *Canadian Journal of Economics* 5 (August 1972): 331–348.

West, E. C. *Canada-United States Price and Productivity Differences in Manufacturing Industries.* Staff Study No. 32 for The Economic Council of Canada, 1971.

Wilkinson, Bruce. "Recent American Tax Concessions to Industry and Canadian Economic Policy." *Canadian Tax Journal* 20 (January-February 1972): 1–14.

Williams, James R. *The Canadian-United States Tariff and Canadian Industry: A Multisectoral Analysis.* Toronto: University of Toronto Press, 1978.

Wilton, David. "An Econometric Model of The Canadian Automotive Manufacturing Industry and The 1965 Automotive Agreement." *Canadian Journal of Economics* 5 (May 1972): 157–181.

Wonnacott, Paul. *The Floating Canadian Dollar: Exchange Flexibility and Monetary Independence.* Washington, D.C.: American Enterprise Institute, 1972.

Wonnacott, Ronald J. *Canada's Trade Options.* Ottawa: Information Canada, 1975.

Wonnacott, Ronald J., and Wonnacott, Paul. *Free Trade Between The United States and Canada: The Potential Economic Effects.* Cambridge, Mass.: Harvard University Press, 1967.

Young, John H. *Canadian Commercial Policy.* Ottawa: The Queen's Printer, 1957.

INDEX

INDEX OF NAMES

INDEX OF SUBJECTS

Mining
  industry, 88, 101–103, 154
  sectors, 83
Mobility of labor (migration), 105–107
Monetary policy, 169–171, 174
Monopoly, 2, 13, 23, 33–34, 90, 128,
  138, 175. *See also* Excess
  profits; Rents

National Policy, 166
Neoclassical model (paradigm), 4, 105,
  109–110, 157, 173, 177
Neoclassical socialism, 109
Net present value, 47, 51, 56, 58
New Democratic Party, 129
Noneconomic goals, 3, 31, 133, 138,
  140
Noranda, 95–96

Offshore assembly, 60
Oil
  cartel, 116, 119
  embargo, 68, 117
  prices, 116–120
Oil firms
  and risk of earnings, 66–71, 117
Oligopoly, 26, 45
OPEC, 116–118
Opinion polls, 27, 127, 174
Optimal tax, 3, 120
Optimum tariff, 160

Pareto optimal, 2, 4, 137, 160. *See
  also* Efficiency; General
  equilibrium
Patents, 35–36, 55, 57. *See also*
  Knowledge advantage
Patino, 95–97
Petrofina, 66
Pharmaceuticals, 88–89, 92
Political economy, 2–3, 24, 41, 176
Portfolio, 17, 19
  theory, 25, 65, 99
Positive economics, 7

Pressure groups, 24
Price discrimination, 35–36, 38, 44–45,
  58
Production (function), 11–12, 33–34,
  113, 162. *See also* Marginal
  product
Productivity, 161–163, 165–166
Profits, 22–24, 26–27, 32, 51, 65, 148,
  174–175
  excessive, 66, 138–139
  rates, 1–2, 5, 75, 88, 95, 112
Property rights, 34–36, 44
Proprietary information, 45. *See also*
  Knowledge advantage
Public good(s), 35, 39, 44, 49, 81. *See
  also* Knowledge advantage

Quotas, 33

Random innovations, 26
Random walk, 93
Reading, University of, 94
Regional income disparities, 60,
  104–109, 126, 175
Regions, 34, 114, 156, 159, 169
Rents, 26, 44, 54, 74, 111, 116–117,
  175. *See also* Excess profits
Research and development, 34–36, 38,
  54, 59–61, 113, 124, 155, 164,
  166, 176. *See also* Knowledge
  advantage
Rio Algom, 72, 95–99
Risk, 19, 22–25, 41, 139, 144, 148,
  157, 162, 166
  of profits, 5, 13–14, 65–68, 74, 96,
  174
  standard deviation as a measure of,
  19, 68, 71, 95, 99, 106

Scale, economies of, 15, 21, 23, 33–34,
  82, 139–142, 153–168
Science Council of Canada, 61
Science policy, 60–61, 113–114
Self-sufficiency, 116–118